FOREWORD

The UNECE/FAO Team of Specialists on Forest Products Markets and Marketing advises the UNECE Timber Committee and the FAO European Forestry Commission on forest products markets structures, policies and opportunities in the UNECE region. Our work is premised on sustainable and rational growth of forest products markets in the region. In order to accomplish this, we examine a myriad of social, economic and environmental influences and factors that influence forest products markets and marketing. The members of the Team are authors, contributors and reviewers of the *Forest Products Annual Market Review, 2006-2007*.

Global changes in forest-based sectors including forest management, harvesting, processing, distribution and end-use demand continue to be dynamic and significant, even in the last 12 months since the 2006 *Review* was published. In this *Review*, we discuss this changing landscape, associated policies, and their effects on sustainable wood and paper product markets in the UNECE.

The *Review* analysis of market and policy developments is based on first-available statistics supplied by official country correspondents and is the first comprehensive analysis available each year for the UNECE region. It covers all primary wood-processing and value-added wood-products sectors.

In addition to providing information to participants at the Timber Committee market discussions the *Review* is a valuable resource for market specialists, Government policymakers, economists and other forest-sector stakeholders. It supports UNECE and FAO priorities by providing an objective

analysis of market and policy developments and a stimulus for meaningful policy discussion in international forums.

The *Review* highlights market developments for the following sectors:
- Wood raw materials
- Wood energy
- Sawn softwood
- Sawn hardwood
- Panels
- Paper, paperboard, and woodpulp
- Certified forest products
- Value-added wood products
- Tropical timber

In addition, the *Review* highlights emerging policy developments:
- Policy dilemmas due to rising bioenergy demand
- Trade trends and policy issues
- Reducing the forest sector's global footprint through certification and corporate social responsibility
- Russian forest-sector reform: a new forest code and export regime
- Research and development policies

I wish to express my appreciation to the Team members, the secretariat review team and to all the other persons who contributed information and statistics. I believe that the *Forest Products Annual Market Review* continues to be a unique and valuable source of information for Government officials, industry members, educators and other stakeholders throughout the UNECE region and in the global forest products community.

Dr. Richard Vlosky
Leader of the UNECE/FAO Team of Specialists
on Forest Products Markets and Marketing

PREFACE

The aim of the United Nations Economic Commission for Europe (UNECE) is to promote economic integration of the 56 countries within its region. It provides analysis, policy advice and assistance to Governments within the UN global mandates in the economic field, in cooperation with other global players and key stakeholders, notably the business community.

The *Forest Products Annual Market Review, 2006-2007* implements these objectives by analysing forest products market developments and the government and industry policies with which they interact. The *Review* addresses topical issues within the forest and forest industries sector, as well as cross-sectoral influences, especially in energy and environment. Since the UNECE region is the major producer, consumer and trader of forest products in the world, it has the responsibility to ensure sustainability, both in forest management and in the downstream part of the forest sector.

A major issue today is climate change, which is present throughout this *Review*. In 2006 and 2007, the forests in the UNECE region have sustained damage from windstorms, fire and insects, all of which can be attributed at least partly to climate change. Even if the forest sector may be well positioned to mitigate climate change, for example by providing wood-based renewable energy, policies must be considered in a holistic manner, taking into account the current needs of the wood and paper industries, the forest environment and the people dependent on forests.

Wood energy demand is having an effect throughout the forest sector. Although the UNECE region's forests produce more wood than is harvested, in the short term there are constraints to the volumes which can be mobilized for the rising needs of both the wood-processing industries and the energy sector.

This *Review* is a key background document for the annual market discussions of the Timber Committee, which for the first time will hold joint market discussions together with the International Softwood Conference on 8-9 October 2007. The interaction between industry, government and international organizations should lead to better mutual understandings about the market and policy developments.

The Review like much of UNECE work, is a collective effort. It is produced within the integrated programme of work of the UNECE Timber Committee and the FAO European Forestry Commission. It is based on statistics supplied by official country statistical correspondents and is the earliest comprehensive analysis of the sector available each year for the UNECE region.

I take this occasion to express my sincere appreciation to our partner in FAO. I thank the 150 experts, partners, information suppliers and secretariat who have worked to produce this *Review*.

The *Review* is prepared for government policymakers, industry analysts and marketing specialists in the sector, as well as in other sectors. I hope it will achieve its objectives of providing a factual and neutral analysis of market and policy developments and providing a stimulus for meaningful policy discussion in international forums.

Marek Belka
Executive Secretary
United Nations Economic Commission for Europe

United Nations Economic Commission for Europe/
Food and Agriculture Organization of the United Nations

UNECE

Timber Section, Geneva, Switzerland

ECE/TIM/SP/22

Geneva Timber and Forest Study Paper 22

FOREST PRODUCTS ANNUAL MARKET REVIEW 2006-2007

UNITED NATIONS
New York and Geneva, 2007

NOTE

The designations employed and the presentation of material in this publication do not imply the expression of any opinion whatsoever on the part of the secretariat of the United Nations concerning the legal status of any country, territory, city or area, or of its authorities, or concerning the delimitation of its frontiers or boundaries.

Please note that the Timber Bulletin series was discontinued in 2005. The present publication was issued under the Geneva Timber and Forest Study Paper series starting in 2006.

ABSTRACT

The UNECE/FAO *Forest Products Annual Market Review, 2006-2007* provides general and statistical information on forest products markets and related policies in the UN Economic Commission for Europe region (Europe, North America and the Commonwealth of Independent States). The *Review* begins with an overview chapter, followed by a description of government and industry policies affecting forest products markets. After a description of the economic situation and construction-related demand in the region, five chapters based on annual country-supplied statistics, describe: wood raw materials, sawn softwood, sawn hardwood, wood-based panels, and paper and paperboard. Additional chapters discuss markets for wood energy, certified forest products, value-added wood products and tropical timber. In each chapter, production, trade and consumption are analysed and relevant material on specific markets is included. Tables and graphs provided throughout the text present summary information. Supplementary statistical tables may be found on the Market Information Service website within the UNECE Timber Committee and FAO European Forestry Commission website.

KEYWORDS

Forest products markets, wood markets, market analysis, forest policy, consumption, production, imports, exports, forestry industry, forestry trade, forestry statistics, Europe, North America, Commonwealth of Independent States, China, corporate social responsibility, climate change, housing market, construction, timber, wood industry, pulp and paper industry, wood fuels, certification, wood products, tropical timber, forestry trade, sustainable forestry, sawnwood, sawn softwood, hardwood, lumber, wood-based panels, particle board, fiberboard, fibreboard, OSB, MDF, plywood, paperboard, cardboard, woodpulp, pulpwood, sawlogs, pulplogs, roundwood, industrial roundwood, value-added, wood energy, fuelwood, certified forest products

ECE/TIM/SP/22

$40

UNITED NATIONS PUBLICATIONS
Sales No.E.07.II.E.18
ISBN 978-92-1-116971-3
ISSN 1020-2269

CONTENTS

LIST OF TABLES

LIST OF GRAPHS

LIST OF FIGURES

ACKNOWLEDGEMENTS

Once again it is a pleasure to thank the Geneva-based Review Team and the extended network of authors, statistical correspondents and contributors to the *Forest Products Annual Market Review, 2006-2007* on behalf of the UNECE Timber Committee and the FAO European Forestry Commission. While we mention some specific people below, we also acknowledge the support of their companies, institutions, organizations, associations and Governments that made it possible for contributions of their time and travel.

The *Review's* analysis is based on statistics received from official country correspondents, who are listed separately. Some information in the chapter on certified forest products is from the Timber Committee and European Forestry Commission Network of Officially Nominated Country Correspondents on Certified Forest Products Markets and Certification of Sustainable Forest Management. Our sincere appreciation goes to these people whose efforts made it possible to produce the *Review*.

By chapter we recognize the valuable efforts of the authors and contributors, many of whom are participating again. Most of the authors are members of the UNECE/FAO Team of Specialists on Forest Products Markets and Marketing. We express our gratitude to these experts for their work and our hope for continuing collaboration.

Chapter 1, an overview of market and policy developments, was written by Mr. Ed Pepke, Forest Products Marketing Specialist, UNECE/FAO Timber Section, drawing mainly on information from the following experts.

Chapter 2 on policy issues was written by Dr. Jim Bowyer, Director of Responsible Materials Program, Dovetail Partners, and Professor Emeritus, Department of Bio-based Products, University of Minnesota, US. He was assisted by Dr. Helmuth Resch, Emeritus Professor, University of Natural Resources, Austria. Ms. Franziska Hirsch, Policies and Institutions Specialist, UNECE/FAO Timber Section, Geneva, contributed from her international perspective. The corporate social responsibility section was written by Ms. Natalia Vidal, PhD candidate, and Dr. Robert Kozak, Associate Professor, University of British Columbia, Canada, both specialists in this important field.

Chapter 3 on economic and construction developments begins with a new author, Dr. Robert Shelburne, Senior Economic Affairs Officer, UNECE, who analysed the economic framework for market developments. The construction section was written by Dr. Al Schuler, Research Economist, Northeast Forest Experiment Station, USDA Forest Service, and Mr. Craig Adair, Director, Market Research, APA–The Engineered Wood Association, US.

Chapter 4 on wood raw materials, benefits from the perspective and experience of Mr. Håkan Ekström, President, Wood Resources International, US. He is Editor-in-Chief of *Wood Resource Quarterly* and the *North American Wood Fiber Review*, two publications tracking worldwide wood fibre markets and prices.

Chapter 5 on sawn sawnwood is provided thanks to the continued collaboration of three authors: Mr. Russell Taylor, President, International WOOD MARKETS Group Inc., Canada, coordinated the chapter and wrote the North America analysis; Mr. Jarno Seppälä, Senior Consultant, Pöyry Forest Industry Consulting, Finland, analysed European markets; and Dr. Nikolai Burdin, Director, OAO NIPIEIlesprom, Russia, wrote the Russia analysis.

Chapter 6 on sawn hardwood was made possible with the support of the American Hardwood Export Council (AHEC), and especially Mr. David Venables, European Director. The analysis was done by Mr. Rod Wiles, Broadleaf Consulting, UK and assisted by Mr. Rupert Oliver, Forest Industries Intelligence Limited, UK.

Chapter 7 on panels markets was coordinated by Dr. Ivan Eastin, Director, Center for International Trade in Forest Products, University of Washington, US, who produced the North American analysis. Ms. Bénédicte Hendrickx, Economic Advisor, European Panel Federation, Belgium, analysed the European panel markets. They had input on the Russian market from Dr. Burdin.

Chapter 8 had four authors who analysed the paper, paperboard and woodpulp markets: Professor Eduard L. Akim, PhD, Saint Petersburg State Technological University of Plant Polymers and the All-Russian Research Institute of Pulp and Paper Industry; Dr. Peter J. Ince, Research Forester, Forest Products Laboratory, USDA Forest Service; Mr. Bernard Lombard, Trade and Competitiveness Director, Confederation of European Paper Industries (CEPI), Belgium, with statistical assistance from Mr. Eric Kilby and Ms. Ariane Crèvecoeur, CEPI; and Mr. Tomás Parik, Managing Director, Wood and Paper A.S, Czech Republic.

Chapter 9 analysis of wood energy markets was coordinated by Dr. Bengt Hillring, Associate Professor, and Mr. Olle Olsson, Research Assistant, both from the Swedish University of Agricultural Sciences (SLU). This year they were joined by Dr. Christopher Gaston, National Group Leader, FPInnovations-Forintek Division and Dr. Warren Mabee, Research Associate, University of British Columbia, for the Canadian analysis and Dr. Kenneth Skog, USDA Forest Service, for the US analysis. Dr.

Tatiana Stern, Associate Professor, SLU, brought in the Russian developments. The chapter was possible thanks to financial support from the Swedish Ministry of Industry, Employment and Communications, facilitated by Mr. Peter Blombäck, Head, International Division, Swedish Forest Agency, and Ms. Birgitta Naumburg, Ministry of Industry, Employment and Communications. Mr. Blombäck is Vice-Chairman of the FAO European Forestry Commission.

Chapter 10 on certified forest products markets is by Mr. Florian Kraxner, Research Scholar, International Institute for Applied Systems Analysis, Austria. He was assisted by the co-authors: Dr. Catherine Mater, President, Mater Engineering, US; and Dr. Toshiaki Owari, Lecturer, University of Tokyo, Japan, who provided subregional perspectives.

Chapter 11 on value-added products chapter has two sections, the first written by Mr. Tapani Pahkasalo, Market Analyst, Indufor Oy, Finland. Dr. Adair and Mr. Schuler wrote the second section on engineered wood products markets.

Chapter 12 on tropical timber was written by our colleagues in ITTO: Dr. Steve Johnson, Statistician and Economist; Dr. Jairo Castaño, Market Information Service Coordinator; Mr. Jean-Christophe Claudon, Statistical Assistant; and Mr. James Cunningham, Consultant. They based their analysis on the ITTO *Annual Review and Assessment of the World Timber Situation 2006.*

Once again we express our appreciation to the University of Helsinki's Department of Forest Economics for sending us two assistants during the *Review* production: Mr. Olli Kaukonen and Ms. Leila Räsänen. They conducted market research and produced all the graphics. They also revised our *Graphics Production System, Review Production Manual, Review Planning System* and websites associated with the *Review*. They are critical to the quality and timeliness of the publication. These annual internships from the University of Helsinki were facilitated thanks to Dr. Heikki Juslin, Professor, and Mr. Tomi Amberla, Assistant.

This year's *Review* was produced with direct input by 53 people. Mr. Alex McCusker, UNECE/FAO Timber Section, collected, validated and produced the statistics. Mr. Ronald Jansen, United Nations Statistics Division, provided the latest forest products trade statistics from Comtrade and Mr. Bruce Michie, Senior Researcher, European Forest Institute, validated the trade data and produced the database for trade flow graphs and tables. Thanks to them we had the most up-to-date, global, statistical database possible.

Mr. Matt Fonseca, UNECE/FAO Timber Section, was responsible for the publication layout. Ms. Cynthia de Castro, UNECE/FAO Timber Section, performed all administrative duties. Ms. Sefora Kifle, UNECE/FAO Timber Section, prepared price data and supported authors with documents and journals. Editors were Ms. Barbara Hall, Consultant, Ms. Christina O'Shaughnessy, Editor, Trade and Timber Division, UNECE and Ms. Line Konstat, Associate Information Officer, Transport Division, UNECE. Ms. Lindsey Farquharsen, UNECE/FAO Timber Section, assisted with proofreading. Thanks to all of them.

Initial technical reviews in the UNECE/FAO Timber Section were done in chronological order by Mr. Pepke, Mr. Douglas Clark and Mr. Kit Prins. We appreciated the second reviews by Mr. Arvydas Lebedas, Forest Products and Industry Division, FAO Forestry Department. Other reviewers from the Timber Section included Mr. Sebastian Hetsch and Mr. Jan-Eirik Kjeldsen.

This manuscript was completed on 23 July 2007. It is my pleasure to thank all members of the Team, the authors, and the many other contributors, for their dedicated work in producing this *Forest Products Annual Market Review.*

Ed Pepke, Project Leader
Forest Products Marketing Specialist
UNECE/FAO Timber Section
Trade and Timber Division
United Nations Economic Commission for Europe
Palais des Nations
CH - 1211 Geneva 10, Switzerland
E-mail: info.timber@unece.org

CONTRIBUTORS TO THE PUBLICATION

The secretariat would like to express our sincere appreciation for the information and assistance received from the following people in preparation of the *Forest Products Annual Market Review*. The base data for the *Review* were supplied by country statistical correspondents, who are acknowledged in a separate listing. We regret any omissions.

Martti Aarne, Finnish Forest Research Institute, Finland
Craig Adair, APA – The Wood Engineered Association, United States
Yngve Abrahamsen, Euroconstruct, Swiss Economic Institute, Switzerland
Eduard L. Akim, Saint Petersburg State Technological University of Plant Polimers, Russian Federation
Tomi Amberla, University of Helsinki, Finland
Harry Bagley, Lumber Quality Consulting, United States
Peter Blombäck, Swedish Forest Agency, Sweden
John Bolles, Plum Creek Timber, United States
Jim Bowyer, University of Minnesota, United States
Steve Bratkovich, USDA Forest Service, United States
Michael Buckley, World Hardwoods, United Kingdom
Nikolai Burdin, OAO NIPIEIlesprom, Russia
Jairo Castaño, International Tropical Timber Organization, Japan
Jean Christophe Claudon, International Tropical Timber Organization, Japan
Roger Cooper, University of Wales, United Kingdom
Ariane Crevecoeur, CEPI, Belgium
Guillaume Daelmans, Fédération Belge du Commerce d'Importation du Bois, Belgium
Pierre-Marie Desclos, Forest Products Consultant, Italy
Matthias Dieter, University of Hamburg, Germany
Ralf Dümmer, Ernährungwirtschaft, Germany
Ivan Eastin, Center for International Trade in Forest Products, University of Washington, United States
Håkan Ekström, Wood Resources International, United States
Chris Gaston, FPInnovations – Forintek Division, Canada
Carl-Éric Guertin, Quebec Wood Export Bureau, Canada
Lindsey Farquharson, University of Wales, United Kingdom
Ben Gunneberg, Pan European Forest Certification Council, Luxembourg
Riitta Hänninen, Finnish Forest Research Institute, Finland
Eric Hansen, Oregon State University, United States
Bénédicte Hendrickx, European Panel Federation, Belgium
Aimee Herridge, UN Library, Geneva
Sebastian Hetsch, Consultant, Germany
Bengt Hillring, Swedish University of Agricultural Sciences, Sweden
Yanjie Hu, Chinese Academy of Forestry, China
Peter Ince, USDA Forest Service, United States
Filip de Jaeger, CEI-Bois, Belgium
Hans Jansen, UNECE, Switzerland
Ronald Jansen, UN Statistics Division, United States
Heikki Juslin, University of Helsinki, Finland
Emiko Kato, Japan Wood-Products Information & Research Center, Japan
Olli Kaukonen, University of Helsinki, Finland
Nick Kent, North American Wholesale Lumber Association, United States

Eric Kilby, CEPI, Belgium
Jan-Eirik Kjeldsen, Ecole Superieur du Bois, France
Line Konstat, UNECE, Switzerland
Robert Kozak, University of British Columbia, Canada
Igors Krasavcevs, Latvian Forest Industry Federation, Latvia
Florian Kraxner, International Institute for Applied Systems Analysis, Austria
Arvydas Lebedys, FAO, Italy
Nico Leek, Probos, Netherlands
Fengming Lin, Chinese Academy of Forestry, China
Bernard Lombard, CEPI, Belgium
Wenming Lu, Chinese Academy of Forestry, China
William Luppold, USDA Forest Service, United States
Warren Mabee, University of British Columbia, Canada
Elina Maki-Simola, Eurostat, Luxembourg
Bruce Michie, European Forest Institute, Finland
Markie Muryawan, UN Statistical Division, United States
Birgitta Naumburg, Ministry of Industry, Employment and Communications, Sweden
Sten Nilsson, International Institute for Applied Systems Analysis, Austria
Michael O'Halloran, Western Wood Products Association, United States
Rupert Oliver, Forest Industries Intelligence Limited, United Kingdom
Lars-Göran Olsson, Swedish Wood Association, Sweden
Olle Olsson, Swedish University of Agricultural Sciences, Sweden
Toshiaki Owari, University of Tokyo, Japan
Tapani Pahkasalo, Indufor, Finland
Heikki Pajuoja, Metsäteho, Finland
Tomás Parik, Wood and Paper, A.S., Czech Republic
Ewald Rametsteiner, Institute of Forest Sector Policy and Economics, Austria
Leila Räsänen, University of Helsinki, Finland
Craig Rawlings, Smallwood Utilization Network, United States
Helmuth Resch, University of Natural Resources, Austria
Al Schuler, USDA Forest Service, United States
Jarno Seppälä, Pöyry Forest Industry Consulting, Finland
Robert Shelburn, UNECE, Switzerland
Kunshan Shi, Chinese Academy of Forestry, China
Ken Skog, USDA Forest Service, United States
Mike Smith, Forest Information Update, New Zealand
Florian Steierer, University of Hamburg, Germany
Tatiana Stern, Swedish University of Agricultural Sciences, Sweden
Kiwami Tamamoto, Japan Wood-Products Information & Research Center, Japan
Xiufeng Tan, Chinese Academy of Forestry, China
Russell Taylor, R.E. Taylor & Associates, Ltd., Canada
Jukka Tissari, Indufor, Finland
Endre Varga, European Federation of the Parquet Industry, Belgium
David Venables, American Hardwood Export Council, United Kingdom
Rebecca Westby, USDA Forest Service, United States
Roderick Wiles, Forest Industries Intelligence Limited, United Kingdom
Nelson Y. S. Wong, International Forest List, Malaysia

STATISTICAL CORRESPONDENTS

The national statistical correspondents listed below are the key suppliers of data for this publication. We are grateful for their essential contribution and their significant efforts in collecting and preparing the data. Complete contact information for the correspondents is provided in the publication *Forest Products Statistics*.[1]

Ashot Ananyan, National Statistical Service, Armenia

Ramazan Bali, Ministry of Environment and Forestry, Turkey

Anna Margret Björnsdottir, Statistics Iceland

Aija Budreiko, Ministry of Agriculture, Latvia

Nikolai Burdin, OAO NIPIEIlesprom, Russian Federation

Josefa Carvalho, Direcçao Geral dos Ressoursos Florestais, Portugal

Guillaume Daelmans, Fédération Belge du Commerce d'Importation de Bois, Belgium

Mira Dojcinovska, State Statistical Office of the Republic of Macedonia

Simon Gillam, Forestry Commission, United Kingdom

Branko Glavonjic, Belgrade State University, Serbia

Hanne Haanaes, Statistics Norway - Statistisk sentralbyrå, Norway

Johannes Hangler, Federal Ministry of Agriculture, Forestry, Environment and Water Management, Austria

Eugene Hendrick, COFORD (National Council for Forest R&D), Ireland

James L. Howard, USDA Forest Service, United States

Aristides Ioannou, Ministry of Agriculture, Natural Resources and Environment, Cyprus

Constanta Istratescu, National Institute of Wood, Romania

Surendra Joshi, National Board of Forestry, Skogsstyrelsen, Sweden

Peter Kottek, State Forest Service, Hungary

Nico Leek, Probos, Netherlands

Angelo Mariano, Ministry of Agricultural and Forest Policies, Italy

Anthony Mifsud, Agricultural Research and Development Centre, Malta

Michel-Paul Morel, Ministère de l'Agriculture et de la Pêche, France

Darko Motik, University of Zagreb, Croatia

Mika Mustonen, Finnish Forest Research Institute, Finland

Yuri M. Ostapchuk, State Committee on Statistics of Ukraine

Tatiana Pasi, Swiss Federal Office for the Environment

Birger Rausche, Federal Ministry of Food, Agriculture and Consumer Protection, Germany

Annie Savoie, Natural Resources Canada

Václav Stránský, Ministry of Agriculture, Czech Republic

Wladyslaw Strykowski, Wood Technology Institute, Poland

Rafael S. Suleymanov, State Statistical Committee of Azerbaijan Republic

Verena Surappaeva, State Forest Service, Kyrgyzstan

Roman Svitok, Forest Research Institute, Slovakia

Irena Tomsic, Statistical Office of the Republic of Slovenia, Slovenia

Mati Valgepea, Estonian Center of Forest Protection and Silviculture, Estonia

Roberto Vallejo Bombin, Ministry of Environment, Spain

Darius Vizlenskas, State Forest Survey Service, Lithuania

Frank Wolter, Forest Administration of Luxembourg

---

[1] *Forest Products Statistics* is available at: www.unece.org/trade/timber/mis/fp-stats.htm

DATA SOURCES

The data on which the *Forest Products Annual Market Review* is based are collected from official national correspondents[2] through the FAO/UNECE/Eurostat/ITTO Joint Forest Sector Questionnaire, distributed in April 2007. Within the 56-country UNECE region, data for the 29 EU and EFTA countries are collected and validated by Eurostat, and for other UNECE countries by UNECE/FAO Geneva.

The statistics for this *Review* are from the TIMBER database system. As the database is continually being updated, any one publication's analysis is only a snapshot of the database at that particular time. The database and questionnaires are in a state of permanent development. Data quality differs between countries, products and years. Improvement of data quality is a continuing task of the secretariat, paying special attention to the CIS and south eastern European countries. With our partner organizations and national correspondents, we strongly believe that the quality of the international statistical base for analysis of the forest products sector is steadily improving. Our goal is to have a single, complete, current database, validated by national correspondents, with the same figures available from FAO in Rome, Eurostat in Luxembourg, ITTO in Yokohama and UNECE/FAO in Geneva. We are convinced that the data set used in the *Review* is the best available anywhere as of July 2007. The data appearing in this publication form only a small part of the total data available. *Forest Products Statistics* will include all of the data available for the years 2002-2006. The TIMBER database is available on the website of the joint Timber Committee and European Forestry Commission at http://www.unece.org/trade/timber/mis/fp-stats.htm#Database

The secretariat is grateful that correspondents provided actual statistics for 2006 and, in the absence of formal statistics, their best estimates. Therefore all statistics for 2006 are provisional and subject to confirmation next year. The responsibility for national data lies with the national correspondents. The official data supplied by the correspondents account for the great majority of records. In some cases, where no data were supplied, or when data were confidential, the secretariat has estimated figures to keep region and product aggregations comparable and to maintain comparability over time. Estimations are flagged within this publication, but only for products at the lowest level of aggregation.

Despite the best efforts of all concerned, a number of significant problems remain. Chief among these problems are differing definitions, especially when these are not mentioned, and unrecorded removals and production. In certain cases, for example woodfuel removals, the officially reported data can be only 20% of actual figures. Conversions into the standard units used here are also not necessarily done in a consistent manner.

In addition to the official statistics received by questionnaire, trade association and government statistics are used to complete the analysis for 2006 and early 2007. Supplementary information came from experts, including national statistical correspondents, trade journals and internet sites. Most of these sources are cited where they occur in the text, at the end of the chapters, on the list of contributors and in the annex reference list.

EXPLANATORY NOTES

"Apparent consumption" is calculated by adding a country's production to imports and subtracting exports. Apparent consumption volumes are not adjusted for levels of stocks.

"Net trade" is the balance of exports and imports and is positive for net exports, i.e. when exports exceed imports, and is negative for net imports, i.e. when imports exceed exports. Trade data for the twenty-five European Union countries include intra-EU trade, which is often estimated by the countries. Export data usually include re-exports. Subregional trade aggregates in tables include trade occurring between countries of the sub-region.

For a breakdown of the regions please see the map in the annex. References to EU refer to the 25 countries members of the EU in 2006. The term CIS refers to the 12 countries of the Commonwealth of Independent States.

The term "softwood" is used synonymously with "coniferous". "Hardwood" is used synonymously with "non-coniferous" or "broadleaved". More definitions appear in the electronic annex.

All references to "ton" or "tons" in this text represent the metric unit of 1,000 kilograms (kg).

Please note that all US and Canadian softwood lumber production and trade are in solid m^3, converted from nominal m^3. An explanation of this is provided in the Forest Products Annual Market Review, 2001-2002, page 84.

The use of the term "oven-dry" in this text is used in relation to the weight of a product in a completely dry state, e.g. an oven-dry metric ton of wood fibre means 1,000 kg of wood fibre containing no moisture at all.

---

[2] Correspondents are listed with their complete contact details at www.unece.org/trade/timber/mis/fp-stats.htm

SYMBOLS AND ABBREVIATIONS USED

(Infrequently used abbreviations spelled out in the text may not be listed again here.)

…	not available
€	euro
$	United States dollar unless otherwise specified
ATFS	American Tree Farm System
B.C.	British Columbia, Canada
BJC	builders' joinery and carpentry
CFP	certified forest product
CIS	Commonwealth of Independent States
CO_2	carbon dioxide
CoC	chain-of-custody
CSA	Canadian Standards Association
EFI	European Forest Institute
EFTA	European Free Trade Association
EQ	equivalent of wood in the rough
EU	European Union
EWPs	engineered wood products
FSC	Forest Stewardship Council
GDP	gross domestic product
GHG	greenhouse gas
GWh	giga watt
ha	hectare
IMF	International Monetary Fund
ITTO	International Tropical Timber Organization
kWh	kilowatt hour
LVL	laminated veneer lumber
m.t.	metric ton
m^2	square metre
m^3	cubic metre
MDF	medium density fibreboard
NGO	non governmental organization
OSB	oriented strand board
PEFC	Programme for the Endorsement of Forest Certification Schemes
PJ	petajoule
PoC	Province of China
SAR	Hong Kong Special Administrative Region of China
SFI	Sustainable Forestry Initiative
SFM	sustainable forest management
STEM	Swedish Energy Agency
VAWPs	value-added wood products

Chapter 1
Wood energy policies and markets reshaping entire forest sector: Overview of forest products markets and policies, 2006-2007[3]

Highlights

- In 2006, United States house construction fell sharply, dragging down North American forest products markets, notably for sawnwood; however, stronger European and CIS markets pushed UNECE region consumption of wood and paper products to record volumes.

- Responding to climate change and energy security concerns, government policies in Europe and North America are accelerating woodfuel demand to meet targets for renewable energy.

- Rising demand for wood energy, in addition to the wood and paper industry's increasing demand for wood raw materials, necessitates mobilizing more wood, which is reshaping the entire forest sector, with long-term opportunities and short-term consequences.

- Certified forest area reached 292 million hectares worldwide by mid-2007, with most in the UNECE region, where in addition to wood, other products are being certified, including woodfuel and non-wood forest products.

- China now leads the world in both roundwood imports and furniture exports, which has stimulated imports of roundwood and sawnwood from the UNECE region, and is an existential threat for some of the region's furniture manufacturers.

- In Europe, strong growth in both production and consumption of sawn softwood occurred in 2006, with increased prices for sawlogs and sawnwood; conversely, North American markets fell and prices dropped.

- Investments in European wood processing capacity, at times with EU assistance and at times by multi-national companies, have created greater demand for industrial roundwood and more production of wood products for both domestic and export markets.

- Russia implemented a far-reaching Forest Code to improve the whole sector, and then initiated rising export taxes on roundwood in mid-2007; however, there were numerous start-up complications.

- A longstanding US-Canada Softwood Lumber Agreement was resolved with a new seven-year trade agreement in 2006, but it remains controversial.

- Germany became Europe's largest sawnwood producer in 2004, and its production of sawn softwood escalated again in 2006, by 12%; together with higher demand for wood for energy and other wood products, roundwood removals continued their rapid climb in 2006, by over 9%.

---

[3] By Mr. Ed Pepke, UNECE/FAO Timber Section, Switzerland.

1.1   Introduction

This overview chapter of the *Forest Products Annual Market Review, 2006-2007* (*Review*) provides a summary analysis of forest products markets and policy developments in the UNECE region and its three subregions: Europe, North America and the Commonwealth of Independent States (CIS). The chapter first presents the market developments and then the policy developments, yet it is impossible to completely separate their interactions.

Two themes permeate this *Review*: wood energy and mobilization of more wood raw materials, and softwood markets. The first theme is in line with the UNECE/FAO Policy Forum scheduled on 10 October 2007 titled, "Opportunities and impacts of bioenergy policies and targets on the forest and other sectors." The second theme is in preparation for the first joint UNECE Timber Committee and International Softwood Conference Market Discussions to be held on 8 and 9 October 2007.

Since this chapter can only summarize the key findings of this year's analysis, readers are encouraged to seek further market and policy details in the following 11 chapters, which begin with an analysis of policy issues, and then the economic developments affecting forest products markets. A chapter is devoted to each primary wood products market sector, including wood raw materials, sawn softwood, sawn hardwoods, panels, paper, paperboard and woodpulp, wood energy and tropical timber. Two additional chapters cover certified forest products markets and value-added wood products.

Considerable additional information may be found in the *Review's* electronic annexes of statistical tables available on the UNECE Timber Committee and FAO European Forestry Commission website.[4]

The second chapter of this *Review*, "Forest product market and policy interactions, 2006-2007", analyses the following policies areas, which are summarized in this chapter:

- Policy dilemmas due to rising bioenergy demand, including sustainable mobilization of more wood.
- Trade trends and policy issues.
  - o China's growing influence on world markets as wood consumer and trader.
  - o Measures to tackle illegal logging and trade.
  - o US and Canada Softwood Lumber Agreement.
  - o Reducing the forest sector's footprint worldwide: Corporate social responsibility.
- Russian forest-sector reform: a new forest code and export regime.
- Research and development policies.

_____

[4] www.unece.org/trade/timber/mis/fpama.htm.

1.2   Market developments

1.2.1   *Regional and subregional developments*

Forest products markets in the UNECE region moved up slightly in 2006 to remain at a record level of consumption (table 1.1.1). However, trends were far from consistent between the three subregions (graph 1.1.1). Currently, consumption in North America, the largest consuming subregion, fell by 1.8% in 2006, primarily due to a severe downturn in US housing construction, by 13% in 2006; another 18% drop is forecast for 2007. In turn, Canada's wood products production, most of which is destined for US markets, also fell, compounded by reduced harvests in some provinces, the strengthening currency and insect outbreaks. In North America, these problems together have resulted in panel, paper and sawmill closures and reduced output and profitability for those that have stayed in production. In certain localities and product sectors, market analysts have termed the situation catastrophic.

GRAPH 1.1.1

Consumption of forest products in the UNECE region, region, 2002-2006

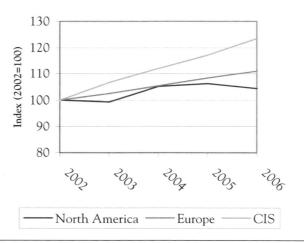

Source: UNECE/FAO TIMBER database, 2007.

TABLE 1.1.1

Apparent consumption of sawnwood[a], wood-based panels[b] and paper and paperboard in UNECE region, 2002-2006

	Thousand	2002	2003	2004	2005	2006	Change 2005 to 2006	
							Volume	%
Europe								
Sawnwood	m³	107 807	110 692	114 636	116 485	120 389	3 904	3.4
Panels	m³	55 382	57 968	62 716	65 328	67 347	2 019	3.1
Paper and paperboard	m.t.	89 582	91 002	91 721	94 592	96 272	1 680	1.8
Total	m³ EQ[c]	564 786	578 351	594 699	611 568	626 740	15 172	2.5
of which: EU25								
Sawnwood	m³	93 905	96 471	99 382	100 440	102 926	2 487	2.5
Panels	m³	49 593	51 424	55 214	56 341	57 983	1 642	2.9
Paper and paperboard	m.t.	82 470	83 770	84 349	85 585	87 292	1 707	2.0
Total	m³ EQ[c]	509 169	520 612	533 298	540 982	553 375	12 394	2.3
CIS								
Sawnwood[d]	m³	13 217	12 319	12 443	11 591	10 584	-1 007	-8.7
Panels	m³	6 740	8 212	9 132	10 197	11 879	1 681	16.5
Paper and paperboard	m.t.	5 706	6 432	6 763	7 444	8 075	630	8.5
Total	m³ EQ[c]	51 276	54 653	57 445	60 098	63 314	3 216	5.4
North America								
Sawnwood	m³	144 148	140 129	155 488	157 372	149 815	-7 558	-4.8
Panels	m³	60 106	62 580	66 524	69 070	69 577	507	0.7
Paper and paperboard	m.t.	97 248	96 570	98 614	98 603	98 298	-304	-0.3
Total	m³ EQ[c]	656 476	651 708	689 521	696 571	684 257	-12 314	-1.8
UNECE region								
Sawnwood	m³	265 172	263 140	282 568	285 449	280 788	-4 661	-1.6
Panels	m³	122 229	128 761	138 372	144 595	148 802	4 207	2.9
Paper and paperboard	m.t.	192 536	194 003	197 098	200 639	202 645	2 006	1.0
Total	m³ EQ[c]	1 272 538	1 284 712	1 341 666	1 368 237	1 374 311	6 074	0.4

Notes: a. Excluding sleepers; b. Excluding veneer sheets; c. Equivalent of wood in the rough; d. The CIS sawnwood decrease is not accurate. 1 m³ of sawnwood and wood-based panels = 1.6 m³, 1 m.t. paper = 3.39 m³.
Source: UNECE/FAO TIMBER database, 2007.

The different products sectors are no longer moving upwards together in the region. The downturn in North American sawnwood demand registered a divergent trend in 2006, which continued in 2007 (graph 1.1.2).

In contrast to North America, wood and paper markets in Europe have risen again for the fifth straight year as measured by consumption volumes. Economies have strengthened over the last year, and in mid-2007, market indicators suggest continued growth. Sawnwood consumption moved up by 3.4%, with all of the increase for softwood, as hardwood remained steady. Panel and paper manufacturers had higher production and exports in 2006 over 2005 and received higher prices for their products.

Strongest overall growth in consumption, by over 5.4%, occurred in the CIS in 2006. This increase is certainly understated since the largest component of consumption, sawn softwood, is calculated as another year of falling consumption. However, all market analysts believe that sawnwood consumption increased in 2006, and has been increasing for years, contrary to the official statistics. The main reason given for the statistical anomaly is that most sawmills are small- and medium-size enterprises, which produce for the local market and do not report their production. In Russia, the 400 largest sawmills are export market-oriented, and therefore customs declarations show high exports, which have been growing much faster than the official production statistics.

GRAPH 1.1.2

Consumption by wood products sector in Europe and North America subregions, 2002-2006

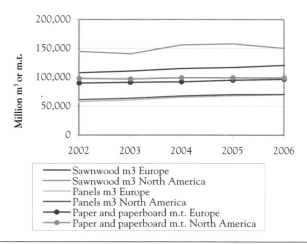

Source: UNECE/FAO TIMBER database, 2007.

Wood energy markets accelerated in 2006 and 2007, driven by record-high fossil fuel prices and government policies to achieve energy security and to mitigate climate change. The entire forest sector was affected, from forest owners to wood-based energy and wood and paper products producers. Competition for wood raw material resulted in local shortage and higher prices. While advantageous for landowners and by-product producers, panel and paper product manufacturers were impacted, especially in Europe.

Currency exchange rate changes have been dramatic in 2006 and 2007, and have influenced many wood sectors' trade and profitability. The US dollar continued falling, reaching a new low level in the summer of 2007 of approximately $1.40 against the euro. Canada experienced compounding complications due to a stronger Canadian dollar, which rose to its highest levels by mid-July, gaining 10% against the US dollar. The currency valuations had direct effects on the prices in dollars and changed trade patterns: European sawn softwood exports to the US fell dramatically; US sawnwood exports benefited from the weak dollar and rising sawnwood prices in Europe; and both softwood and hardwood sawnwood exports rose in the first half of 2007.

Thus, in contrast to the previous *Review* analysis of 2005-2006, when all subregions grew to record levels, a dichotomy exists between the UNECE subregions. Although as a whole, the UNECE region's consumption advanced slightly, North America shed 12.3 million m³ of consumption, which by chance is approximately equal to the EU25 gain in consumption. All of these 2006 trends will be reviewed and 2007 and 2008 forecasts analysed at the October 2007 joint Timber Committee and International Softwood Conference Market Discussions.

1.2.2   Wood raw material markets

Increased production of sawnwood, panels and pulp and their subsequent value-added products, as well as rapidly rising wood energy in the UNECE region required greater wood raw material. However, in 2006 forest harvests actually shrank by 1.4%, down to 1.4 billion m³, since remaining storm-felled roundwood[5] from 2005 was used. Approximately 75% of the industrial roundwood is softwood species converted to sawnwood.

With climate change recognized by governments in both Europe and North America, policies are being implemented to use more biofuels, including wood. EU Member States have been introducing policies to reach the new EU target of 20% renewable energy by 2020, with consequences for the forest sector, both positive and negative, depending on viewpoints.

Climate change is blamed for a number of disasters in forests in the region in 2006 and 2007. The unusually mild 2006/2007 winter hindered harvests in Europe and Russia. In 2007, storms damaged forests in Europe. In addition, forest fires occurred in France, Greece, Switzerland, US and other countries.

Part of the reason for roundwood prices in Europe escalating to record levels in mid-2007 was the competition for wood resources between the wood processing industries and the wood energy producers. European sawmillers and pulp and panel manufacturers faced shortages of logs in 2006, despite well-documented surpluses in growing stock and annual growth in forests. Calls for greater wood mobilization led to a series of high-level meetings, which will continue at the October 2007 Policy Forum. The 2006 log shortage eased when a disastrous windstorm ripped through northern Europe in January 2007. Nevertheless, the mild European winter of 2006/2007 constrained harvesting and the storm clean-up in many European countries, as well as Russia.

The European wood industry has been tapping the forest resources of neighbouring Russia, as evidenced by record Russian industrial roundwood export levels in 2006. However, the rapid increase in primary material exports has not escaped government policy-makers, who placed a new export tax on roundwood starting in July 2007, which is scheduled to increase to a possibly unprofitable €50 per cubic metre in 2011. This tax is of such great concern for importers of Russian logs that complaints have been taken to the European Commission and the World Trade Organization (WTO). The Russian Government also enacted a new Forest Code (discussed later), which together with these export taxes, has the goal of improving the entire forest sector,

---

[5] Roundwood is divided into industrial roundwood and fuelwood. A breakdown of terminology appears in the annex of this *Review*.

and the wood and paper industry in particular, by promoting greater value-added production. As a reference, the Russian forests have annual growth of 900 million m³, in addition to the growing stock of 82 billion m³. In terms of area, they represent 25% of the global softwood forests.

North American industrial roundwood production increased despite a downturn in sawmilling and pulping demand. Log exports to Asia increased. Harvests of beetle-killed Ponderosa pine in British Columbia, and now Alberta, intensified to prevent the spread of the insects and to use the wood before it is degraded or burned.

Source: J. Bolles, 2007.

1.2.3 Wood energy markets

Climate change is the one issue creating the greatest sensation in the UNECE region forest sector, both in the forests and in the wood processing industries. Forest owners and managers benefit from the option of selling previously pre-commercial thinnings and other forest residues from timber stand improvement. Some countries have experience in harvesting forest residues and converting them into heat and electrical energy. For example, in Finland approximately 20% of their energy needs are derived from woody residues, including a large percentage of combustible industrial by-products.

The wood processing industry is not homogeneous in its views of expanding wood energy. Currently in Europe, about half of the harvests are eventually used for energy, although often as by-products from higher value processing (Steierer *et al.*, 2007). Sawmillers welcome new markets and higher prices for their residues. Panel manufacturers fear reductions in raw material and higher wood prices. Pulp manufacturers are also concerned about their raw material availability and prices, but also see potential for producing energy in addition to pulp and paper.

These developments are not yet universal across the UNECE region. Where wood energy demands are less than the available wood supply, new trade channels are being

established. For example, Sweden, which some time ago established taxes and incentives to promote wood-based energy, has been importing wood for energy, increasingly as pellets, from destinations well beyond Europe, including British Columbia, Canada. Currently, ocean freight costs are affordable for long distance shipping; however, with the record-high petroleum prices, truck transport is prohibitive for long distances, even within Sweden.

Modern, efficient wood combustion units are proving cost-competitive compared to fossil fuels, especially for municipalities and district heating. Nevertheless, concern has been raised about particulate emissions from low-efficiency combustion units without filters, and some countries have established pollution standards and regulations for new stoves.

1.2.4 Sawn softwood markets

As well documented in Chapter 3, the economic and construction overview, following the peak in late 2005 and early 2006, the dramatic downturn in US housing construction has had ramifications throughout the UNECE forest products markets and beyond, extending to other exporters to the US (graph 1.2.1). Especially hard hit were the North American sawn softwood and panels sectors. As demand plummeted, prices fell to break-even levels and mills reduced capacity or closed if they could no longer support the unprofitable situation. Mill reductions and closures have a chain of unfortunate effects on local employment, economies and forest resources management.

GRAPH 1.2.1

United States housing starts, 2004-2007

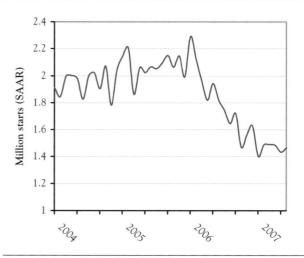

Note: SAAR = Seasonally adjusted annual rate.
Source: US Bureau of the Census, 2007.

In striking opposition to the North American situation, sawn softwood markets were strong in Europe in 2006 and early 2007. Production rose to a new record level of 110.5 million m³, consumption recorded a new high of 110.4 million m³, and Europe remained a net exporter with a yet higher level of 49.6 million m³. Demand for sawnwood was strong for both new construction and remodelling. Prices rose dramatically, increasing approximately 25% over the last two years through mid-2007. The rising prices helped sawmillers' profitability faced with rising log and energy costs.

In 2006, large sawmill capacity increases occurred in central European countries, including Germany, Czech Republic and Switzerland. Germany's demand for sawlogs and wood for energy resulted in shortages in 2006 despite rising prices and greater harvests (graph 1.2.2). The severe windstorm in northern and central Europe in January 2007 relieved the sawlog shortage, yet prices remained high (graph 1.2.3).

GRAPH 1.2.2

Industrial roundwood, fuelwood and sawnwood production in Germany, 1996-2006

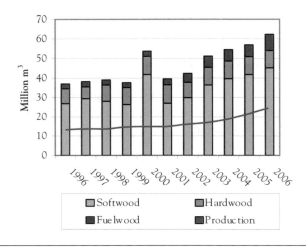

Notes: The authors believe that the official fuelwood statistics underestimate the actual production. The abnormally high production in 2000, which has now been surpassed, resulted from the windstorms in December 1999.
Source: UNECE/FAO TIMBER database, 2007.

European exporters quickly left the formerly lucrative US market and expanded markets in Asia and the Middle East. On the other hand, the weak US dollar enabled North American exporters to penetrate European markets where sawnwood prices were higher. Russian exports grew again to new record levels as new capacity was added. Foreign direct investment in Russian forest products industries, especially sawmills, panel mills, and pulp and paper mills, is taking place due to greater political and economic stability. In western Russia, joint ventures have been established by European-based multi-national companies for both a booming domestic market

and export. In eastern Russia, Chinese investors have built mills to convert logs before export.

GRAPH 1.2.3

Delivered softwood sawlog prices in Europe and Russia, 2003-2007

Source: *Wood Resource Quarterly*, Wood Resources International, 2007.

Tremendous sawmilling capacity was added in Europe in 2006 and more is scheduled for 2007 and beyond. Some of these expansions and new mills were planned before the downturn in the US market, but it is improving demand in Europe and export markets other than the US that is driving these developments. With the millions of cubic metres of capacity being added, there is renewed concern for affordable sawlogs in the short term. However, capacity is built for the long term and Europe's forests are continuously growing far more than harvests. It has become difficult for market reporters to attribute production and trade to one country when multi-national corporations are responsible.

The longstanding US-Canada Softwood Lumber Agreement entered a new phase in October 2006 when the former agreement was ended and replaced by a new seven-year trade agreement. Resolution included a return of 80% on the duties paid by Canada (about US$ 4 billion), and the remaining 20% was divided evenly between the US Government and the US sawmilling industry. Advantages for Canada with the new agreement were claimed to be: certainty of seven years of US market access; protection from decreased market share due to other countries' exports, e.g. from European countries; and freedom for British Columbia to manage its timber pricing system to take into account the mountain pine beetle epidemic. The new agreement still has export taxes based on sawnwood prices and quotas. By mid-2007, disputes have already arisen on interpretation of the agreement's trigger mechanisms and funding procedures for Canadian federal and provincial forestry programmes.

1.2.5   Sawn hardwood markets

Sawn hardwood production rose in Europe by 3.2% to reach 16.0 million m³. With stable consumption in Europe, however, more sawnwood was exported. Greater value-added processing is occurring in eastern Europe and in Asia, where much of the sawnwood was exported. Hardwood flooring has been increasingly popular since 2004.

Most of the sawn hardwood in the UNECE region is produced and consumed in the US. For a number of years, imported furniture, cabinets and component parts, sometimes produced from US species, have grown rapidly to the detriment of the hardwood industry. Severe restructuring has taken place in the furniture, flooring and sawnwood manufacturers, and capacity has been curtailed. In the face of less expensive imported furniture, US furniture companies have maintained their strength in marketing and have invested in production outside the US, for example in Mexico and Asia. Currently, 60% of the furniture exports from China are produced by US joint ventures in China, 43% of which go to the US.[6]

US exports of sawn hardwood rose, with more volume going to Asia. CIS hardwood exports increased strongly on smaller volumes. European prices also climbed higher, as did US white oak prices; however, many other US species prices fell.

1.2.6   Panel markets

Despite the divergence again in the subregions' market movements, with strength in Europe and the CIS and weakness in North America, one similarity is increased production costs for wood raw materials, resins and energy.

In Europe, production, exports and consumption all rose by about 3% from 2005 to 2006. Non-structural boards, such as MDF, advanced the most, by 12.3% to a new record volume of 11.7 million m³. In contrast to other panels, Europe is a net importer of plywood, with imports growing primarily from Russia, China and Brazil. However, in 2006, Brazilian plywood lost market share in both Europe and the US because of decreased production, a port strike, competition with Chinese exports, higher log and therefore plywood prices, and a government clampdown on illegal logging which reduced harvests.

European panel manufacturers have experienced competition from the wood energy sector for their wood raw materials. Wood costs as well as other manufacturing costs, such as resins and energy, have risen, and the industry is seeking solutions to mobilize more wood.

Profitability was assisted by rising prices for plywood, particle board and OSB in 2006 and early 2007.

In North America the overall 2006 results show little change from 2005. But linked to the US housing slump, panel markets weakened in the second half of 2006 and have been falling in 2007. Despite a drop in consumption, some panel capacity is scheduled to come on stream, which could reinforce the drop in prices. While less than Europe, there is some competition for raw materials with the energy sector.

Russian panel manufacturing has benefited from foreign direct investment and strong domestic and export markets. Russia is currently a net importer of panels, but this could change with new capacity.

1.2.7   Paper, paperboard and woodpulp markets

In 2006 in the UNECE region, paper, paperboard and woodpulp markets grew; nevertheless, there were diverging developments in the subregions: Europe and the CIS generally improved, while North American markets weakened.

North American manufacturers have reduced capacity, and with demand down marginally and a weak US dollar, prices rose to ten-year highs in early 2007. Prices also rose in Europe.

The climate change issue has put the spotlight on the pulp and paper industry, because they are the largest producer and user of renewable energy sources based on wood. Projects to produce woodfuels could eventually lead to manufacturers producing more value in energy than in pulp and paper. Governments are supporting R&D in integrated biorefineries.

The International Council of Forest and Paper Associations issued a sustainability report in 2007, which shows continued environmental progress, and rising paper recovery targets.

Russia's paper consumption climbed 11.1% on a per capita basis, and production continues to increase due to joint ventures with multi-national corporations. Despite more production and exports, Russia's paper trade deficit continued growing in 2006.

1.2.8   Certified forest products

The area of forests certified for sustainable forest management grew slower in 2006, reaching 292 million ha by mid-2007 (graph 1.2.4). Approximately 84% of the certified forests are in the northern hemisphere, indicating that most are in the UNECE region. Most of the certified area is in North America and Europe, and Russia is starting to apply limited certification. Despite the continued growth in certification, only 8.3% of the world's forests have been certified during the last 12 years.

---

[6] *China Forest Products Market Information.* April 2007. ITTO and the Tropical Forest Products Information and Consultation Center of China.

The original target of certification, tropical deforestation, continues at an alarming rate.

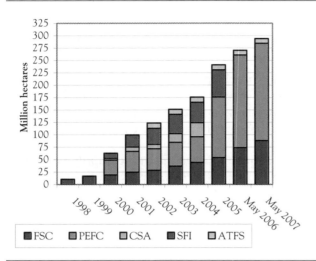

GRAPH 1.2.4

Forest area certified by major certification schemes, 1998-2007

Notes: As of May 2007, approximately 2.3 million ha have been certified by more than one scheme. The graph therefore shows a slightly higher amount of total forest area certified than in reality.

FSC=Forest Stewardship Council; PEFC=Programme for the Endorsement of Forest Certification Schemes; CSA=Canadian Standards Association Sustainable Forest Management Program (endorsed by PEFC in 2005); SFI=Sustainable Forestry Initiative (endorsed by PEFC in 2005); ATFS=American Tree Farm System.

Sources: Individual certification systems and the Canadian Sustainable Forestry Certification Coalition, 2007.

In addition to wood, other products are being certified, including woodfuel and non-wood forest products. Plantation-produced wood is a driver for certification, and approximately half of certified forests are classified as plantations, mixed plantations and semi-natural forests.

The major challenge for certification systems is building demand for certified forest products. Due to low consumer awareness, and therefore demand, as well as the lack of incentive for the producer, the vast majority of certified forest products are marketed without any reference to certification. The Timber Committee believes that one of certification's attributes is communication from seller to buyer, an opportunity missed by non-labelled products.

As there is no mutual recognition between the two major international certification systems, a growing trend is dual certification of the same forest. This enables producers to sell to both markets.

1.2.9 Value-added wood products markets

Some changes are occurring in UNECE region forest products markets, with sawnwood and panels being "consumed" within countries and processed into value-added wood products (VAWPs) for export. The development of the Baltic countries is a good example of a rapid evolution from sawnwood export-orientation to production of more profitable VAWPs.

Four of the five largest importers of VAWPs are in the UNECE region: US, Germany, France and UK (the fifth being Japan). Imports rose slightly in 2006 for the three products tracked in this *Review*: furniture, builders' joinery and carpentry and profiled wood. Rising imports are controversial for domestic manufacturers who have occasionally succeeded in obtaining anti-dumping duties in some cases. A more long-term approach is the proposed creation of the World Furniture Federation, expected in September 2007.

Manufacturers of engineered wood products (EWPs), including glulam, laminated veneer lumber and I-beams, suffered a setback when their major market, residential construction, turned steeply down in the US. From 60 to 75% of all EWPs are destined for house construction.

1.2.10 Tropical timber markets

Production of tropical timber products increased in 2006: for logs, by 10.6%; for sawnwood, by 13.0%; for plywood, by 10.2%; and for veneer, by 2.9%. Consumption increased in tropical countries, and exports fell for logs and sawnwood, but rose for plywood. Log exports have been falling due to government policies for forest conservation and value-added production promotion.

Tropical countries imports, including within tropical regions, remain stable, with all of the above products remaining net imports, with the exception of plywood. Half of Brazilian softwood plywood is exported to the US despite an 8% import tax and an unfavourable exchange rate. With the downturn in the US market, however, exporters are seeking other markets, for example in the EU. China is the largest importer of tropical logs, most of which is used for plywood production, which was forecast by the International Tropic Timber Organization (ITTO) to double between 2004 and 2007. Brazilian export markets faced heavy competition from Chinese exporters. Prices for most tropical timber products strengthened in 2006, especially plywood.

Tropical value-added products continue their long-term upward trend, breaking the $10 billion mark in 2005. In value terms, 55% is furniture. Tropical producers face stiff competition from Asian producers for the two main markets, US and Japan. With the elimination of China's furniture import tariffs, tropical VAWP producers expect to establish a new export channel.

1.3   Policy developments

In 2006 and 2007, the most important policies affecting forest products markets are those related to mitigation of climate change through increased use of renewable energy. In the forest products sector, policies related to climate change have the main impact on wood energy. A number of other national and international policies interact to affect forest products markets in 2006 and 2007, as well as in the future. One notable development is the new 2007 Russian Forest Code and export taxes, which will have international ramifications.

1.3.1   *Wood energy policies*

The record-high oil price in 2007, which reached $77 per barrel for Brent crude in mid-July, has driven policy-makers, wood products producers and individuals to seek alternatives. In addition to the high prices, other incentives include reducing climate change and energy security.

In early 2007, the UN Intergovernmental Panel on Climate Change declared that the evidence of a warming trend is "unequivocal," and that human activity has "very likely" been the driving force in that change over the last 50 years (Intergovernmental Panel on Climate Change, 2007). US business groups have joined together to call for federal regulation of greenhouse gases. The public interest was raised by the Oscar-winning documentary, "An Inconvenient Truth," by former US Vice President Al Gore.

Wood energy production is not new, and the technology for efficient, clean combustion exists in the UNECE region. What is new are the promotional policies, sometimes with incentives and subsidies, to stimulate achievement of targets such as the EU 20% renewable energy by 2020. Countries such as Sweden enacted legislation years ago to promote wood energy, with the result of totally new trade channels, for example importing woodfuel pellets from British Columbia, Canada. Ocean freight costs are sufficiently low to enable shipping great distances, yet truck transport costs are too high to allow shorter hauls by land. R&D is intensely seeking new fuels from wood that could be transported greater distances or that could economically replace gasoline and diesel fuels.

In the short term, it is difficult to simply increase harvests and use of by-products to satisfy growing energy demand. Competition for raw material to produce wood and paper products as well as energy is therefore increasing, especially in Europe. Along with steep increases in energy and transport costs, this is one more factor that has led to the current record-high roundwood prices in Europe.

The forest products industry has always been a producer and user of wood energy, and much of the nearly 50% of roundwood equivalent used for energy in Europe is by the wood industries for process heat, steam and increasingly electricity. In both Europe and North America, the industry can find support to invest in wood energy, including loan guarantees and subsidies.

While the US Government has not set targets to reduce greenhouse gas (GHG) emissions, many states have targets. Some states have established mandatory trading mechanisms for carbon credits and others have voluntary mechanisms. The US Environmental Protection Agency estimated sequestration of over 10% of the US GHG emissions via such schemes in 2006.

Encouragement of bioenergy development is occurring in many countries through subsidies and other fiscal measures. This new market provides outlets for forest owners for woody biomass and for wood products manufacturers for by-products. However, such actions have increased raw material costs in some regions, placing pressure on longstanding wood industries that are vital in providing rural employment. Thus, it is important that strategies for developing wood energy take a comprehensive, multi-sector approach. They must consider enhancement of overall market and revenue potential of the entire sector, without compromising the future of wood-using industries. National forestry programmes should be reconciled with biomass action plans to avoid market distortions through the contradictory use of fiscal measures. Specific subregional, national and sub-national conditions need to be respected when developing bioenergy strategies, which should support the achievement of global commitments. A guiding principle is that all strategies and measures must be within the limits of sustainable forest management, a reality that warrants continual reassessment against emerging policies and guidelines (UNECE Timber Committee and FAO European Forestry Commission, 2007).

1.3.2   *Policies for mobilization of wood*

To meet the targets for wood energy and the increasing demand from other wood processing industries, more wood will need to be harvested and recovered. Most processing by-products are already used. Increased harvests while remaining within sustainability are possible in the UNECE region. There is a short-term constraint in infrastructure that will prevent rapid developments. In the medium term, more harvesting equipment and transportation means are anticipated. For the medium- and long-term goals, more research is needed on the balance between supply and demand; UNECE/FAO and partners initiated such a study in 2007.

The UNECE/FAO Workshop on Wood Mobilization, held in January 2007, concluded with these strategies for implementation of policies to mobilize more wood:[7]

- Governments, with the participation of all stakeholders, should take the lead to develop policies and strategies that are holistic and inclusive, coordinated with frameworks for other sectors, that address issues at the appropriate level (local, subnational, national regional), and that are based on sound information.

- There is an urgent need for reliable information on the realistic potential for and consequences of increased wood mobilization.

- There is a need to empower forest owners to form "clusters" and improve wood-supply capacities through cooperation and servicing professional units (cooperatives).

- Education and training should play a central role in mobilizing wood resources.

- Governments and industry should facilitate access to and utilization of the resource

- Governments, the research community and industry should stimulate knowledge development, identification and transfer, as well as innovation.

- The potential of forest certification systems requires analysis to secure a level playing field for wood and woody biomass markets.

Source: Finnish Forest Research Institute, 2007.

1.3.3 China's forest products markets

It is fruitless to repeat the superlatives concerning China's rapid rise as an importer of primary forest products and an exporter of processed wood products (graphs 1.3.1-1.3.4). China is both an importer of wood raw materials from the UNECE region as well as increasingly an exporter of finished and semi-finished products to UNECE region markets.

www.unece.org/trade/timber/workshops/2007/wmw/recomm.htm#top

GRAPH 1.3.1

Chinese forest products output, 1997-2006

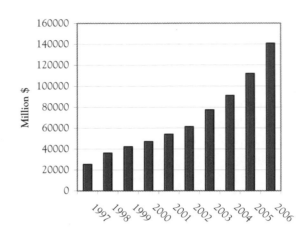

Note: Includes roundwood, sawnwood, panels, paper and pulp.
Source: Lu, W., 2007.

In June 2007, China's trade surplus for all products, not just wood products, was 83% greater than in the first six months of 2006. Economists forecast that the 2007 trade surplus could be $250 to $300 billion, compared with the record $177 billion in 2006 (*Wall Street Journal Europe*, 2007).

GRAPH 1.3.2

Chinese forest products production, 1997-2006

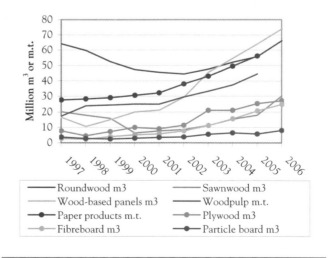

Source: Tan, X. *et al.*, 2007.

GRAPH 1.3.3

Chinese forest products exports, 1997-2006

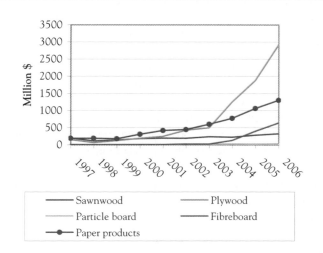

Source: Tan, X. *et al.*, 2007.

GRAPH 1.3.4

Chinese forest products imports, 1997-2006

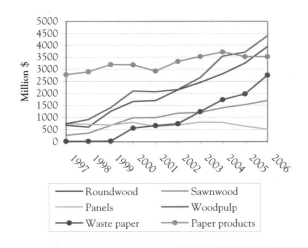

Source: Tan, X. *et al.*, 2007.

Much of China's early roundwood imports were tropical logs and China remains the leading importer of tropical timber. However, tropical countries initiated policies to promote domestic value-added processing and forest conservation laws. To support its seemingly insatiable need for industrial roundwood and paper furnish, today most of China's logs come from Russia and other CIS countries. China's increasing paper production is based in part on huge imports of recovered paper, mostly from the US. China is also the top importer of US sawn hardwood.

The Chinese Government has successfully attracted foreign investment through generous promotional policies. The weak yuan has been advantageous for their exports. Importing countries are frequently divided on the benefits and detriments of the new trade channels. For example, in the US, half of imported wooden furniture imports came from China in 2006, mainly from US joint ventures. Many other countries are investing in China due to the low manufacturing costs.

Import tariffs and anti-dumping duties have been placed on a variety of Chinese products by importing countries within the UNECE region. Furniture and panel products were previously or are currently targeted. In March 2007, the US placed tariffs on Chinese glossy paper.

Source: FAO, 2007.

1.3.4   Policies combating illegal logging and trade

In all three of the subregions, governments at federal and lower levels are enacting policies to eliminate illegal logging in their countries and prevent trade of illegally derived forest products. Within the CIS region, an acknowledged 10-30% illegal log export to China is the focus of policies on both sides of the border.

For the first time, US Congress introduced a bill to ban the import and use of illegally harvested timber and wood products of illegal origin.[8] The intent is similar to the EU Forest Law Enforcement, Governance and Trade (FLEGT).[9] These measures in the US and the EU are supported by a broad coalition of forest industry representatives, environmental organizations and government agencies.

Under the EU Timber Trade Action Plan (TTAP), members of the Timber Trade Federation (TTF) and representatives of EU Countries committed to source only verified legal timber and to harmonize purchasing policies with other European trade organizations. The TTAP works to establish chain-of-custody systems and verify legality of products. In December 2006, TTAP issued a review of codes of conduct and purchasing policies of individual TTF members. These codes of

---

[8] www.theorator.com/bills110/text/hr1497.html

[9] ec.europa.eu/environment/forests/flegt.htm

conduct are part of corporations' and timber trade associations' policies on corporate social responsibility, as discussed below.

In June 2007, the illegal logging issue was again discussed at the G8 Summit of the leaders of the wealthiest nations. The G8 Summit Declaration links illegal logging, deforestation and climate change, stating that the world leaders will "support existing processes to combat illegal logging", noting that it is "one of the most difficult obstacles to further progress in realising sustainable forest management and thereof, in protecting forests worldwide."[10]

The Timber Committee and the FAO European Forestry Commission have also discussed this serious problem in a number of forums and concluded with a number of options for actions, which remain valid, to combat illegal logging and trade at their 2004 workshop.[11]

1.3.5 Russian forest sector policies

The collapse of the Soviet Union was catastrophic for the Russian forest sector with unprecedented drops in consumption, production and trade of all forest products. Since the mid-1990s, unprocessed roundwood exports have been growing to reach one-third of harvested volumes. Although not all products have regained pre-transition levels, industrial roundwood exports are at record level, a fact that does not escape the government's attention.

GRAPH 1.3.5

Russian forest products exports evolution, 1998-2006

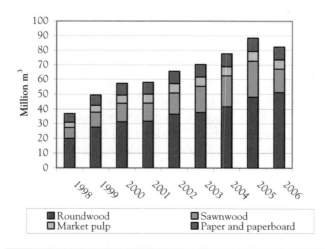

Notes: Market pulp is woodpulp produced for sale and not used by the manufacturer to make their paper. Volumes in cubic metres converted to roundwood equivalents using factors in Table 1.1.1.
Source: UNECE/FAO TIMBER database, 2007.

[10] www.g-8.de/Content/DE/Artikel/G8Gipfel/Anlage/2007-06-07-gipfeldokument-wirtschaft-eng,property=publicationFile.pdf

[11] www.unece.org/trade/timber/docs/sem/2004-1/sem-2004-1.htm

Many years of internal debate between various levels of government and the forest sector culminated in these two landmark policies in 2007: a new Forest Code and increased tariffs on roundwood exports. The Russian Forest Code adopted in January 2007 is based on "principles of rational use, conservation, protection and reproduction of forests, and enhancement of their ecological and resource potential". The new Code sets out a unified national forest policy and promotes structural reform, granting regional governments basic rights and powers in forest management, and charging them with the responsibility of managing, protecting, using and regenerating forests. As of mid-2007, many regulations were not yet implemented and many new regulations were awaiting adoption by the federal Government.

The introduction of the new Forest Code was followed by levying new duties on roundwood exports in July 2007. With 82% of the volume of all Russian exports in the graph above in logs and sawnwood and at least 40% of global softwood log exports, importers are dependent on this trade channel. The value-added processing into both primary and secondary products is thus captured outside of Russia. Russia abolished export taxes on sawnwood in May 2007. However, the higher roundwood export taxes of minimum €15 ($20) per m³, which are proposed to increase up to €50 ($68) per m³ in 2009, will completely restructure roundwood trade.

These new policies in Russia affect most of the market sectors analysed in this *Review*. Competitors and trading partners with Russia have different viewpoints, which could change from the present if the long-term restructuring takes place as planned. In mid-2007, Russian industry associations described the situation within Russia as "chaotic", with negative consequences for the wood and paper processing industries and their trade associations.

While these new policies go into effect in mid-2007, with their high expectations, it is impossible to predict whether they will achieve their objectives.

1.3.6 Corporate social responsibility policies

Forest products companies and their trade associations, especially in western Europe and North America, have established corporate social responsibility (CSR) policies. They protect the interests of their members and address public concerns about the social and environmental impacts of the sector. While some codes of conduct provide general guidelines, others require members to take more defined action.

A number of guidelines and even legislation have been enacted by Governments within the UNECE region, e.g. the UK and by the EU, by organizations such as the World Business Council for Sustainable Development; even the International Organization for Standardization is expected to launch a standard for CSR in 2008. One example of an area within these policies is sound procurement practices of legal and sustainable wood and paper products, and certification of supply sources is frequently mentioned. Many trade associations, e.g. the American Forest and Paper Association, make implementation of certification on members' forestlands a requirement for membership. While certification is not the only way of demonstrating responsibility with respect to environmental and social impacts, it is a way to verify responsible corporate behaviour.

The first UN Global Compact Leaders Summit was held in July 2007 in Geneva, Switzerland. The UN Global Compact,[12] signed by a thousand leaders of corporations, governments and international organizations, launched major public-private initiatives on climate, education, investment and water. The Secretary-General announced the establishment of a new international movement of companies dedicated to advancing responsible business practices. Most of the corporate participants held positions in corporate social responsibility. Forest products companies were among the signatories, yet currently, they represent only 1% of over 3,000 companies that participate in this programme, which "asks companies to embrace, support and enact, within their sphere of influence, a set of core values in the areas of human rights, labour standards, the environment, and anti-corruption" (UN Global Compact, 2007).

CSR has become an important marketing tool for wood and paper companies and their associations who are engaged in an increasingly environmentally and socially conscious marketplace. The Timber Committee and its Team of Specialists on Forest Products Markets and Marketing have brought attention to the inequity of uneven implementation of CSR policies across the UNECE region.

1.3.7 *Research and development policies*

Strong R&D is essential for the forest sector to continually produce competitive and innovative products that meet clients' current and future needs. A current example related to the above policies is the work carried out by universities and research institutions on biofuels, especially conversion of cellulosic fibre to liquid fuels as substitutes for fossil fuels.

A major development in forest products research occurred in 2007 in Canada. A reorganization combined three previous institutes into a new institute, FPInnovations. The intent is to provide Canada's forest industry with one of the world's largest forest sector research institutes and enhance the Canadian forest industries' ability to face global competition and associated economic and environmental challenges. FPInnovations works with a network of universities. Funding is provided by member companies, Natural Resources Canada, Environment Canada and provincial governments.

In Europe, forest products R&D is supported by national programmes and internationally by the EU's Seventh Framework Programme for Research and Technological Development (FP7) and the Cooperation in the field of Scientific and Technological Research (COST). COST has 29 separate programmes related to the forest sector. The Forest-based Sector Technology Platform is also operational in Europe and has agreed on a Strategic Research Agenda. All of these R&D programmes involve public-private partnerships and are aimed at improving the competitiveness of the sector.

1.4   References

FAO Forestry Newsroom. 2007. Available at: www.fao.org/forestry/newsroom/en/news/index.html

International Tropical Timber Organization and Tropical Forest Products Information & Consultation Center of China. 2007. *China Forest Products Market Information.* Research Institute of Forestry Policy and Information, Chinese Academy of Forestry, Beijing, China.

FAO. 2007. InfoSylva. Press Reviews via FAO Listserver. Available at: www.fao.org/forestry/site/22449/en

Global Forest Information Service. 2007. Available at: www.gfis.net/gfis/home.faces

Intergovernmental Panel on Climate Change. 2007. Climate Change 2007: Mitigation. Contribution of Working Group III to the Fourth Assessment Report of the Intergovernmental Panel on Climate Change. Edited by B. Metz, O. Davidson, P. Bosch, R. Dave and L. Meyer. Cambridge University Press, Cambridge, United Kingdom and New York, NY, USA. Available at: www.ipcc.ch/SPM040507.pdf

Lu, W. 2007. Chinese forest products statistical information. Chinese Academy of Forestry. Beijing, China.18 July 2007. Unpublished.

Martin, C. 2007. "The Environmental Third Way – Independent Certification." *Partnerships for the Planet, Stories from Geneva.* Swiss Federal Department of Foreign Affairs, the World Business Council for Sustainable Development, UN Environment Programme and the World Conservation Union. pp. 32-33. Available at: www.partnerships4planet.ch

---

[12] www.unglobalcompact.org

Steierer, F. & Fisher-Ankern, A. 2007. *Wood Energy in Europe and North America: A new estimate on volumes and flows*, UNECE/FAO/IEA/EU. Study in progress. Available at: www.unece.org/trade/timber /docs/stats-sessions/stats-29/english/report-conclusions-2007-03.pdf

Tan, X., Shi, K. & Lin, F. 2007. *The Production and Trade of Wood Products in China During 1997-2006*. Chinese Academy of Forestry. Beijing, China. (in press)

UN Comtrade/EFI. 2007. UN Comtrade database validated by European Forest Institute. Comtrade available at: comtrade.un.org; EFI available at: www.efi.fi

UN Global Compact. 2007. Available at: www.unglobalcompact.org

UNECE/FAO TIMBER Database. 2007. Available at: www.unece.org/trade/timber

Wall Street Journal Europe. 2007. "China trade surplus rises despite quality concerns." 11 July 2007.

Chapter 2
Policy issues related to forest products markets in 2006 and 2007[13]

Highlights

- Increased production of energy from woody biomass is generating intense interest on both sides of the Atlantic, with major incentives undertaken at all levels of government in North America and Europe to stimulate bioenergy investment and industry growth.

- The forestry and energy sectors are increasingly entering into joint ventures to realize potential synergies in bioenergy and biochemicals development.

- The emergence of the biomass energy industry presents an opportunity for forest owners and wood products manufacturers to diversify income sources; however, public policy development must balance both the established wood products sector and the new bioenergy sector.

- Russia enacted a new Forest Code in early 2007, which marks a fundamental shift in forest policy and brings sweeping changes to the control and management of forests.

- A Russian government decree in March 2007 dramatically increased duties on the export of logs, which could lead to significant realignment of current trading patterns, especially with China, Japan and Finland.

- Meeting increasing demands for wood raw materials throughout the UNECE region requires mobilizing additional wood resources consistent with principles of sustainable forest management.

- Chinese wood imports continued to rise in 2006, confirming China's status as the largest log importer, with the volume rising 9.5%, with over two thirds of which being imported from Russia, and one fourth from tropical forests.

- Corporate social responsibility (CSR), a little-known concept as yet in the global forestry arena, except as expressed through some forest certification programmes, is gaining traction, driven in part by the environmental standard of the International Organization for Standardization and the CSR standard.

- A January 2007 merger of Canada's principal forest products research organizations created one of the world's largest forest-sector research institutes.

- Universities within the UNECE region are increasingly teaming up with the energy sector in the conduct of bioenergy and liquid biofuels research.

---

[13] By Dr. Jim L. Bowyer, Dovetail Partners, Inc., USA; Dr. Helmuth Resch, University of Natural Resources, Austria; and Ms. Franziska Hirsch, UNECE/FAO Timber Section, Switzerland.

Secretariat introduction

The *Forest Products Annual Market Review* links market and policy developments in individual market sectors. This chapter analyses the higher policies which are influencing the production, trade and consumption of forest products. A number of market developments mentioned here are further analysed in the subsequent chapters.

Some of the categories of policy issues are the same as last year, but with significant developments. Other issues are new, raised by the authors because of their present or future impact on the forest sector. The authors will present the policy issues analysed in this chapter at the 8-9 October 2007 joint Timber Committee and International Softwood Conference Market Discussions. One theme throughout this *Review* and of the Market Discussions is wood mobilization for both wood industry processing and energy needs in the UNECE region, and the authors discuss that issue in this chapter.

The secretariat would like to express its sincere appreciation to Dr. Jim Bowyer,[14] Director of the Responsible Materials Program, Dovetail Partners Inc., and Professor Emeritus, Department of Bioproducts and Bioprocess Engineering, University of Minnesota, USA, who was again the lead author and chapter coordinator. He was joined for the second year by Dr. Helmuth Resch[15], Emeritus Professor, University of Natural Resources and Applied Life Sciences, Vienna, Austria, who provided a valuable European perspective. Ms. Franziska Hirsch[16], Policies and Institutions Specialist within the UNECE/FAO Timber Section, Geneva, provided contributions to several sections from her international perspective, as well as reviewing the entire chapter. The corporate social responsibility section was written by Ms. Natalia Vidal[17] and Dr. Robert Kozak,[18] both specialists in

this important field. Drs. Bowyer, Resch and Kozak are members of the UNECE/FAO Team of Specialists on Forest Products Markets and Marketing.

2.1 Chapter overview

This chapter focuses on the principal policies that influence markets for forest products, on the market forces most influential in driving change in established global markets and in public policy, and on new and emerging technologies that are likely to have an impact on both markets and forest-related policy.

Included in this year's report are:

2.2 Policy dilemmas due to rising bioenergy demand.

2.3 Trade trends and policy issues.

2.4 Reducing the forest sector's footprint worldwide.

2.5 Russian forest-sector reform: a new Forest Code and export regime.

Because of space limitations the reader is referred to last year's *Forest Products Annual Market Review*[19] for further discussion of some other relevant topics.

2.2 Policy dilemmas due to rising bioenergy demand

National and sub-national energy, environment and forest sector policies are accelerating wood energy developments. This analysis focuses on policy developments, and describes their general market effects, especially with regard to the near term. Chapter 10 on wood energy markets takes the opposite approach, describing market developments that are often triggered by policy developments.

2.2.1 Rising demand for wood energy

Wood is being increasingly used for energy, driven by high fossil fuel prices and new energy and environmental policies in both the developed and the developing world. In developing countries wood has long been known to be a major source of energy, often for heating and cooking. Less widely known is that the use of wood for energy production in developed countries has always been high, and in fact much higher than generally realized because of inadequate statistical systems.[20] Thus, energy production

[14] Dr. Jim L. Bowyer, Director of the Responsible Materials Program, Dovetail Partners Inc., 528 Hennepin Avenue, Suite 202, Minneapolis, Minnesota, 55403, USA and Professor Emeritus, Department of Bioproducts and Bioprocess Engineering, University of Minnesota, USA, tel: +1 612 333 0430, fax: +1 612 333 0432, e-mail: jimbowyer@comcast.net, www.dovetailinc.org.

[15] Dr. Helmuth Resch, Emeritus Professor, University of Natural Resources, Gregor Mendel Str. 33, A-1180 Vienna, Austria, tel: +43 147654 4254, fax: +431 476 544 295, e-mail: resch@boku.ac.at, www.boku.ac.at.

[16] Ms. Franziska Hirsch, Policy and Institutions Specialist, UNECE/FAO Timber Section, Trade and Timber Division, UNECE, Palais des Nations, CH-1211 Geneva 10, Switzerland, tel: +41 22 917 2480, fax: +41 22 917 0041, e-mail: Franziska.Hirsch@unece.org, www.unece.org/trade/timber.

[17] Ms. Natalia Vidal, PhD Candidate, Faculty of Forestry, University of British Columbia, Vancouver, Canada, V6T 1Z4, tel: +1 604 822 2685, fax: fax: +1 604 822 9104, e-mail: nvidal@interchange.ubc.ca, www.forestry.ubc.ca.

[18] Dr. Robert Kozak, Associate Professor, Faculty of Forestry, University of British Columbia, Vancouver, Canada, V6T 1Z4, tel: +1 604 822 2402, fax: +1 604 822 9104, rob.kozak@ubc.ca, www.forestry.ubc.ca.

[19] www.unece.org/trade/timber/docs/fpama/2006/fpamr2006.pdf, (pp. 17-29).

[20] *European Timber Trends Study V* (1996) and *European Forest Sector Outlook Study* (2005) pointed out that energy has always been the single largest end use for wood in Europe, by volume.

from wood in developed countries is not new. What is new is a high degree of policy interest and the expectation of dramatic growth in energy production from wood over the next several decades. The promotion of bioenergy policies is driven by interest in energy security and diversification as well as by the climate change commitments of the Kyoto Protocol and beyond.

In Europe and North America, harvested wood volumes for energy production are significantly higher than reported in official international statistics, based on the outcome of a study led by UNECE/FAO and published in 2007 (Steierer et al., 2007).[21] Private households increasingly consume very high volumes, especially in some countries, e.g. France and Germany, and are more often than previously realized the major consumers. In addition wood used for energy arises during wood-based industries' processing, or afterwards when wood products are recovered for energy use after their in-service life. The study concludes that while there are technical and sustainable production limits, expansion is possible for wood for energy (see chapter 9 on wood energy markets).

In Europe, electricity is generated from large-scale plants that use woody biomass or a coal/wood mixture (such as in Austria – see 2.2.4); steam and electricity from wood and black-liquor-fired boilers and cogeneration facilities for internal use by the forest products industry; ethanol made from corn (1.56 billion litres in 2006); biodiesel made primarily from rapeseed (about 4.6 million tons in 2006); pellets made of wood and other forms of biomass for home heating and electricity production (4.7 million tons in 2006); and heat from district heating systems fuelled by woody biomass. A variety of monetary incentives and subsidies are driving biofuel industry development, with impressive results. European production of ethanol, biodiesel and fuel pellets rose 71%, 45%, and 38%, respectively, in 2006 compared with the previous year. Although wood plays an important role in district heating and electricity generation, it is not yet a part of liquid fuels production, but this is likely to change as cellulosic ethanol and biodiesel technologies reach commercialization within the near future.

In North America, the bioenergy mix is much different from that in Europe, with differences largely attributed to traditional energy use patterns and the emphasis of various government incentives for biofuels development. For instance, biodiesel is not as prominent in North America as in Europe, whereas ethanol production is far greater in North America. In 2006 US production of biodiesel (primarily from soybeans) was about 1.0 million tons, only 22% that of Europe, but

ethanol production (from corn) exceeded 19 billion litres, over 12 times that of Europe. Wood fuel pellets enjoy only limited regional markets in the US and Canada, with a significant portion of annual production (1.56 million tons in 2006) exported to Europe.

In North America, as in Europe, the forest products industry is a significant producer of bioenergy for internal use. Now, however, as a result of loan guarantees, subsidies, and other incentives from the federal and state governments, along with policy changes that allow sales of power to regional grids at prevailing prices, wood products manufacturers and others have made significant investments in small (3-10 megawatt) wood-fuelled electric generating facilities in forested areas of the northern and western US, with a number of new facilities in place and under development As in Europe, biofuels production is rising rapidly. US production of biodiesel quadrupled in 2006, while ethanol and fuel pellet production each rose by about 25%.

In Europe and North America, further growth of both large- and small-scale electricity generation from wood is likely, as is continued growth in reliance on fuel pellets, particularly in Europe. It can be expected that production of ethanol and biodiesel will continue to increase, and that alternative fuels such as biobutanol will become more common. Assuming a breakthrough in cellulosic ethanol technology, cornstarch-based ethanol production will shift to cellulosic ethanol as new technologies become available. The technology shift will allow wood to become a significant contributor to liquid fuels production in both regions, though dedicated energy crops. Agricultural crop residues will continue to dominate.

2.2.2 Bioenergy as a vehicle for GHG emission reduction

Beyond the framework of reducing greenhouse gas (GHG) emissions by 8% below 1990 levels by 2012 as set out in the Kyoto Protocol, EU countries in March 2007 committed to reducing emissions by 20% by 2020, and up to 30% if other countries follow European ambitions. The EU Emissions Trading Directive began in 2005 for a trial period through 2007, instituting a mandatory "cap and trade" scheme to facilitate emission reductions before the onset of the first Kyoto commitment period 2008-2012 which foresees emissions trading as one of its flexible mechanisms for implementation.

In January 2007, the European Commission established a target of 20% of energy from renewable sources by 2020, topping the 2010 target of 12%, established through the 1997 White Paper on "Energy for the Future: Renewable Sources of Energy". The EU 2003 Directive on Biofuels, the 2005 Biomass Action Plan and the 2006 Biofuels Strategy reinforced the overall strategy

---

[21] www.unece.org/trade/timber/docs/stats-sessions/stats-29/english/report-conclusions-2007-03.pdf

of increasing renewable fuels use by setting concrete targets for energy production from biomass. The EU Forest Action Plan, promulgated in 2006 and based on the Forest Strategy of 1998, encourages the promotion of the use of forest biomass for energy generation. It recognizes the need to gather information on wood and residue availability and the use of wood for bioenergy, and to investigate the mobilization of small-diameter, low-value timber and residues for energy production.

Whereas such ambitious environmental leadership is commendable, the question arises as to the extent to which these commitments can realistically be met. Since the March 2007 decision by the European Climate Change and Energy Summit to establish new reduction (for the EU as a whole), no agreement has yet ..hed on how the 20% GHG emission reduction ..divided among the 27 EU Member States. As ...vledged by the European Commission, there is a danger of missing the EU targets for 2010, and biomass energy development in particular is lagging behind. According to the European Commission, at this point it appears that only about one half of the targeted amount of biomass utilization will be reached by 2010.

At the June 2007 G8 Summit of the world's wealthiest industrial nations[22], climate change and reduction of GHG emissions was one of the issues. Led by host Germany, the intention was to set targets of 50% reduction by 2050. However, the US agreed to "consider seriously" the targets. The Summit Declaration[23] states an agreement "that resolute and concerted international action is urgently needed in order to reduce local GHG emissions and increase energy security". The Declaration recognizes halting deforestation, especially in developing countries, as "a significant and cost-effective contribution toward mitigating GHG emissions and toward conserving biological diversity, promoting sustainable forest management and enhancing security of livelihoods". It agrees to "continue to support existing processes to combat illegal logging [which] is one of the most difficult obstacles to further progress in realising sustainable forest management and thereof, in protecting forests worldwide". The Declaration does not specifically mention wood, but refers to alternative energy sources, including biomass and cellulosic biofuels for transportation. The Summit ended with a unanimous call by G8 leaders to establish a post-2012 agreement (post-Kyoto) within the UN framework by 2009.

Source: M. Fonseca, 2007.

2.2.3 Potential impacts of carbon trading markets on forest management and wood availability

Although the US federal Government has not established targets for GHG emission reduction, recent moves on the part of several states, and most notably the northeastern states led by New York (New York, New Jersey, Vermont, Connecticut, Maine, Massachusetts, New Hampshire, Delaware and Maryland) provide a basis for future action. Under the ten-state agreement, 188 million tons of carbon credits are to be apportioned among each of the participating states. The states, in turn, will auction all or some of the credits to the 230 power plants larger than 25MW located within the region. The programme is mandatory and carries high penalties for non-compliance. The goal is to stabilize emissions through 2008, and to then begin a programme of planned reductions. Other states that have set targets for reduction of GHG emissions include California, Illinois, Minnesota, New Mexico and Washington, Other than the new northeastern states programme, all initiatives to reduce or mitigate GHG reductions are voluntary at this point. Accordingly, voluntary registries related to forestry have been established by the US Department of Energy, the State of California, and the Chicago Carbon Exchange. All of the forestry registries recognize reforestation, afforestation, forest conservation, and responsible forest management that preserves forest stocks. The Chicago and US Department of Energy registries, in addition, recognize management of urban forests. Though voluntary, the programmes appear to be having a positive effect. Examining GHG emissions related to Land Use, Land Use Change, and Forestry (LULUCF) within the US in 2004, the US Environmental Protection Agency found that sequestration of 780 million tons of CO_2 equivalent, equal to 13% of US CO_2 emissions or 11% of US GHG emissions overall, resulted from domestic LULUCF (and primarily forestry) actions (USEPA, 2006). A new forest

---

[22] Canada, France, Germany, Italy, Japan, Russia, UK and US.

[23] www.g-8.de/Content/DE/Artikel/G8Gipfel/Anlage/2007-06-07-gipfeldokument-wirtschaft-eng,property=publicationFile.pdf

carbon registry being developed as part of a carbon reductions initiative of seven northeastern states will become operational in 2009 as a mandatory programme (Ruddell et al., 2006).

EU member countries ratified the Kyoto Protocol and set up an emissions trading system (ETS) to achieve targets for reduction of CO_2 as the major GHG. The EU scheme during its first implementation period 2005-2007 covers over 11,500 energy-intensive installations across the EU, which represent close to half of Europe's emissions of CO_2, including industrial plants for the production of pulp from timber and other fibrous materials and paper and board, with a production capacity exceeding 20 tons per day. Additional installations included are combustion plants, oil refineries, coke ovens, iron and steel plants, and factories producing cement, glass, lime, brick, and ceramics. All 27 EU Member States are now in the process of preparing their national allocation plans for the ETS second commitment, coinciding with the first Kyoto commitment period 2008-2012, fixing the total of emission allocations available in each Member State and the allocation made to each installation covered by the scheme. By placing a cap on the total number of emission allowances, the objective of the scheme is to develop a functioning market in allowances, with this, in turn, enabling companies to limit or reduce their emissions at least cost.

There have, however, been significant problems with the ETS since its inception in 2005, especially due to a significant drop in carbon trading prices. Some EU Member States have allocated a higher amount of carbon emission allowance than their industry could use up. In mid-2006, trading prices collapsed, from over €30 ($40) per ton to almost €10 ($13), following reports from five countries that actual emissions were lower than expected. Most of the EU's major "polluters" emitted significantly less CO_2 than allocated; Germany, for example, was left with 44.1 million tons additional CO_2 allowances for 2006. This prompted calls for the inclusion of allocations tighter than forecasted during the upcoming second phase of the scheme beginning in 2008. In June 2007 a review of the ETS was to be presented to the Council of the European Union and the European Parliament, which will consider whether further sectors and greenhouse gases should be included. The European Commission had adopted a legislative proposal for the inclusion of the aviation sector from 2011 onwards.

In the context of the ETS, companies are allowed to use credits from Joint Implementation (JI) and the Clean Development Mechanism (CDM), up to a certain proportion of their allocation of emission allowances, to cover their emissions. Current EU and United Nations Framework Convention on Climate Change (UNFCCC) legislation also does not allow reforestation

projects to be included in Kyoto's flexible mechanisms, clean development and joint implementation. Some believe that inclusion of the forestry sector in the ETS could be achieved after the completion of the second commitment period from 2013 onwards. The European Parliament mandated the European Commission to find ways to include forestry. The Conference of the Parties to the UNFCCC agreed in November 2006 to further explore a proposal that would provide incentives to reduce deforestation emissions in developing countries; a decision on the matter can be expected during the Conference of the Parties (COP 13) in December 2007. A number of countries and coalitions such as the Coalition of Rainforest Nations have been mandating an inclusion of the recognition of emissions from deforestation as a major driver of global warming, contributing to approximately 18% of GHG emissions worldwide.

2.2.4 *Biofuels potential stimulating forest industry investment and new cooperation between forest and energy sectors*

A number of initiatives focused on bioenergy development have been mounted by forest products firms in recent years. Two examples are the late October 2006 UPM-Kymmene announcement that it will "invest strongly" to become a major second generation biodiesel producer using wood-based biomass as raw material, and a January 2007 Flambeau River Paper Company announcement that it will develop a cellulosic ethanol biorefinery facility in Park Falls, Wisconsin.

The forestry and energy sectors are also increasingly entering into joint ventures to realize potential synergies. One example of a forward-looking and innovative collaboration is perhaps Europe's largest wood biomass power plant that went on stream in the third quarter of 2006 in Vienna, Austria. Two years ago Wien-Energie (Vienna-Energy) and the Austrian Federal Forests Inc. formed a joint venture and subsequently invested €52 million ($69.1 billion) in the power plant project. When fully operational, approximately 625,000m³ of forest biomass per year will be converted to produce electricity for about 48,000 apartments, as well as hot water heating for 12,000 families. The project provides a possible template for how the forest industry can work in partnership, rather than in competition, with other sectors to realize bioenergy goals. Another example of forest industry and energy sector cooperation is reflected in an April 2007 announcement by the Chevron Corporation and the Weyerhaeuser Company. The two firms will jointly assess the feasibility of commercializing the production of economical, clean-burning second-generation biofuels for cars and trucks from cellulose-based sources.

The development of a second generation of biofuels is receiving interest by the pulp and paper industry globally. In contrast to producing ethanol through fermentation, a thermo-chemical approach achieves decomposition by means of heating and then synthesis by means of chemical engineering. Biomass can be gasified to a synthesis gas that may be further converted to a number of products such as methanol, dimethyl ether, and Fischer-Tropsch diesel. The goal is to develop commercially viable second-generation biofuels that can compete in the marketplace without subsidies. According to reports by STFI-Packforsk AB, the production costs for the second generation biofuels could be considerably less than for ethanol today. This is but one example of emerging biofuel technologies that do not rely on the use of enzymatic reactions – a current limiting factor in cellulosic ethanol commercialization.

These and similar developments could signal that bioenergy development may soon reach a stage in many UNECE region countries at which further government intervention to stimulate development is unnecessary. However, where wood energy is underdeveloped, or used inefficiently, such as in the Balkans, continued promotion of wood energy may be warranted for some time to come.

2.2.5 Sustainable mobilization of additional wood resources

Rising demand for wood energy and higher prices for wood raw materials are increasing the economic attractiveness of wood and strengthening the viability of forestry management. However, wood-processing industries face added pressure because of competition for raw materials from bioenergy producers. To meet increasing demands for wood raw materials throughout the UNECE region, it is recognized that there is a growing need for mobilization of additional wood resources consistent with principles of sustainable forest management.

There appears to be significant potential for increased wood supply if every component is developed and the supply base broadened. Potential strategies include expansion of the forest area harvested annually, further development of short rotation tree plantations, and better use of post-consumer recovered wood products (UNECE Timber Committee and FAO European Forestry Commission, 2007).

UNECE/FAO forest resource assessments have consistently shown that annual forest growth in Europe and North America far exceeds harvests. The Joint Wood Energy Enquiry, conducted by UNECE with FAO, IEA and the EU, has validated the importance and enormous potential of wood for energy. However, there is an urgent need for improved information to assess the realistic potential of wood and fibre available for mobilization as

noted by experts during the recent wood mobilization workshop (UNECE, 2007).

As identified in the EU Forest Action Plan (June, 2006), actions that might be taken to encourage the mobilization of additional wood resources include:

- Empowerment of forest owners to form "clusters" and improve supply capacities, by facilitating cooperation and the servicing of professional units.

- Facilitation of access to and utilization of forest resources on the part of Governments and industry through enhancement of infrastructure and logistics.

- Providing greater opportunity for education and training of forest owners, the workforce, and enterprises involved in forest operations.

- Involvement of the entire wood supply chain in development and implementation of appropriate policies for promoting renewable energy sources.

Source: A. Korotkov, 2006.

2.2.6 Policy challenges

The growing demand for wood for use in energy production brings new policy challenges as forests now need to satisfy not only environmental and social needs of society, and provide an economic basis for industry but also to increasingly supply an increasing part of the energy mix while contributing to climate change mitigation.

While encouragement of bioenergy development in many regions through subsidies and other fiscal measures provides new opportunities for forest owners and wood products manufacturers, such actions have increased raw material costs in some regions, placing pressure on longstanding wood industries that are vital in providing rural employment. It is thus becoming increasingly important that strategies for development of wood energy focus on enhancement of overall market and revenue potential without compromising the future of traditional wood-using industries. The objectives of forest and energy policies should, moreover, be aligned and coherence ensured with related agricultural, environmental and other policies. National forestry programmes should therefore be reconciled with biomass action plans to avoid market distortions through the contradictory use of fiscal measures. Specific regional, national and sub-national conditions need to be respected when developing bioenergy strategies, which should support the achievement of global commitments. A guiding principle is that all strategies and measures must be within the limits of sustainable forest management, a reality that warrants continual reassessment against emerging policies and guidelines (UNECE Timber Committee and FAO European Forestry Commission, 2007).

Although the present situation may be perceived as a particular challenge to part of the industry faced with steep increases in raw material prices, it can also represent a major opportunity for the sector as a whole. Bioenergy producers can seize new market opportunities. At least some of the wood-processing industries can optimize their use of raw materials, increase the efficiency of their production of energy from wood, possibly expand their businesses into bio-refinery operations, and perhaps in the process become net energy suppliers to society, as noted in the recent International Seminar on Energy and the Forest Products Industry (FAO, Rome, 2006).

As liquid fuels based on wood and other forms of cellulose will probably play an important role in the future energy mix, there may be a marked effect on markets for lower-valued wood, and this will present both significant opportunities and challenges for forest managers. Rational policy development will be needed to ensure a smooth transition to wood markets that include a substantial energy component. Policy attention is needed for the development of harvesting guidelines for forest biomass on public and private lands. Guidelines are needed for harvesting of agricultural crop residues, considering social parameters vis-à-vis food and fibre vs. energy production.

One concern regarding biofuels is the environmental impact of promotion of such fuels on global demand for palm oil. For instance, it has been noted that the recent adoption by EU Governments of a 5.75% renewable fuels goal as a percentage of all vehicle fuels has increased demand for palm oil used in biodiesel and increased investment in oil palm plantation development. The US has specifically identified palm oil as a feedstock for biodiesel in its tax code, translating to a tax credit for its use. Oil palm plantation establishment in Malaysia and Indonesia has long been linked to clearing of natural tropical forests (see photos). The apparent link between market growth for bio-based transportation fuels and conversion of natural tropical forests suggests a need for caution in developing biofuels trade policies.

There is concern about a possible increase in air pollution and its ecological and health impacts if wood combustion expands. In particular, wood combustion installations without sufficient filters or with incomplete combustion, release fine particulate matter, which is an acknowledged health hazard. Fine particles arise from many sources other than wood combustion, e.g. diesel motors. Some countries have burning device standards, but the best intentions can be compromised by low fuel quality, e.g. wet wood, and ineffective burning techniques.

Source: J. Bowyer, 1994.

Source: J. Bowyer, 1994.

Evidently, potential air pollution should receive attention in discussion of wood energy policies. As there are major consequences of increased biomass combustion, many of which are interlinked, a holistic approach is necessary when setting targets and making policies to combat climate change.

2.3 Trade trends and policy issues

With globalization, trade among nations has increased, occasionally raising concerns about raw material availability, magnifying trade issues, and triggering environmental concerns. This section highlights several current issues and concerns as well as approaches to problem resolution.

2.3.1 *China log imports continue to rise*

The volume of raw logs imported by China rose by 9.5%, to 32.15 million cubic metres, in 2006; 68% of imported volumes came from Russia, while 24% were of tropical species. The value of log imports increased more than twice as fast as import volume, reflecting supply issues and competitive pressures, and weak statistics. Given the substantial reliance on Russia for log supplies, announced increases in Russian log export duties (see 2.5.2) will substantially increase the cost of China's log supply, creating a strong incentive for developing new sources of supply or moving processing operations nearer the source of the raw material e.g. in Russia. In view of the magnitude of Chinese demand and limitations on low-cost supply resulting from Russia's actions, a significant realignment of global wood trade flows is a possibility. In March 2007, China and Russia signed a trade agreement that included provisions for cooperation on timber processing.

2.3.2 *China's rising recovered paper imports impact global markets and raise environmental concerns*

China's imports of recovered paper from North America rose by 15% in 2006 to over 9.1 million tons. The quantity of recovered paper imported from North America amounted to almost one third of the volume of recovered paper recycled into paper products within North America. European recovered paper exports to China rose by about 12% in the past year, exceeding 5 million tons for the first time. Overall, China's recovered paper imports have increased 40-fold since 1990 and have more than doubled in just the past four years. China's exports of paper and paperboard have increased as well, with export volume rising 44% in 2006 alone. From a policy perspective, the long shipping distances now common in recovered paper supply chains raise the question of whether use of recycled paper necessarily translates to lower environmental impact. It might, for example, make more sense to use recovered paper for energy production that avoids consumption of fossil fuels (Pearce, 1998).

2.3.3 *US Congress focuses on illegal timber trade*

On 14 March 2007, a bill was introduced in the US House of Representatives to ban the use of illegally harvested timber and wood products of illegal origin. Similar to language under EU Forest Law Enforcement, Governance and Trade (FLEGT)[24], the law would make it illegal to bring into the United States any timber that is taken, transported, or sold without the authority required by, or in violation of, any law that applies at the place where harvest occurs. Supported by a broad coalition of forest industry representatives, environmental organizations, and government agencies, the draft legislation[25] represents the first US attempt to legislatively address the illegal logging problem.

2.3.4 *EU FLEGT measures being prepared for implementation*

The regulation to implement the FLEGT licensing scheme was adopted by the Council of the European Union in December 2005, and further development is expected in 2007. The system will be built on a series of voluntary partnership agreements between the EU and tropical producer countries. It is hoped that the first agreements will be signed in 2007: negotiations are advancing with Cameroon, Ghana, Indonesia and Malaysia. A potential additional option under consideration is to make it illegal to import, purchase or market timber produced illegally in foreign countries (a principle similar to that of the Lacey Act in the US).

2.3.5 *EU Timber Trade Action Plan issues review of codes of conduct and purchasing policies*

Under the EU Timber Trade Action Plan (TTAP), members of the Timber Trade Federation (TTF), with representatives of EU Countries, have committed to source only verified legal timber and to harmonize purchasing policies with other European trade organizations. TTAP, in turn, is working with suppliers of European timber trade companies in establishing chain-of-custody systems and verifying the legality of their products. In December 2006, TTAP issued a review of codes of conduct and purchasing policies of individual TTF members. Findings showed that while only a few TTFs can demonstrate active implementation of purchasing commitments, two thirds have codes of conduct that commit their members to trade in legal timber and to promoting sustainable forest management, 42% require members to take specified actions toward these ends, and 25% view codes of conduct as binding on all members. The federations of Belgium, France, the Netherlands, Spain, and the UK are recognized as having made the most progress towards meeting TTAP goals, with the Netherlands' and the UK's efforts aided by government funding to support development of purchasing policies related to a broad goal of responsible

---

[24] http://ec.europa.eu/environment/forests/flegt.htm

[25] http://www.theorator.com/bills110/text/hr1497.html

purchasing. Findings also indicate that work by TFFs to develop purchasing policies has often involved environmental non-governmental organizations (ENGOs) and others, and that the process appears to have enhanced cooperation and engagement with both ENGOs and civil society. An interesting development among TFFs is that most have moved beyond environmental purchasing goals, while they continue to work on them, and have begun providing advice and services to their members regarding environmental issues in general. From a policy perspective, the TTAP model of working through industry-led national organizations and encouraging inclusive participation in standards development may provide a useful model for broader application in seeking to address issues such as illegality.

2.3.6 US and Canada Softwood Lumber Agreement may be unravelling

In October 2006, the US/Canadian Softwood Lumber Agreement went into effect, apparently ending a long-simmering trade dispute between the two countries. Now US trade officials are expressing concern about forest industry support programmes of the provinces of Quebec and Ontario, and of the federal Canadian Government, citing a provision of the agreement that prohibits "any grants or other benefits of any public authority that offset, in whole or in part, the basis for the exemption [from export measures]." The US position is that such programmes constitute subsidies, while Canada's position is that the programmes are simply intended to ensure long-term competitiveness of its forest industry and do not violate the agreement. Failure to resolve new concerns through direct consultation would result in referral of the issue to the London Court of International Arbitration for a binding ruling.

2.3.7 China paper exports trigger tariffs

In March 2007, the US announced duties on Chinese imports of high-gloss paper. Citing alleged subsidies in the form of government-financed discounts on imported manufacturing equipment and low-interest loans, countervailing duties of 10.9% and 20.35% were imposed against two specific manufacturers, with duties of 18.16% levied against all other Chinese glossy paper imports. Though imposition of the tariffs was immediate, the action is subject to administrative review; final action is expected in October. China has indicated that it will appeal the ruling in the US Federal court and the WTO. The actions vis-à-vis glossy papers follow the imposition of anti-dumping duties by the US in 2005 on Chinese crepe and tissue papers.

2.3.8 Unique suit seeks to invoke trade laws as rebuke to lax environmental enforcement

The Sierra Club and the United Steelworkers recently requested the US Department of Commerce to consider whether lax enforcement of logging laws on the part of paper-exporting countries constitutes an unfair trade subsidy. A favourable response could open the door to the use of trade law to pressure exporting countries regarding environmental performance.

Source: H. Bagley, 2007.

2.4 Reducing the forest sector's footprint worldwide

2.4.1 Russia moves to bolster national forest certification programmes

In anticipation of the implementation of mandatory certification of wood supplies and secondary forest resources through the new Forest Code, leaders of several forest certification initiatives – the Russian National Council for Forest Certification (RNCFC), an initiative supported by the Russian Ministry for Natural Resources and the World Bank, and the National Council of Voluntary Forest Certification in Russia, announced in mid-September 2006 a cooperative effort to seek PEFC endorsement. Meanwhile, the forest area certified within the Russian Federation by the Forest Stewardship Council (FSC) increased considerably in 2006, from 6.7 to 14.7 million hectares, with FSC accounting for most of the certified area within the country. The Russian Forest and Trade Network association of 33 timber companies who have committed to avoiding sourcing of timber from high conservation value forests and from illegal harvests, established under the aegis of the World Wide Fund for Nature (WWF) in 2000, account for 67% of the FSC-certified area.

2.4.2 Corporate social responsibility in the forest sector

More and more companies, from all sectors, wish to show that they are socially and environmentally responsible, and industry associations, along with others such as accountants, are drawing up standard procedures to increase uniformity and credibility. The new standards are generally referred to in terms of Corporate Social Responsibility (CSR). In addition to companies and industry associations, Governments and the EU are also contributing to the establishment of CSR procedures and norms.

CSR practices in the forestry sector currently translate into adoption of both forest certification strategies and sound procurement policies. For over a decade, forest certification has been considered one of the better indicators of responsible behaviour within the forest sector. While it is not the only way of demonstrating responsibility with respect to environmental and social impacts, it remains an important means of verifying responsible behaviour, legality and claims of sustainable practice. In addition, it has become a well-established marketing tool for companies engaged in an increasingly environmentally conscious marketplace.

Increasingly, social as well as environmental impacts are considered in raw material procurement. Industry and trade associations, especially in Europe, have been developing codes of conduct and/or purchasing policies as a way of protecting the interests of their members and addressing public concerns about the social and environmental impacts of the sector. While some codes of conduct provide general guidelines, others require members to take more defined action. Voluntary or required compliance with such codes and policies can also vary among industry organizations (Hentschel, 2006), and several – as outlined below – are currently being developed and implemented in the UNECE region.

In 2007, the World Business Council for Sustainable Development (WBCSD) is expected to publish its Responsible Procurement Guide for Customers. Concurrently, CEOs of all member companies involved in the Sustainable Forest Products Industry working group of this organization are expected to adopt a set of membership principles and responsibilities for forestry companies. These principles lay out the sustainability aspirations of member companies and reinforce their commitment to sustainable practices. Companies are expected to report progress against these principles in their regularly published sustainability reports (WBCSD, 2007).

In February 2007, the Forest Products Association of Canada (FPAC) released its first Sustainability Report. This biannual initiative reports on the progress of FPAC members against a set of environmental, social and economic indicators. FPAC members also adopted a statement on illegal logging in 2006, and as part of this commitment have agreed to purchase and use wood only from legal sources and to "trace their fibre back to the forest area of origin by the end of 2008" (FPAC, 2007).

The UK CSR policy and legislation and the European Commission CSR policy also have the potential to influence best practices in the forestry sector. The UK CSR policy and legislation aim at promoting the adoption and reporting of CSR practices. In July 2001, the Pensions Act Amendment came into effect requiring trustees of occupational pension plans to provide transparency on policies related to the social, environmental and ethical impacts of their investments. The European Commission published a Green Paper in 2001 and additional communications on CSR in 2002 and 2006. In October 2002, the Commission established the European Multi-Stakeholder Forum on CSR with a similar intent of promoting responsible practices, while the March 2006 Communication advocated targeted actions to promote CSR and announced backing for a European Alliance for CSR. The latter "is a political umbrella for new or existing CSR initiatives" by companies of all sizes and their stakeholders with the intent of increasing CSR adoption among European enterprises (European Commission, 2006).

In the UK, a provision of the "Companies Act" passed through the House of Commons and received Royal Assent in November 2006. Under this Act, UK companies will have to file corporate social responsibility reports. The measure requires business to report anything concerning the welfare of employees, community, environment and the company itself, allowing shareholders and the general public to judge the performance of companies in all three areas. The law imposes controls on companies in regard to environmental and social issues, but was designed so as not to jeopardize commercial confidentiality. A proposed addition to the bill would force businesses to include information about their supply chains, raising concerns that, indeed, companies might have to report confidential information. Forest products companies often face the difficulty of tracing an entire supply chain, especially for composites and paper. The Companies Act, which comes into force in October 2008, may be seen as a precursor for similar laws in other countries.

The International Organization for Standardization (ISO) will be releasing a new set of standards on social responsibility in 2008. The ISO 26000 standards will not be a certification standard per se, but rather will provide guidelines for social responsibility. Given the wide acceptance of other ISO standards such as the 14000 and 9000 series, the upcoming ISO 26000 standards may just be what is required to provide traction on issues of social responsibility in the forestry sector.

Finally, in November 2006, the UN Global Compact office and ISO signed a memorandum of understanding to increase their collaboration in the development of the ISO 26000 standards. The memorandum will help to ensure consistency between the 10 Global Compact principles and ISO 26000 and may result in increased participation by forest companies in the Global Compact initiative. Currently, forest companies represent only 1% of the 3,056 companies that participate in this programme, which "asks companies to embrace, support and enact, within their sphere of influence, a set of core values in the areas of human rights, labour standards, the environment, and anti-corruption" (UN Global Compact, 2007).

2.5 Russian forest-sector reform: a new forest code and export regime

Subsequent to the collapse of the Soviet Union, the Russian forest sector experienced a major decline. What followed was increasing export of unprocessed wood as well as increasing dissatisfaction with forest-sector contribution to regional and local economies within Russia. Years of discussion culminated in two landmark decisions in 2007: one that fundamentally changed the ground rules for management of forests and one that markedly increased tariffs on the export of unprocessed wood. Both of these measures are discussed here.

2.5.1 *Russia enacts new Forest Code*

A new Russian Forest Code was adopted in January 2007, based upon "principles of rational use, conservation, protection and reproduction of forests, and enhancement of their ecological and resource potential". The new Code sets out a unified national forest policy and promotes structural reform, granting regional governments basic rights and powers in forest management, and charging them with responsibility for managing, protecting, using and regenerating forests. Provisions of the code shift the main responsibility for forest management closer to forest lessees and users. Forest-use regulations are yet to be implemented, with a reported 60 new regulations still awaiting adoption during the second half of 2007.

While public ownership of forests is retained within forest federal lands, the Forest Code allows for the privatization of some forest parcels. Major emphasis is placed on forest lease agreements. Provisions reduce the maximum lease period from 99 to 49 years, specify that leases will be awarded through auctions only, and place no limitations on the acquiring of leases by foreign legal

entities. The minimal lease term of 10 years can be extended (without auction) for a new term, which may make forest usage more attractive for investors. Russian industry fears increasing forest lease expenses and inconsistency in decision-making and notes that the maximum lease term reduction from 99 to 49 years leaves little incentive to reforest harvested lands when rotation ages are longer than the lease period.

Auctioning will increase competition as well as the possibility for private companies becoming involved, but may reduce the quality of forest management and sylvicultural activities performed by third parties because of the absence of requirements for licensing and accreditation. Bidding may favour large-scale commercial and foreign enterprises, placing small-scale community-based businesses at a disadvantage, leading to reduced opportunities for local communities to make a sustainable living from forestry.

The new legislation expands the rights and responsibilities of enterprises leasing forest lands. Lease rights for forest parcels can be used as collateral and can be sub-leased. In addition, lessees are charged with forest management responsibilities, including reforestation. Because of these changes, PriceWaterhouseCoopers (2006) expects that the level of reforestation may increase as much as threefold. In contrast, the ENGOs World Wide Fund for Nature (WWF), Greenpeace, and the Taiga Rescue Network observe that no obligations are placed on lessees related to sustainable forest management, biodiversity conservation and resolution of social issues. This coalition of ENGOs fears that this can eventually lead to a rise in illegal and unsustainable logging, as opportunities for forest leasing for commercial logging businesses have increased and obligations to leasees, with regard to sustainable forest management, reduced.

The Code introduces the legal framework for forest infrastructure development. As stipulated in the Code, forest resources shall be made available under investment agreements related to wood-processing projects which are coordinated with infrastructure development. The new Code aims to create an enabling environment for investment in wood-processing industries, including pulp and paper, in order to accrue the benefits of value-addition to domestic producers rather than to foreign importers. Accordingly, forest leaseholders are encouraged to supply wood for domestic processing. Included within the Code are provisions designed to remove obstacles to harvesting timber, increase forest utilization levels and income, encourage domestic and foreign investment in the sector as well as partnerships between the State and business, and to discourage export of unprocessed logs. The measure also streamlines permitting processes and provides tax incentives. Its introduction was followed by an announcement of sharp increases in log export duties, which will be phased in over a two-year period (see 2.7.1).

In an apparent attempt to provide balance to the strong emphasis on forest infrastructure and industrial development, one provision of the Forest Code stipulates that "the preservation of the ecological functions of production forests must be ensured in the procurement of wood," while another mandates certification of wood supplies and secondary forest resources by the Federal Forest Agency (see 2.4.1). Despite these provisions, WWF Russia considers the new legislation to be pro-industry rather than forestry oriented.[26] With an expanded list of forest-use types (including mineral resource extraction, construction, roads and pipelines), the Code expands the territory of forest use and appears focused on industrial exploration, reducing limitations on construction and development in forest areas. Environmental impact assessments are no longer a mandatory requirement for developments in forested areas.

ENGOs are furthermore concerned with the reclassification of forest-use types into protection, reserve and production, claiming that as a result, several categories of protected forest types (e.g. watershed forest protection) no longer exist or have been placed to lower levels of protection. Moreover, the designation of protected areas is likely to become more complicated, as areas crossing regional boundaries will be governed by several regional authorities, and non-forested areas governed at the federal level. ENGOs, along with industry, expect a period of difficult and unregulated transition ahead and fear that the reorganization of forest management structures could lead to a large number of job losses in rural areas, along with an increase in social problems and illegal logging.

2.5.2 Russia export tax increase shakes world log trade

Unprocessed timber has dominated Russian export figures in recent years, with logs and sawn timber representing 70% of all forest products exports. Russia is in particular a major exporter of softwood logs, providing about 40% of such exports globally, and a large percentage of the softwood log volume imported by China, the Republic of Korea, Japan, Finland, Sweden and, more recently, the Baltic States. Higher value-added exports such as plywood, pulp and newsprint amount to approximately one quarter of total export values. The

Russian forest products industry has thus been a global market player only in the lower value-added market segments, the economic benefits of the value-addition being accrued mostly to the importing countries. There would appear to be significant potential for the expansion of wood processing within Russia. While Russian annual exports of unprocessed timber (50 million m³ in 2006) have increased 2.5-fold in the past decade, all wood-processing volumes, with the exception of plywood, are at significantly lower levels than during the Soviet era.

In recent years, a number of resolutions were passed by the Government of the Russian Federation to give preferential rates to exports of value-added processed timber, while raising duties on unprocessed forest products. In January 2006, a single export duty for unprocessed forest products was established at the rate of 6.5% of the customs value of timber. A revision of this "very liberal export regime," as seen by the Russian administration,[27] was announced in December 2006, in order to encourage development of domestic wood-processing industries, promote the export of higher-value added products and reduce reliance on imports. Russian President, Vladimir Putin, echoed these thoughts in a February 2007 speech.

Under the newly enacted legislation, the current export tax of 6.5% on roundwood, sawn softwood, and veneer logs is scheduled to rise to 20% (and not less than 10/m³ ($13/m³)) as of 1 July 2007, to 25% (and not less than 15/m³ ($20/m³)) in April 2008, and to 80% (and not less than 50/m³ ($65/m³)) by January 2009. Custom duties on pulp and paper products are also included, but mostly with 6.5% and 10% as of 1 July 2007, increases thus not being as significant. As part of the strategy to promote domestic value-added processing, import tariffs on high-tech wood-processing equipment will be reduced.

Russian wood-processing industries, in particular, are expected to benefit from the new export regime as well as from other legislative measures that aim at promoting more significant domestic value-added processing, while ensuring an abundant supply of forest resources to domestic and foreign markets. Conversely, the effects of the higher export tariffs on unprocessed timber are likely to greatly affect current importers of Russian timber and their wood-processing industries. This, in turn, could lead to diversion towards other markets and negatively affect existing demand for Russian logs. Finland, for example, which obtains about 17% of the timber for its domestic mills from Russia, has indicated that it may decide to import timber from the Baltic States and Latin America

[26] Ms. Elena Kulikova. Forest Program Director, WWF Russia, during the FAO Committee on Forestry, Information session "Russian forests: National and international dimensions", 13 March 2007.

[27] Mr. Valery P. Roshchupkin, Chief Federal Forest Agency, Russian Federation, during the FAO Committee on Forestry, Information session "Russian forests: National and international dimensions", 13 March 2007.

by 2010, when the announced duties are to reach their highest level. Representatives of the Finnish company Stora Enso commented that given a current cost of about 45/m³ ($60/m³), the effect of an export tax of 50/m³ ($65/m³) would be to more than double the cost and to "ruin the economics of wood imports from Russia."

While the new customs duties may lower foreign demand for logs, the expected development of Russian wood-processing industries, facilitated through infrastructure investments, preferential export rates for value-added processed timber and other measures, may result in increasing domestic demand for raw materials. Although this may partly offset the expected decrease in demand from foreign markets, price levels for unprocessed Russian timber could fall, thus affecting the economic viability of forestry management.

The new customs duties are intended to induce investors to establish processing facilities in Russia. It remains to be seen whether this new strategy will work as intended. In the several months since passage of the tariff measure, significant numbers of foreign timber processors have not stepped forward to invest in the Russian timber industry, partly due to uncertainties associated with the new Forest Code. Should significant new investment and new domestic timber demand not develop within the period of increasing tariffs, Russian logging firms would almost certainly be adversely affected, particularly in 2009, when export duties will reach their peak. The Chairman of the Russian company Ilim Pulp has indicated that Russia's current annual exports of unprocessed timber would no longer be profitable under the new export duties. According to some observers, the Russian move regarding unprocessed timber appears somewhat similar to its energy policy that seeks to achieve a rapid shift from a role as a primary raw material supplier to a finished goods exporter.

Concern with the new export stance on the part of affected countries such as Finland, which view the introduction of prohibitive new customs duties as "contrary to the spirit of the WTO", may eventually slow Russia's accession if taken up in the ongoing negotiations. Finland approached the EU pointing out that the increases violate a standstill agreement Russia signed with the EU ahead of its planned WTO accession, agreeing there would be no tariff increases before it joins.

2.6 Research and development policies

Research investment in the near term will play a significant role in determining successes and failures in the forest sector over the longer term. Hence, an examination of recent trends in research organization and activity are briefly examined below.

2.6.1 Funding of R&D

In January 2007 the three primary forest products research institutes of Canada – Forintek Canada Corporation, the Forest Engineering Research Institute of Canada (FERIC), and the Pulp and Paper Research Institute of Canada (PAPRICAN) – were merged into a new single institute, "FPInnovations". Under the new structure FPInnovations will also provide technical direction to the Canadian Forest Service's Fibre Centre. The stated intent is to provide Canada's forest industry with one of the world's largest forest sector research institutes, and enhance the ability to face global competition and associated economic and environmental challenges. The separate budgets of the now-combined institutes totalled about CDN$60 million in 2006. Other entities involved in forest products research within Canada include a network of universities and Natural Resources Canada. Funding is provided by member companies of research institutions, Environment Canada, and by provincial governments. Additional funding in areas related to bioenergy is provided by the Programme for Energy Research and Development.

Within the United States, forest products research is conducted primarily by the US Forest Service, and in the past decade has received funding from 12 different federal agencies. For instance, the Federal Departments of Energy, Housing and Urban Development, Agriculture (in addition to the Forest Service) and Defense have also provided significant forest products research funding in recent years. There is no institutionalized cooperation with the forest industry at the federal level as there is in Canada. In total, federal funding in support of forest products research totalled $54 million annually in 2004 and 2005 (GAO, 2006). State governments also fund forest products research through a network of universities and various state-level research organizations.

Forest products research is funded differently within Europe. The Seventh Framework Programme for Research and Technological Development (FP7) is the European Union's main instrument for funding research in Europe. The current-funding round will run from 2007 to 2013, with a seven year budget of €50.5 billion ($67.1 billion) to support selected research areas, in which the EU wishes to become or remain a world leader, as well as to respond to Europe's employment needs and competitiveness. The broad objectives of FP7 have been grouped into four categories: cooperation, ideas, people and capacities: a) cooperation between industry and academia to gain leadership in key technology areas; (the largest subprogramme, with €32.4 billion ($43.1 billion) seven-year budget support); b) ideas to support basic research at the scientific frontiers; c) support of researchers' mobility and career development for both within and outside Europe; and d) development of capacities that Europe needs to be a thriving knowledge-based economy.

One programme is the European Cooperation in the field of Scientific and Technological Research (COST), with its main objective to stimulate new, innovative and interdisciplinary scientific networks in Europe, including the domain of forests, their services and products.

The relevant COST Domain has 29 separate actions on a wide variety of topics in the sector, including innovative timber elements (E29), recovered wood (E31), timber bonding (E34), enhanced wood durability (E37), innovative use of large-dimensioned timber (E40), wood-processing strategy (E44), wood-based panels (E49), integrating innovation and development policies for the forest sector (E51), quality control (E53) and biotechnology for lignocellulose biorefineries (FP0602). The Competitiveness and Innovation Framework Programme is another focus of FP7. It is aimed at supporting companies. Also running from 2007 to 2013, it has a budget of approximately 3.6 billion ($4.8 billion) and three specific subprogrammes in its framework, with "Eco-innovation" as a transversal theme across them. One of these subprogrammes – the Intelligent Energy-Europe Programme encourages the wider uptake of new and renewable energies and improvement of energy efficiency. Among the various objectives of this programme, a high priority goal is the production of ethanol as a fuel for transport.

The Forest-based Sector Technology Platform (FTP) is now fully operational, basing its activities on the agreed Strategic Research Agenda (SRA), used to guide and prioritize proposals for research in the sector, notably under the FP7. Four national research agendas are now complete and a FTP project database is operational. FTP also monitors to what extent funding is in line with the agreed priorities of the SRA.

2.6.2 Universities increasingly teaming up with the energy sector to develop biofuels technology

It is not only forest industry that is cooperating with the energy sector in biofuels development (see 2.5.4), but also universities. Three of many examples that could be given are provided by the State of New York, British Petroleum, and Sweden.

The State of New York recently awarded $25.1 million to two companies to develop and construct pilot facilities for the production of commercial cellulose ethanol. Mascoma Corporation is to construct a 1.9 million litre per year (500,000 gallon) plant in Greece, NY. The facility will produce ethanol from wood chips and paper residues using a technology developed in cooperation with Cornell University, Clarkson University and Genencor. Catalyst Renewables Corporation will build a facility in Lyonsdale to produce from wood chips 130,000 gallons of ethanol per year using a process developed by the SUNY's College of Environmental Science and Forestry.

British Petroleum also recently announced that it will invest $500 million over the next ten years to fund the development of new sources of clean and renewable energy through applications of bioscience. The company also indicated that it has joined with the University of California-Berkeley, the University of Illinois, and the Lawrence Berkeley National Laboratory to establish the Energy Biosciences Institute.

In a related development, the ethanol pilot plant at Örnsköldsvik, Sweden, which is owned by two universities, is reported to be working in cooperation with Royal Dutch Shell and British Petroleum. The cooperative venture, dedicated to research and definition of research direction, is focused on production of cellulosic ethanol from spruce. A preliminary conclusion arising from the first trials, conducted in the forth quarter of 2006, is that higher yields can be expected using enzymatic hydrolysis to break down some ligno-cellulose materials than was previously achieved with dilute acid.

2.7 References

Bureau of International Recycling. 2006. Recovered Paper Imports on Course to Increase in China. BIR Autumn Round Table Sessions, Paper Division. Brussels. 31 October. Available at: http://www.bir.org/publications/news/detailednewspage.asp?NewsID=355

Cha, A. and Goodman, P. 2007. US puts tariffs on Chinese paper. Washington Post. 3 April. Available at: http://www.washingtonpost.com/wp-dyn/content/article/2007/04/02/AR2007040201496_pf.html

Chuyko, V., Director of the Board, CEO, RAO BUMPROM. The New Forestry Code and its Impact on the Russian Forestry and Pulp & Paper Enterprises. Presentation in Montreal, Canada, February 2007.

CIBC. 2007. Russia plans to dramatically increase its export tax on logs: a structural change in global wood markets. Industry Update, 22 February.

Directive 2003/87/EC of the European Parliament and of the Council of 13 October 2003 establishing a scheme for greenhouse gas emission allowance trading within the Community and amending Council Directive 96/61/EC. Available at: http://eur-lex.europa.eu/LexUriServ/LexUriServ.do?uri=CELEX:32003L0087:EN:HTML

Euractiv.com. 2006. Forest sector seeks inclusion in emissions trading. 30 November. Available at: http://www.euractiv.com/en/sustainability/forest-sector-seeks-inclusion-emissions-trading/article-160133

European Commission. 1997. Energy for the Future: Renewable Sources of Energy. White Paper for a Community Strategy and Action Plan.COM (97) 599. November. Available at: http://ec.europa.eu/energy/library/599fi_en.pdf

European Commission. 2003. Directive 2003/87/EC of the European Parliament and of the Council of 13 October 2003 establishing a scheme for greenhouse gas emission allowance trading within the Community and amending Council Directive 96/61/EC. Available at: http://eur-lex.europa.eu/LexUriServ/site/en/oj/2003/l_275/l_27520031025en00320046.pdf

European Commission. 2005. Biomass Action Plan COM (2005) 628, December. Available at: http://ec.europa.eu/energy/res/biomass_action_plan/doc/2005_12_07_comm_biomass_action_plan_en.pdf

European Commission. 2006. Biofuels Strategy COM (2006) 34, December. Available at: http://ec.europa.eu/agriculture/biomass/biofuel/com2006_34_en.pdf

European Commission. 2006. Communication to the European Parliament on an EU forest action plan. COM (2006) 302, 15 June. Available at: http://ec.europa.eu/agriculture/fore/action_plan/index_en.htm

European Commission. 2006. Press release. Climate change: Commission proposes bringing air transport into EU Emissions Trading Scheme. 20 December. Available at: http://europa.eu/rapid/pressReleasesAction.do?reference=IP/06/1862&format=HTML&aged=0&language=EN&guiLanguage=en

European Commission. 2007. Action Plan for Energy Efficiency: Realizing the Potential – Saving 20% by 2020. Directorate-General for Energy and Transport. Available at: http://ec.europa.eu/energy/action_plan_energy_efficiency/index_en.htm

European Environment Agency. 2006. How Much Bioenergy Can Europe Produce Without Harming the Environment? Copenhagen: EEA Report No. 7.

European Parliament and Council of the European Union. 2003. Directive 2003/30/EC on the promotion of the use of biofuels or other renewable fuels for transport. Official Journal of the European Union L123/42, 8 May. Available at: http://ec.europa.eu/energy/res/legislation/doc/biofuels/en_final.pdf

European Parliament. 2006. Committee on the Environment, Public Health and Food Safety. Amendments 1-30 19 September. Available at: http://www.europarl.europa.eu/meetdocs/2004_2009/documents/am/630/630845/630845en.pdf

Fairfield, H. 2007. Carbon currency: regional greenhouse gas initiative. When carbon is currency. New York Times, 6 May 2007. Available at: http://environmental-economics.blogspot.com/2007/05/carbon-currency.html

Financial Times. 2007. European climate change and energy summit. 9 March, 2007.

Financial Times. 2007. Finns fear that Russia aims to reduce their mills to pulp resources: ratcheting up export tax on logs brings echoes on Moscow's moves to manipulate oil and gas, 12 April

Foreign Agricultural Service. 2007. Wood Market Update. US Department of Agriculture, FAS, Office of Global Analysis March.

Forest Products Association of Canada (FPAC). 2007. Available at: http://www.fpac.ca/en/who_we_are/sustainability_initiative.php

Hamilton, G. 2007. China scooping up recycled newsprint. Vancouver Sun, 7 February. Available at: http://www.canada.com/vancouversun/news/business/story.html?id=df97ec41-2040-46be-b2f0-a8e063518271

Hentschel, G. 2006. Review of the European Timber Trade Federations' Codes of Conduct and Purchasing Policies. EU Timber Trade Action Plan (TTAP), December. Available at: http://www.timbertradeactionplan.info/uploads/Review_Purchasing_Policies_Final_draft.pdf

IEA, FAO, UNECE, ICFPA, ITTO. 2006. International Seminar on Energy & the Forest Products Industry." Rome, 30-31 October. Available at: http://www.iea.org/dbtw-wpd/textbase/work/workshopdetail.asp?WS_ID=265

Kommersant Online. 2007. Finland walks out from Russian forests. March 19. Available at: http://www.kommersant.com/p750970/Finland_Timber_Export/

Kulikova, E. 2007. Coordinator Forestry Programmes WWF Russia. Presentation during the FAO Committee on Forestry. Information session "Russian forests: National and international dimensions." 13 March. Available at: http://www.fao.org/forestry/foris/data/cofo/2007/kulikova_elena_russian_forests_national_and_international_dimensions.pdf

Kulikova, E. 2007. WWF Russia. Update on Russian Forest Sector: WWF View. London, 26 January. Available at: http://www.illegal-logging.info/presentations/25-260107/Kulikova.ppt

Lichte, Rocio. 2007. Reducing Emissions from Deforestation. Latest Developments within the UNFCCC. Presentation during the FAO Committee on Forestry, March 2007. Available at: http://www.fao.org/forestry/foris/data/cofo/2007/lichte_rocio_reducing_emissions_from_deforestation_in_developing_countries.pdf

Moscow Times. 2007. Timber producers edgy as customs duty looms. 25 May.

Palmer, D. 2007. US sets new duties on China goods. Toronto Star. 30 March. Available at: http://www.atlanticcallcentres.com/printArticle/197812

Patzek, L. and Patzek, T. 2007. The disastrous local and global impacts of tropical biofuel production. Energy Tribune. Available at: http://www.energytribune.com/articles.cfm?aid=403

Pearce, F. 1998. Burn me. New Scientist 156 (2109): 26-30.

PEFC. 2007. Russian forest certification initiatives sign historic agreement. 15 September. Available at: http://www.pefc.org/internet/html/news/4_1154_65/5_1105_1400.htm

PriceWaterhouseCoopers. 2006. Risks & Rewards. Forest, paper & packaging in Russia. October

Roshchupkin, V. P. 2007. Presentation the FAO Committee on Forestry, Information Session "Russian forests: National and International Dimensions", 13 March. Available at: http://www.fao.org/forestry/foris/data/cofo/2007/roshchupkin_valery_p_russian_forests_%20national_and_international_dimensions.pdf

Russian Federation Forest Code. 2007. Federal Act No. 22-FZ. Adopted by the State Duma on 22 January 2007. Available at: http://www.forest.ru/eng/legislation/forestcode.html

SKRIN Market & Corporate News. 2006. Russia opened up for forest privatization 15 December.

SKRIN Market & Corporate News. 2007. New forestry code hard to implement. 5 March.

Society of American Foresters. 2007. Trouble ahead for softwood lumber agreement. Forestry Source 12(4): 20. April.

Softwood Lumber Agreement Between the Government of Canada and the Government of the United States of America. 2006. Available at: http://www.international.gc.ca/eicb/softwood/pdfs/SLA-en.pdf

Steierer, F. and Fischer-Ankern, A. 2007. Wood Energy in Europe and North America: A New Estimate of Volumes and Flows. Study in progress. UNECE/FAO, February. Available at: http://www.unece.org/trade/timber/docs/stats-sessions/stats-29/english/report-conclusions-2007-03.pdf

Stueck, W. 2007. Higher Russian log tax a boon for North American timber operations. Vancouver Globe and Mail, March 5.

Taiga Rescue Network Briefing Note. 2007. Comments on the new Russian forest code. Available at: http://www.taigarescue.org/_v3/files/pdf/201.pdf

UN Global Compact. 2007. Available at: http://www.unglobalcompact.org/AboutTheGC/TheTenPrinciples/index.html

UNECE/FAO/CEPI/MCPFE/EFI. 2007. Workshop "Mobilizing Wood Resources: Can Europe Satisfy the Increasing Demand for Raw Material and Energy Under Sustainable Forest Management?" Recommendations. Available at: http://www.unece.org/trade/timber/workshops/2007/wmw/recomm.htm#top

Wall Street Journal, Asia. 2007. China, Russia sign a trade deal. (29 March)

Wall, J. 2006. "An overview of existing and emerging EU policies relating to energy from biomass and their effects on forest-based industries". Proceedings: International Seminar on Energy & the Forest Products Industry. Rome, October 30-31. Available at: http://www.fao.org/forestry/webview/media?mediaId=11518&langId=1

World Business Council for Sustainable Development (WBCSD.) 2007. Sustainable Forest Products Industry. Executive Briefing. Available at: http://www.wbcsd.org/DocRoot/8qJMUoHCe1fj8ctrHgHD/Forest_200207_proof%204.pdf

WBCSD. 2006. EU carbon trade firms "undershooting 2005 quotas.". Available at: http://www.wbcsd.org/plugins/DocSearch/details.asp?type=DocDet&ObjectId=MTkwMDM

Weisman, S. 2007. In big shift, US imposes tariffs on Chinese paper. New York Times. 31 March.

Chapter 3

United States housing downturn affecting many countries – positive trends in European housing: Economic developments affecting forest products markets, 2006-2007[28]

Highlights

- World economic growth has been quite robust and is expected to remain so although it is likely to slow down moderately in almost all regions in 2007 and 2008.

- Major downside risks to growth include higher interest rates, a depreciating dollar, a crash in global real estate markets, higher oil prices or an unexpected development concerning hedge funds or derivatives.

- Interest rates have been increasing throughout most of the world and this will probably depress the demand for housing.

- US housing starts fell by 13% to 1.8 million units in 2006, and are expected to fall another 18% in 2007, which seriously affects North American economies, and has consequences for the forest industries.

- An upturn in the US residential market is forecast, based on demographics, in 2008.

- There is a dichotomy in US construction markets, as non-residential markets grew 13.4% on a value basis in 2006 and are expected to expand by up to 10% in 2007.

- Prices of building materials in the US reflect these changes – wood products are down substantially from highs in 2004 and 2005; however, non-wood material prices continue to increase.

- European construction markets continue to expand, growing uninterruptedly for 13 years and another three years of growth is forecast, driven by 5.6% growth in new residential activity and 4.2% in civil engineering construction.

- New residential construction in Europe is expected to cool in 2007 and decline modestly in 2008, however, renovation markets will take up some of the slack and civil engineering will be the other growth sector during 2007-2008.

---

[28] By Dr. Robert Shelburne, UNECE, Switzerland, Dr. Al Schuler, USDA Forest Service and Mr. Craig Adair, APA – The Engineered Wood Association.

Secretariat introduction

The secretariat of the UNECE/FAO Timber Section sincerely appreciates the contribution on economic developments by Dr. Robert Shelburne,[29] Senior Economic Affairs Officer, UNECE. His overview provides the essential foundation for the market sector analyses in the following chapters and is equally appreciated by delegates at the annual Timber Committee Market Discussions.

We also express our gratitude for continuing collaboration to Dr. Al Schuler,[30] Research Economist, US Department of Agriculture, Forest Service, and Mr. Craig Adair,[31] Director, Market Research, APA–The Engineered Wood Products Association, for the analysis in the second section of this chapter, focusing on construction developments. Construction of houses and non-residential buildings creates demand for structural wood products, as well as for value-added wood products.

3.1 The economic situation of the UNECE region economies in 2007[32]

3.1.1 *Global context*

World gross domestic product (GDP) increased by an impressive 5.4% in 2006, the largest increase since the early 1970s, and is likely to be only slightly less at around 4.9% in 2007.[33] Since the slowdown in 2001, the world economy has now experienced six years of good growth, with the last four being exceptionally strong. Overall, this is the best extended performance of the global economy since before the first oil shock in 1973. This expansion has been led by the stellar performance of the emerging

---

[29] Dr. Robert C. Shelburne, Senior Economic Affairs Officer, UNECE, Palais des Nations, CH-1211 Geneva, Switzerland, tel. +41 22 917 2484, fax +41 22 917 0107, e-mail: robert.shelburne@unece.org www.unece.org.

[30] Dr. Al Schuler, Research Economist, Northeast Forest Experiment Station, USDA Forest Service, 241 Mercer Springs Road, Princeton, West Virginia, 24740, USA, tel. +1 304 431 2727, fax +1 304 431 2772, e-mail: aschuler@fs.fed.us, www.fs.fed.us/ne.

[31] Mr. Craig Adair, Director, Market Research, APA-The Engineered Wood Association, P.O. Box 11700, Tacoma, Washington, 98411-0700, USA, tel. +1 253 565 7265, fax +1 253 565 6600, e-mail: craig.adair@apawood.org, www.apawood.org.

[32] This section is a condensed version of an UNECE working paper *The Economic Situation and Outlook in Mid-2007 for the UNECE Economies,* which is available at www.unece.org/ead/ead_diss_pe_new.htm.

[33] These growth rates are GDP weighted averages adjusted by using purchasing power parity exchange rates; world growth would be lower at about 4% if based upon market exchange rate measures.

market and developing economies, which account for approximately one half of world GDP, and grew by 7.9% in 2006 as compared with the 3.1% growth rate in the advanced economies. The developing world has outgrown the advanced economies consistently since 1990 and the gap has been slowly increasing through time. The economic performance of the developing world was led by China, which continues to grow at rates above 10%, and by India, whose growth topped 9% in 2006. The Commonwealth of Independent States (CIS) minus Russia also ranks amongst the fastest-growing regions having achieved a 9.5% increase in GDP; growth was strong elsewhere in the developing world, including Latin America and Africa.

In the advanced economies, growth picked up in 2006 in all the major regions including the US, western Europe, and Japan, although growth appears to be moderating in 2007, especially in the United States. In Japan the asset price deflation which has plagued the country appears to have ended, with land prices increasing for the first time since 1990 and equity prices doubling since their 2003 nadir. For the UNECE region overall (i.e. the 52 countries with reported GDP[34]) which accounts for 48.5% of global GDP, growth was 3.7% in 2006 but is expected to fall to 3.1% in 2007, which is about what it has averaged over the last 8 years (table 3.1.1).

Inflation throughout most of the world has been low and averaged just 2.3% in the advanced economies and 5.3% in the developing economies. Unemployment throughout much of the world has also been on a downward trend for the last several years although this is expected to stabilize in 2007. This strong economic growth combined with generally low inflation and unemployment is all the more remarkable given that this has occurred during a time when oil and commodity prices increased substantially. This favourable outcome reflects the changing economic structure of the world economy and the improved performance of economic policymaking since the oil shocks of the 1970s.

Potential threats to the sustainability of the current global expansion include the disruptions that might be caused by the realignment of four important prices:

- The price of the largest traded commodity – oil.

- The price of the major international currency – the exchange rate of the US dollar.

- The price of the largest asset that people own – residential housing.

- The basic price of time preference – the global interest rate.

---

[34] There are no GDP data for four members of the UNECE – Andorra, Liechtenstein, Monaco, and San Marino.

The price of crude oil in 2007 appears to have found a trading range of around $60 to $70 a barrel. This price is not only high in nominal terms but is similar in real terms to oil's all-time high in 1981. The relative ease with which the world economy adjusted to the recent increases has perhaps reduced the perceived risks associated with further price movements in this commodity.

The US current account deficit has been increasing progressively for over a decade and reached 6.5% of GDP in 2006; US imports are now almost twice the value of US exports. Although there has been widespread recognition for several years that a significant dollar depreciation is forthcoming, it has been largely postponed because of the interest rate differential that has favoured US assets. However, with growth slowing in the US and picking up elsewhere, this interest differential has begun and is likely to further decline. The dollar generally declined relative to other currencies in which wood and paper products are traded (graph 3.1.1).

GRAPH 3.1.1

Exchange rates of selected currencies vs the US dollar, 2004-2006

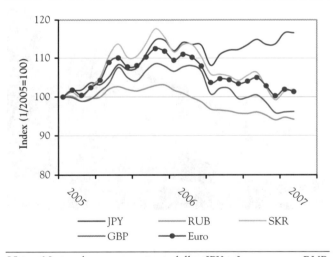

Notes: National currency unit per dollar. JPY is Japanese yen, RUB is Russian ruble, SKR is Swedish krona and GBP is British pound Sterling.
Source: IMF International Financial Statistics, 2006.

There has been a boom in residential real estate prices over the past 10 years in most of the major markets in the world. Since current housing price levels are in excess of a number of longer-term relationships, such as between prices and income and prices and rental costs, there may be a bubble in many of these markets. Analysis of previous housing bubbles has found that a bust occurs after a boom in approximately half of the cases and it is usually preceded by a significant increase in interest rates

(as has recently occurred). A housing bust typically has a more serious impact on the economy than an equity market bust and takes longer to work itself out. Housing prices levelled off and even declined in some regions of the United States during 2006. However, this may be only the tip of the bubble as price appreciation in some European markets such as Ireland, Spain and the UK were twice as much as those in the US between 1997 and 2005.

Over the last several years, there has been a significant increase in interest rates in most of the major economies. Over the last 40 years, whenever interest rates have risen significantly, especially when it has been more global in scope, this has precipitated some form of financial or currency crisis. Thus it would be somewhat atypical if the current increase in interest rates did not result in some form of financial crisis in the coming year; and given the existing vulnerabilities, housing markets would appear to be the prime candidate. In addition to the risks associated with possible changes in the four prices listed above, there are two other areas of risks. The first concerns the explosive growth of hedge fund and derivative markets. The other concerns the possible global implications of an avian influenza pandemic.

Besides the global risks outlined above, the emerging markets of the UNECE region have a more regional vulnerability in regard to the rapid credit growth of both domestic credit and private sector borrowing from abroad. Bank credit, especially to households, has been growing extremely fast over the last several years. Although rapid credit growth is a normal process and characteristic of financial deepening in emerging markets, this rapid growth, even from a relatively small base, raises concerns because the regulatory and financial institutional structure is new and has yet to be seriously tested.

3.1.2 North America

Despite a recent slowdown in the US economy, with a projected 2.1% increase in GDP for 2007 compared to the 3.3% increase in 2006, the economic situation remains generally favourable, with low unemployment and inflation and sound government and household debt levels. The US slowdown is largely the result of the significant increase in short-term interest rates which began in mid-2004 and has now stabilized at 5.25% since June 2006. Inflation in the US is approximately 2.8% year-on-year (y-o-y) for the period ending in March 2007. Unemployment fell to 4.4% in March, which is close to or slightly below what is viewed to be full employment. Given the slowdown in the US housing market, it is somewhat surprising that since March 2006, employment in the construction sector increased by 21,000 owing to the fact that growth in non-residential construction was more than sufficient to compensate for the decline in residential construction. US productivity growth that experienced a revival in the mid-1990s appears to have fallen back to its longer-term trend level as it has only increased at an annual rate of 1.6% since the third quarter of 2004. Investment has also remained sluggish despite the fact that profits as a percentage of GDP reached an all-time high in 2006; housing investment has been particularly low and with the inventory of unsold houses at a rather high level, is likely to stay low for some time.

The two primary areas of concern for the US economy are its housing market with its possible economy-wide implications and the country's large current account deficit. Housing starts increased slightly in February from depressed levels, although permit applications remained weak (see next section on construction developments). The US current account deficit has stabilized at slightly over 6% of GDP and is unlikely to fall much more until there is a further dollar depreciation, which will likely depend on a reduced interest rate differential. In a fundamental way, the housing and current account issues are related from a macroeconomic standpoint in that the current account deficit is due to low national savings, which are in turn due significantly to the fact that housing price appreciation has increased consumer wealth and thereby reduced the need to save.

It remains uncertain what will be the global implications of the slowdown in the US housing market. If the weakness is confined to the housing market, then US imports and thus other countries, exports should be generally unaffected since housing has only a small import component, although the US imports approximately one third of its construction sawnwood from Canada. If, however, declining or stagnant house prices reduce significantly equity withdrawal through refinancing, then consumer spending may be negatively affected and this would likely spill over to other economies by lowering US imports. In addition, if the financial problems in the US subprime mortgage market remain contained within that sector, then the foreign financial implications may be minor; but if the crises should spread to the broader US credit market, this could spill over into global financial markets.

The Canadian economy cooled slightly in 2006 to a growth rate of 2.7% and had a particularly poor fourth quarter, but growth is anticipated to be about 2.5% in 2007. This slowdown is due significantly to the slower growth in the US, which accounts for 84% of Canadian exports. The policy environment in terms of monetary and fiscal policy should remain relatively neutral as growth and inflation are reasonably close to their target levels. Canada, being an exporter of numerous commodities including oil and minerals, has benefited

from the recent price increases for these items. This has produced a trade surplus and appreciated its currency; however, this has harmed its manufacturing sector. The slump in the construction of new houses in the US has had a negative impact on the Canadian timber industry.

3.1.3 Western Europe

Growth picked up considerably in western Europe in 2006 to its best level since 2000; however, it should moderate somewhat in 2007 although it is likely to remain slightly above its longer-run trend level. Eurozone GDP rose by 2.8% in 2006 and was especially strong (3.3% y-o-y) in the fourth quarter of the year before cooling off in the first quarter of 2007. The economic expansion of 2006 was particularly strong in Germany. Euro area growth is likely to moderate in 2007 owing to the continuing appreciation of the euro, higher interest rates, and the slowdown in the US although it seems to have weathered satisfactorily a number of recent shocks including the January increase in the value added tax (VAT) rate in Germany. The non-eurozone economies have recently performed slightly better than that of the eurozone and this is expected to continue, although growth in most of these economies, except perhaps the UK, is likely to moderate some in 2007.

APA – The Engineered Wood Association, 2007.

Euro area unemployment has been on a downward trend for a number of years and fell to 7.2% in March 2007. This is the lowest unemployment for the eurozone since Eurostat began publishing data on this in 1993. Inflation in the eurozone has been moderately above the European Central Bank (ECB) target of slightly less than 2% for the last several years, although it achieved this target during the first quarter of 2007. Inflation in the UK has been over a point higher than in the eurozone and reached 3.1% in March 2007. Interest rates in the euro area continued to increase over most of the last year despite the fact that inflation rates fell below the 2% target for the first time in years. The ECB increased its main refinancing rate to 3.75% in early March 2007 for the seventh time since December 2005, with expectations of a likely further increase to 4% in June and perhaps another increase by the end of the year. The Bank of England's main interest rate has been on an upward trend reaching 5.5% in the first quarter of 2007, with another possible increase sometime in the second quarter. The moderately robust growth in Europe has increased tax revenues in most economies, thus slightly improving their fiscal positions. The overall eurozone fiscal deficit declined from 2.4% of GDP in 2005 to 1.6% in 2006, with a further decline to 1.2% projected for 2007. The budget situation has also improved in most of the other non-eurozone economies.

3.1.4   EU new Member States[35]

Economic growth in the EU new Member States (NMS) continues to be quite high, averaging about 6.4% for 2006, although it should moderate to about 6.1% in 2007. Growth has been particularly high in the Baltic economies, especially Estonia and Latvia; Romania and Slovakia have also performed well. This growth is being driven by domestic demand as a result of rapid credit growth and foreign investment (both foreign direct investment (FDI) and portfolio flows), while the stimulus from external trade has diminished, although it benefited in 2006 from the improvement in growth in western Europe. EU accession for Bulgaria and Romania has generally proceeded smoothly. The major adjustments have involved technical issues surrounding the adoption of environmental, health and safety regulations, adjustments in tax laws and implementing the Intrastat system for VAT payments, and output adjustments in industries that had received some trade protections (i.e. food) up until accession. Unemployment, which has been quite significant in many of the NMS for over a decade, has finally begun to decline substantially. The rapid economic growth in the NMS has put upward pressure on prices, with inflation averaging slightly above 3%. Despite the fact that inflation is currently slightly above that in the eurozone, there has been appreciation pressure on many of the NMS currencies, which has required central bank intervention or an official appreciation, as with Slovakia. Although Slovenia adopted the euro in January 2007, the timetable for accession for the other NMS is progressively being pushed further into the future, owing principally to the difficulty in satisfying the Maastricht criteria; government deficits and inflation appear to present the greatest challenge. An area of potential vulnerability for many of the NMS concerns their relatively large current account deficits. The Baltic States and the two newest EU members, Bulgaria and Romania, have deficits exceeding 10% of GDP.

[35] The new Member States (NMS) are Bulgaria, Cyprus, Czech Republic, Estonia, Hungary, Latvia, Lithuania, Malta, Poland, Romania and Slovakia. Slovenia joined the eurozone in 2007.

3.1.5   Southeast Europe

Despite significant uncertainty surrounding the outcome of a number of important developments such as the future political status of Kosovo or the prospects for EU membership for most of the economies in the region, economic growth and investment have been reasonably high in Southeast Europe. Growth moderated in 2006 to 5.9% and is expected to moderate further in 2007.

Turkey, the largest economy in the region, continued its five-year expansion following the financial crisis in 2001 by growing 6.1% in 2006. This is that country's longest period of stable growth since 1970. The expansion, however, has also resulted in an increasing current account deficit, which reached slightly over 6% in 2006 and relatively high inflation of slightly over 10%. Current account deficits are problematic for some of the other economies including Bosnia and Herzegovina, Serbia and Albania. The fiscal deficits of these economies are in reasonably good condition; Albania's projected deficit of 4.1% of GDP is the largest, while Turkey's budget deficit has recently worsened and is projected at about 2.7% in 2007. Despite solid economic growth, unemployment remains a serious problem for the western Balkan economies, with official rates generally above 10% and above 30% for Bosnia and Herzegovina and the former Yugoslav Republic of Macedonia. The production structures of these economies are slowly shifting from agriculture and industry to services and construction.

3.1.6   Commonwealth of Independent States

Growth in the Commonwealth of Independent States (CIS) increased to 7.6% in 2006 and is expected to remain at about 7% in 2007. However, there is considerable variation in the performance of the individual economies, with several having growth close to or over 10%, while Kyrgyzstan's was only 2.7%. In 2007 growth in the CIS is projected to slow down slightly in Europe and the Caucasus, while increasing or remaining high in Central Asia. Russia, now the world's tenth largest economy, experienced growth of 6.7% in 2006, which is equal to its average growth rate over the last seven years; it has now experienced its longest period of sustained growth since the break-up of the Soviet Union. Political uncertainty is likely to limit growth in several economies, especially in Ukraine during 2007. In order for growth to become more sustainable, it will be necessary to further diversify these economies towards higher value-added manufacturing and services.

The robust economic growth has slowly reduced unemployment throughout the region, reducing it in 2006 to 7.3% in Russia and approximately 8% in Kazakhstan; however, unemployment remains extremely high in Moldova, at above 20%. Inflation in the CIS has been on a downward trend over the last five years but at

9.5% in 2006 remains significant, with several economies having rates above 10%. Given relatively moderate inflation worldwide, this region's inflation remains one of the highest in the world. Inflation in Russia fell to the single digits (9.7%) for the first time since the break-up of central planning. Inflation in the energy exporters is due both to their rapid domestic credit growth and their improved terms of trade. In order to limit capital inflows that would put additional upward pressure on inflation and the exchange rate, Russia has maintained negative real interest rates although nominal rates rose throughout 2006.

TABLE 3.1.1.

UNECE real GDP growth rates, 2005-2007

Country	2005	2006	2007	Country	2005	2006	2007
Albania	5.5	5.0	6.0	Denmark	3.1	3.3	2.5
Bosnia and Herzegovina	5.0	6.0	6.0	Sweden	2.9	4.7	4.3
Croatia	4.3	4.6	4.7	United Kingdom	1.9	2.8	2.7
Macedonia, fYR of	3.8	4.0	4.5	**EU-16**	**1.6**	**3.1**	**2.8**
Montenegro	4.3	6.5	6.5				
Serbia	6.2	5.4	5.0	Bulgaria	5.6	6.2	5.9
Turkey	7.4	6.1	5.7	Cyprus	3.9	3.8	3.9
Southeast Europe (non-EU)	**6.9**	**5.9**	**5.6**	Czech Republic	6.1	6.1	5.5
				Estonia	10.5	11.4	9.9
Armenia	14.0	13.4	9.0	Hungary	4.2	3.9	2.5
Azerbaijan	24.3	31.0	29.2	Latvia	10.2	11.9	10.5
Belarus	9.3	9.9	5.5	Lithuania	7.6	7.5	7.0
Georgia	9.6	9.0	7.5	Malta	2.2	2.5	2.3
Kazakhstan	9.7	10.6	9.0	Poland	3.5	6.1	6.7
Kyrgyzstan	-0.2	2.7	6.5	Romania	4.1	7.7	6.5
Moldova	7.5	4.0	4.5	Slovakia	6.0	8.3	8.7
Russia	6.4	6.7	6.5	**EU NMS-11**	**4.7**	**6.4**	**6.1**
Tajikistan	7.3	6.8	7.2	**EU – 27**	**1.9**	**3.3**	**3.1**
Turkmenistan	9.0	9.0	10.0				
Ukraine	2.7	7.1	5.0	Iceland	7.5	2.9	0.8
Uzbekistan	7.0	7.2	7.7	Norway	2.7	2.9	3.1
CIS	**6.6**	**7.6**	**7.0**	Switzerland	1.9	2.7	2.1
				Israel	5.2	5.1	4.8
Austria	2.0	3.2	3.2	**Europe - 31**	**2.0**	**3.3**	**3.1**
Belgium	1.5	3.0	2.5				
Finland	2.9	5.5	3.0	Canada	2.9	2.7	2.5
France	1.2	2.1	2.2	United States	3.2	3.3	2.1
Germany	0.9	3.0	2.9	**North America**	**3.2**	**3.3**	**2.1**
Greece	3.7	4.2	3.9	**UNECE - 52**	**3.0**	**3.7**	**3.1**
Ireland	5.5	6.0	5.5				
Italy	0.1	1.9	2.0	_Memorandum items_			
Luxembourg	4.0	6.2	4.8	**CIS (without Russia)**	**6.9**	**9.5**	**8.0**
Netherlands	1.5	2.9	2.9	**EU-15**	**1.6**	**2.9**	**2.8**
Portugal	0.5	1.3	1.8	**EU NMS-10+2**	**4.7**	**6.3**	**6.1**
Spain	3.5	3.9	3.6				
Slovenia	4.0	5.2	4.5				
Eurozone	**1.4**	**2.8**	**2.7**				

Sources: IMF, OECD and national central banks, 2007.

Russia and Kazakhstan continue to allocate a significant proportion of their energy export receipts into oil stabilization funds and official reserves both as a way to reduce macroeconomic volatility from the oil-price cycle, as well as a way to provide some intergenerational equity. Consistent with this large increase in official reserves has been Russia's large current account balance, which was approximately 9.8% of GDP in 2006 and its significant fiscal surplus of 5.0% of GDP.

3.2 Construction sector developments

3.2.1 *Introduction*

Last year's *Review* discussed the impending slowdown in the US housing market. It also discussed the strong relationship between the economy, housing markets and building material prices. During the past several years, the strong housing market and related activities have contributed about 20% or more to GDP. Building materials comprise about one third of the sale price of a new home, and the strong demand for most materials has driven prices upward, contributing to increased construction costs. But the current "correction" in the housing market, places severe downward price pressure on some building materials such as lumber and oriented strand board (OSB). Despite this trend, prices have been rising for non-wood materials, such as concrete and steel.

European construction markets are also doing quite well, largely as a result of the booming residential (new housing particularly) sector. This section provides information on the North American and European construction markets.

Source: Wood Focus, 2007.

3.2.2 *US construction market outlook*

The McGraw Hill Construction (MHC) forecast for 2007 provides an analysis of both residential and non-residential construction markets. Although the report is somewhat outdated, as of March 2007 observations, the forecasts remain "on track". Because single-family construction accounts for over half of the dollar volume of all construction, when single family housing weakens (as it has since a mid 2005 peak), this has a large impact on total construction. There is a distinct dichotomy between residential and non-residential markets, which is actually good for the economy as construction markets become better balanced and less susceptible to "bubbles". Several reputable forecasts agree that non-residential markets will fare much better than residential markets through 2008.

For readers that like to follow housing starts instead of value of construction, forecasts in March 2007 called for 1.494 million starts in 2007 (down 18% from 2006) – this is a total drop of 28% between the peak in 2005 and 2007 (National Association of Homebuilders 2007) (graph 3.2.1). The drop is due primarily to weakness in single-family house construction where large inventories must be brought down to more manageable levels before builders get optimistic about building again. Furthermore, the inventory is bigger than it looks because the new home inventory excludes homes left with builders owing to cancellations, which surged in 2006. The inventory of existing homes (single family plus condominiums) was a record 3.6 million in 2006, a 6.5-month supply. Record price appreciation over the past several years has resulted in a rapid decline in housing affordability (lowest in the past 20 years), but, as prices recede, affordability will improve and this will help drive a turnaround in housing demand.

GRAPH 3.2.1

United States housing starts, 2004-2007

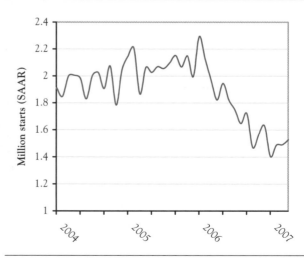

Note: SAAR = Seasonally adjusted annual rate.
Source: US Bureau of the Census, 2006.

The US is not alone with record price appreciation in the housing market. Many global housing markets remain hot, with housing price increases over the period 1997 - 2006 eclipsing those in the US. Some examples include Ireland (252%); Spain (173%); France (127%); Sweden (123%); Denmark (115%); compared with the US being up 100% over the same period. However, there are countries where prices have receded: Germany, for example where prices fell by 1%. Real estate investment was fuelled by the global stock market weakness in the early years of the new millennium (2000-2004), record low interest rates, and aggressive lending practices. The result was real estate bubbles in a number of countries, some of which have burst or may shortly burst, as in Spain.

3.2.2.1 Building material prices

Some building material prices have increased much faster than inflation (as measured by the wholesale price index). In fact, much of the rise in value of construction during 2004-2005 was accompanied by a surge in building material prices. Some building materials are quite volatile while others are relatively tame[36] (graph 3.2.2).

GRAPH 3.2.2

US building material prices, 2003-2007

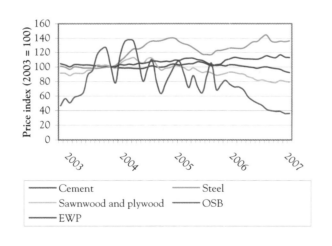

Source: US Department of Labor, 2007.

OSB is the most volatile as prices moved in tandem with single family housing (most of OSB production goes to single family housing) – up dramatically during 2003-2004, cooling off a bit during 2005 as supply caught up

[36] Price volatility is often caused by too much concentration in one market e.g. 70% of structural wood products are consumed in residential construction, so when housing activity changes abruptly, wood product prices will be volatile. Furthermore, when prices continually increase faster than inflation, this is usually a sign of scarcity – which is what is driving steel prices up.

with demand, and then "free-falling" for the past 18 months as residential construction dropped dramatically. Sawnwood and plywood pricing, with demand spread more evenly across residential (both new housing and renovation) and other markets (industrial and non-residential construction), is not nearly as volatile. Non-wood materials – steel and concrete – both increased steadily over the same period, with steel increasing the most, thanks to strong demand from China.

The 2007 outlook for building material prices is mixed. Wood prices are expected to remain weak, while most non-wood materials remain strong, at least in the near term. Wood product prices should remain weak due to excess supply in the face of lower demand from the housing market.

3.2.2.2 Summary of US construction

The economy should experience a "soft landing" in 2007 as a better balance evolves with non-residential construction and business investment growth compensating for the pull back in residential markets. The combination of declining house prices, better balanced inventories, and a continuation of accommodative mortgage rates (between 6 and 7% for the 30-year rate) will help revive the housing market by 2008. Weaker residential markets will mean soft pricing for wood products (and weak earnings for wood product firms) but it will not stop strong pricing for cement, steel, and other non-wood building materials, as strong global growth pressures energy prices, such as oil and natural gas, basic inputs for cement and steel.

3.2.3 Canadian housing market

The Canadian housing market has also been rising; however, prices did not escalate anywhere near what happened in the US. For example, between 1997 and 2006, prices in Canada increased 69% compared with 100% in the US, and 192% in England. Consequently, starts in Canada were up a modest 1.7% in 2006 to 228,000 (in contrast to the downturn in the US) and the consensus forecast from the major Canadian banks is for a modest downturn in 2007 of 10% to 205,000 units. Canadian starts peaked in 2004 with 233,000 units, a year earlier than the US peak.

3.2.4 European construction sector – review of 2006

The European construction sector has grown continuously over 13 years and Euroconstruct forecasts, predict another three years of growth (Euroconstruct, 2006). During the past few years, the booming residential sector (new construction, primarily) has been the primary driver (graph 3.2.3). The residential market is benefiting from low interest rates, favourable demographics including immigration, and sound economies, both domestic and global which fuels exports. Total construction output (either in real terms or inflation adjusted) was estimated to have grown by 3.2% in 2006, double the growth in 2005. This was driven by 5.6% growth in new residential construction and 4.2% growth in new civil engineering construction. Residential construction has been driven over the past few years in large part by growth in Spain, France, Ireland and Italy owing to much lower interest rates following entrance to the eurozone in the late 1990s. Additional stimulation came from population growth from immigration, particularly in Ireland, but also France and Spain. Spain was the real shining star – reaching 700,000 new housing units in 2006, thus accounting for 28% of the eurozone total and almost 40% of the growth in housing production in Europe between 2002 and 2006. The one significant exception to these trends is Germany, where residential growth took place earlier in the1990s following reunification, with a steady downward trend since peaking in 1995.

GRAPH 3.2.3

Construction output in Europe by sector, 2005-2007

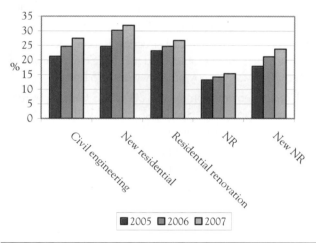

Notes: 2006 and 2007 are Euroconstruct forecasts. NR is non-residential. Total value of all sectors is €1.3 billion in 2005, and forecast to increase by 3.2% in 2006 and by 2.2% in 2007.
Source: Euroconstruct, 2006.

3.2.4.1   *Residential sector outlook*

The residential sector has been booming, led by new housing, but new construction growth will slow in 2007, and then start pulling back modestly in 2008. During this period, renovations will take up some of the slack by providing a steadying influence to the more volatile new construction sector and return to the point where new construction and renovation expenditures are about equal (graph 3.2.4). The pure number and age of housing units in western Europe is where strength in renovations comes from. The largest renovation markets in dollar terms are

Germany, Italy, France, UK, and Spain in that order, but the greatest growth in percentage terms is with the newer members to the European union - eastern countries such as Hungary and Slovakia. By comparison, the residential renovation market in the US is gaining ground on new residential construction – in 2005, renovation expenditures accounted for 40% of total residential expenditures and by 2020, it should be equal to or approaching 50%. In Europe, renovation was 48% of residential expenditures in 2005 i.e. they are already equal.

GRAPH 3.2.4

Housing markets in Europe, 2003-2008

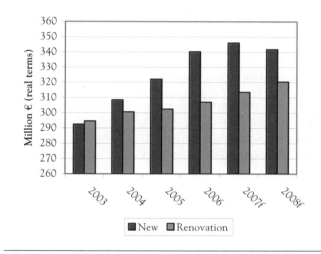

Note: f = forecast.
Source: Euroconstruct, 2006.

3.2.4.2   *Non-residential building construction*

The non-residential market is quite diverse. In 2005, the total market was worth 407 billion euros, split between new construction (58%) and improvements to existing buildings (42%). It is smaller than housing, but larger than civil engineering. It is very important in the Czech Republic, Finland and the UK, but less so in Germany and Sweden in terms of rate of growth. The sectors for new construction varied in size in 2005, from the largest being commercial buildings (45 billion euros) to the smallest being expenditures on health buildings (16.4 billion euros). Growth in the non-residential sector is expected to improve substantially from the -1.7% in 2003, 0.4% in 2004 and 2005 to 2.3% in 2006 and 2.0% in 2007. This will help to compensate for the slowdown in the residential market – similar to what is happening in the US.

3.2.4.3   *Western Europe versus eastern Europe*

In Europe the major differences between east and west is in the relative importance of residential markets and total size of construction outlays. For example, 96% of construction expenditures in Europe are in the west. Of the total construction market outlay, 48% is residential with the bulk of course being in the western countries. In fact, the western countries account for about 95% of the total expenditures on residential construction (new and renovation sectors). Furthermore, five western countries – UK, Spain, France, Germany and Italy account for 75% of residential expenditures. This sort of dichotomy will continue for quite some time as the east is integrated with the western economies. The rate of growth in the eastern countries is substantially higher than the growth rate in the west (table 3.2.1). This is particularly true for civil engineering or infrastructure spending. The west builds and maintains houses, whereas the east is building infrastructure (civil engineering) and non-residential buildings such as factories and stores (graph 3.2.5).

TABLE 3.2.1

European construction sector developments, 2005-2007

(% change, volume basis)

Western countries	2005	2006	2007
Total residential	3.0	3.6	1.8
Total non-residential	0.3	2.1	2.0
Civil engineering	0	2.8	2.6
Total	0.1	2.4	1.6
Eastern countries[1]			
Total residential	3.1	5.6	5.9
Total non-residential	3.1	4.6	3.0
Civil engineering	15.1	11.9	7.8
Total	5.4	6.2	4.4

Note: f = forecast. [1] Czech Republic, Hungary, Poland, Slovakia.
Source: Euroconstruct, 2006.

GRAPH 3.2.5

Western versus eastern European construction sectors, 2006

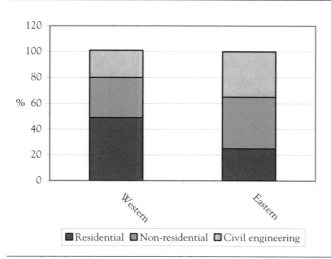

Source: Euroconstruct, 2006.

3.3   References

APA – The Engineered Wood Association. 2007. Economics Report E73. Regional Production and Market Outlook. Tacoma, Washington.

Bank of Nova Scotia. 2007. Real Estate Trends, March 2007. Available at: http://www.scotiabank.com/cda/content/0,1608,CID8339_LIDen,00.html

Euroconstruct. 2006. Munich Conference, December 2006. Summary Report. Available at: www.euroconstruct.org

McGraw-Hill Construction. 2006. Engineering News Record. Special report – Forecast 2007 – Growth Pulse Weakens but the Patient is still Healthy. Authored by Tim Grogan. Available at : www.enr.com

Moody's Economy.com. 2007. The Dismal Scientist, Economic analysis subscription service. Available at: http://www.economy.com/dismal/

National Association of Homebuilders. 2007. Housing Economics. Available at: http://www.nahb.org/generic.aspx?sectionID=140&genericContentID=26009

National Association of Realtors. 2007. Inventory of existing homes for sale. Available at: http://www.realtor.org/research/index.html

The Economist. 2006. Bubble and Squeak. 7 December 2006 issue. Available at: http://www.economist.com/

US Census Bureau. 2007. Construction Reports, Series C-25, New One Family Homes Sold and For Sale. Available at: http://www.census.gov/prod/www/abs/c25.html

US Department of Commerce. 2006. US Census Bureau. Construction Spending. Available at: http://www.census.gov/const/www/c30index.html

US Department of Labor. 2007. Bureau of Labor Statistics. Producer price series. Available at: http://data.bls.gov/cgi-bin/srgate

Chapter 4

Strong sawnwood and pulp markets push roundwood prices to record highs: Wood raw material markets, 2006-2007[37]

Highlights

- Wood raw material costs for the manufacture of sawnwood have shot up in many regions around the world in 2006 and 2007, with the global average softwood sawlog price reaching an all-time record high of $82/m³ in 2007.

- During 2007, the average global wood fibre prices reached their highest levels in 12 years as a result of strong pulp and paper markets and a number of events that impacted the wood fibre supply, including but not limited to increased competition for raw material from the energy sector, weak US sawnwood markets and unfavourable weather conditions.

- The total harvest in the UNECE region in 2006 was estimated at 1.4 billion m³, which was down 1.4% from the exceptional level of 2005, but 10.0% higher than five years ago.

- Almost 1.2 billion m³ of total removals were utilized for industrial purposes; 75% consisted of softwood species, a large share of which was used by an expanding sawmilling sector.

- The apparent sharp decrease of 9% in consumption of softwood roundwood is misleading, as large volumes of damaged timber from the 2005 storm in northern Europe were inventoried and actually consumed during 2006.

- Roundwood consumption by the pulp industry in Europe increased by 8% from 2005, reaching a total of 120 million m³ in 2006, which was 76% of their total wood fibre consumption.

- The Russian Federation has increased harvests of industrial roundwood by 22% over the past five years, reaching 144 million m³ in 2006, of which 65% was used domestically and the remainder exported mainly to China, Japan and the Nordic countries.

- Roundwood consumption fell in Canada, as the forest industry was negatively impacted by the slump in US housing during 2006 and 2007, and the strengthening of the Canadian dollar.

- Removals of fuelwood have gone up substantially in the past few years, reaching 27% of total removals in 2006, due to higher wood energy consumption driven by government policies, higher costs of fossil fuels and greater supply of storm-damaged timber.

- Mobilization of more roundwood while both wood energy and wood industry demands mount, especially in Europe, is of greater concern in light of new Russian export taxes.

---

[37] By Mr. Håkan Ekström, Wood Resources International, US.

Secretariat introduction

This chapter benefits from the expertise in global wood raw material markets of Mr. Håkan Ekström,[38] President, Wood Resources International. The secretariat sincerely appreciates the continued collaboration with Mr. Ekström for his valuable perspective on roundwood, chip and wood energy markets. He is the Editor-in-Chief of two publications that follow global wood fibre markets, including prices: *Wood Resource Quarterly* and *North American Wood Fiber Review*. Mr. Ekström is a member of the UNECE/FAO Team of Specialists on Forest Products Markets and Marketing. He is scheduled to present this chapter to the joint Timber Committee and International Softwood Conference Market Discussions in October 2007.

We thank his contributors, in alphabetical order, beginning with Dr. Nikolai Burdin, Director, OAO NIPIEIlesprom, Moscow, who is also our statistical correspondent for Russia. Dr. Burdin has been chairman of the Timber Committee and the FAO/UNECE Working Party on Forest Economics and Statistics, and is also a member of the Team of Specialists. We also thank Mr. Ralf Dümmer, Ernährungswirtschaft, Germany, Dr. Riitta Hänninen, Finnish Forest Research Institute, and Mr. Bernard Lombard, Confederation of European Paper Industries and contributing author to chapter 8 on paper and pulp markets.

A schematic diagram of the roundwood breakdown into different subcategories appears in the annex to this *Review*.

4.1   Introduction

The UNECE region is the world's leading producer of softwood-based forest products, with softwood species dominating the forests in this region. An estimated 80% of the world's softwood log production occurs in Europe, Russia and North America, which has remained fairly stable over the past five years. Production of hardwood roundwood in this region accounts for approximately half of the world's total and a large share of the temperate hardwood removals.

The total harvest in the UNECE in 2006 was estimated at 1.37 billion m³, which was down 1.4% from 2005 but 10.0% higher than five years ago. Almost 1.16 billion m³ were utilized for industrial purposes, of which 75% consisted of softwood species used mainly by the sawmilling sector. The remaining 25% was hardwood species predominantly consumed by the pulp and paper

industry in the Nordic countries and in the Iberian Peninsula.

Bearing in mind that woodfuel data are unreliable, recorded removals of fuelwood increased by 2% from 2005 to 205 million m³ in 2006. Chapter 9 of the *Review* is on wood energy, and will therefore not be analysed in detail in this chapter.

In 2006, the total consumption of softwood roundwood in the UNECE region fell for the first time in six years (graph 4.1.1), falling by as much as 9% in Europe. This decrease was mainly the result of a substantial reduction in apparent consumption in Sweden in the aftermath to the big storm in 2005.[39] The total consumption of hardwood roundwood in the UNECE region has been practically unchanged in the past five years (graph 4.1.2).

GRAPH 4.1.1

Consumption of softwood roundwood in the UNECE region, 2002-2006

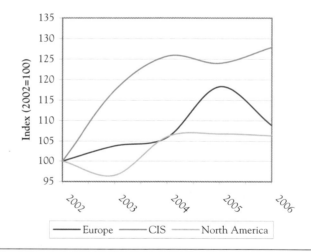

Source: UNECE/FAO TIMBER database, 2007.

An estimated 8.5% of softwood industrial roundwood removals and over 10% of hardwood roundwood are not being processed by domestic manufacturers in the UNECE region, but rather exported to pulpmills and sawmills in neighbouring countries. This is up from 7.9% and 8.9%, respectively, from five years ago.

---

[38] By Mr. Håkan Ekström, President and Editor-in-Chief, Wood Resources International, P.O. Box 1891, Bothell, Washington 98041, US, tel: +1 425 402 8809, fax: +1 425 402 0187, website: www.woodprices.com and email: hekstrom@wri-ltd.com

[39] The sharp reduction in industrial roundwood consumption in Sweden in 2006 (see electronic annex for detailed country statistics) is misleading as large volumes of damaged timber from the 2005 storm Gudrun were inventoried in 2005 and actually consumed in 2006. As roundwood consumption by the pulp industry and the sawmill sector increased in 2006 from the previous year, the actual roundwood consumption in Sweden was higher in 2006 than in 2005.

GRAPH 4.1.2

Consumption of hardwood roundwood in the UNECE region, 2002-2006

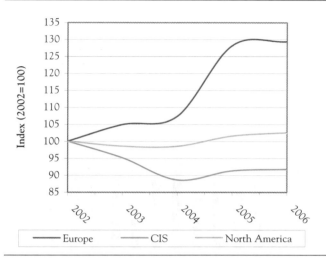

Source: UNECE/FAO TIMBER database, 2007.

Almost all of this increased trade has been in softwood logs shipped from eastern Russia to non-UNECE regions (predominantly China and Japan) and hardwood (birch and aspen) logs from western Russia to the Nordic countries (graph 4.1.3). This trend is likely to be interrupted, as the Russian authorities are planning to implement escalating log export taxes to encourage more processing domestically.

GRAPH 4.1.3

Industrial roundwood trade flows, 2001-2005

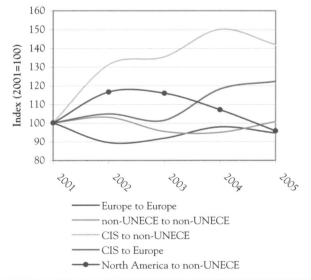

Note: Corresponding trade flow table in electronic annex.
Source: UN Comtrade/EFI, 2007.

4.2 Europe subregion

Europe was again hit by two devastating storms, Kyrill and Per in January 2007. These seemingly annual events impacted mostly central Europe, with the worst damage occurring in Germany, southern Sweden and the Czech Republic. The storms also had an impact on the forests in France, Belgium, Austria and Poland, but reportedly to a much lesser degree. According to recent estimates, over 50 million m³ of timber were damaged by Kyrill, of which over half (35 million m³) was in Germany. Hurricane Per, which hit southern Sweden, was estimated to have damaged approximately 12 million m³ of timber. The storm hit Europe at a time when sawmills and pulpmills had been struggling to find adequate raw material to supply their mills, so there was no difficulty finding buyers for the damaged timber. Further, roundwood prices were generally not affected by the storms as the forest industry geared up to process the excess volumes.

Source: E. Pepke, 2007.

In 2006, the estimated total roundwood removals in Europe were 472 million m³, of which 370 million m³ were for industrial purposes and an estimated (but very uncertain) 101 million m³ for energy uses (table 4.2.1). Softwood industrial roundwood removals, which account for 77% of total industrial removals, were down by 9% from 2005, but still 6% higher than five years ago. Much of the decline occurred in Sweden because of the previously mentioned hurricane-induced storm damage, as well as in Finland, where a new forest tax reform has been dampening private landowners' motivation to harvest timber. Rather than taxing the annual growth of a landowner's forest, the new tax is assessed on the actual timber volume sold. Initially, the new system resulted in limited interest in logging by small landowners who do not necessarily require periodic revenue from their forests. In 2006, the industrial roundwood removals in Finland were down for the third year in a row, to 45.5 million m³ which was the lowest level in ten years. Consumption of roundwood by the Finnish forest industry fell almost 5% in 2006 to the lowest level in six years.

TABLE 4.2.1

Roundwood balance in Europe, 2005-2006

$(1,000 \ m^3)$

	2005	2006	Change %
Removals	497 235	471 856	-5.1
Imports	69 439	66 767	-3.8
Exports	39 768	38 345	-3.6
Net trade	-29 671	-28 421	...
Apparent consumption	526 906	500 278	-5.1
of which: EU25			
Removals	433 580	408 470	-5.8
Imports	62 996	60 817	-3.5
Exports	35 951	33 636	-6.4
Net trade	-27 045	-27 181	...
Apparent consumption	460 625	435 651	-5.4

Source: UNECE/FAO TIMBER database, 2007.

Germany and the Czech Republic, however, have experienced substantial increases of 51% and 24%, respectively, in their removals of industrial roundwood over the past five years. The additional wood supply has mainly benefited an expanding sawmill sector in the two countries. The developments in Germany are of particular interest as the removals in 2006 of over 60 million m³ were almost 65% higher than the average level in the 1990s (graph 4.2.1). One reason that it has been possible to increase harvests is the higher growing stock showed in the 2004 *Second National Forest Inventory* and a higher net annual increment than previously measured. As a result of the new inventory data, annual harvesting potential has been raised to as much as 85 million m³. This German example clearly shows that reliable and updated inventory information is a valuable tool and may be a good investment when countries around the world are trying to mobilize wood supply and calculate harvesting potentials.

The major timber supply developments in the past five years include the increased logging levels in central Europe and the reduced harvests in the Nordic countries. This should not necessarily be seen as a trend, but rather as the result of a number of special events: a number of devastating storms, strikes in the Finnish forest industry, a new timber tax system in Finland and mobilization of the wood supply in Germany. Over the next few years, logging activities are expected to increase in the Nordic countries, while levelling off in central and southwest Europe. Swedish forest owners will likely return to pre-storm harvest levels and potentially higher removals as the result of a spruce bark beetle infestation. The Finnish

forest industry will encourage higher logging activities domestically, as the log imports from Russia will become increasingly prohibitively expensive with the new Russian export taxes.

GRAPH 4.2.1

Industrial roundwood production in Germany, 1996-2006

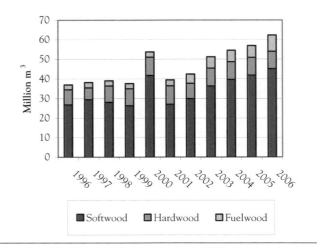

Source: UNECE/FAO TIMBER database, 2007.

In 2006 and 2007, the demand for wood raw material, both roundwood and residues, has been strong, since pulpmills, sawmills and panel manufacturers have been running at high operating rates and all sectors have reached record-high production levels.

Roundwood consumption by the pulp industry increased by 8% from 2005 and by 17% from 2002, reaching a total of 120 million m³ in 2006. This sector relied on over 76% roundwood for its total wood fibre needs, while the remaining 24% were chips from sawmills and plywood mills. The total wood fibre consumption of 158 million m³ in 2006 was 4.8% higher than in the previous year. The general trend over the past five years has been an increased reliance on roundwood rather than wood chips, and higher imports of both softwood and hardwood logs.

The competition for wood fibre in Europe is intensifying as sawmills, pulpmills and bioenergy facilities are expanding capacity and need additional raw material. This has been particularly true in Germany and Sweden recently, resulting in substantially higher costs for sawlogs, pulplogs and wood chips. In much of central and southern Europe, wood fibre costs for the pulp industry have been rising as competition from the bioenergy sector has increasingly had an influence on the pricing structure of hardwood pulpwood. Pulpwood costs rose 10-25% in 2006, both as the result of increased competition and higher transport costs, and in some regions reached historic highs. Although Germany is a small consumer of hardwood pulpwood, the pulp producers have been hit hard, with an almost doubling of costs over the past three years.

Much uncertainty surrounds the national fuelwood data. Nevertheless, it is still worth noting that recorded removals of fuelwood reached 101 million m³, which amounted to 27% of the total removals in 2006. The higher consumption of fuelwood is not only the result of government policies and higher costs of fossil fuels but also of the higher supply of storm-damaged timber during 2005 through 2007. (Readers are directed to chapter 9 for a detailed analysis of wood energy.)

Europe continues to be a net importer of wood chips. In 2006, it imported 24.7 million m³, while exporting 21.1 million m³. The net import volumes were the lowest since 2003. The major destinations were pulpmills and composite panel plants in Italy, Finland, Sweden, Belgium and Germany, while major exporters were countries in central Europe, including Germany, Latvia, France, Estonia and Austria. Increasingly, European countries are importing sawdust and wood pellets for energy consumption.

4.3 CIS subregion

Removals of industrial roundwood in the CIS subregion continue to set new records and reached 160 million m³ in 2006, 4.5% higher than the previous year (table 4.3.1). The Russian Federation accounted for 90% of the removals in this subregion, while Ukraine and Belarus combined had an 8.9% share of the total reported removal volume. The Russian Federation has increased harvests of industrial roundwood by 22% over the past five years, reaching 144 million m³ in 2006. The country is still the largest exporter of logs in the world, exporting a large share of its roundwood removals from both the western and eastern regions of the country.

TABLE 4.3.1

Roundwood balance in the CIS, 2005-2006

(1,000 m³)

	2005	2006	*Change %*
Removals	210 044	216 305	3.0
Imports	1 432	1 221	-14.8
Exports	52 493	55 322	5.4
Net trade	51 060	54 101	6.0
Apparent consumption	158 984	162 204	2.0

Source: UNECE/FAO TIMBER database, 2007.

In 2006, the log export share accounted for 35% of the total harvest. This share is up from 31% five years ago and is based on official statistics. In addition to the official harvest levels, there has been an acknowledgement by the Russian Government that there is another estimated 10% of "undocumented" timber harvest, much of which is exported to China. Other studies in recent years have estimated that 15-20% of timber harvest may be defined as illegal (Wood Resources International LLC and Seneca Creek Associates, 2004). At the October 2006 Timber Committee Market Discussions, the Russian delegation indicated that up to 30% of the roundwood exports to China could be illegal for various reasons. Exports of both softwood and hardwood logs continued to go up in 2006, reaching another record of almost 51 million m³. The major destinations were China (44%), Finland (26%), Japan (10%) and Sweden (4%).

The Russian Government adopted export tariffs for roundwood for the next five years. The overall goal is to sharply reduce exports of raw material and to increase the domestic manufacturing of forest products. Simultaneously with the higher export taxes, the Government has reduced import taxes on machinery to encourage investments in the processing sector.

Exported softwood logs will be taxed at a minimum of €15 ($20) per m³ by April 2008 and will then be increased to a minimum of €50 ($68) per m³ by 2009. Initially, birch logs were to be taxed at such a high level that it would eliminate exports by 2011. However, after protests from both the Swedish and Finnish Governments, the Russian authorities decided to suspend the tax hikes on birch logs smaller than 15 cm top diameter until 2011 and only increase softwood and aspen taxes, at least for now. There is still much uncertainty regarding future log tariffs, and it is possible there will be downward adjustments as the European Commission is currently in discussion with the Russian Government representatives. The Finnish and Swedish Governments have raised this issue with the World Trade Organization (WTO), claiming that Russia is violating the treaty that it has signed.

Due to the lack of satisfactory improvement of the Russian forest sector, the Government approved a new Forestry Code to be implemented in January 2007. This new code is meant to decentralize the decision-making to regional governments, increase transparency of the forest management system and reduce corruption through public auctions for forest leases. These leases will be for 49 years and are planned to be extendable. While it is still too early to conclude how this new Forestry Code will impact wood supply and timber pricing in the medium term, the expected short-term disruptions are described in the earlier policy chapter.

4.4 North America subregion

North America produces more industrial roundwood than Europe and CIS combined. In 2006, this subregion harvested 631 million m³ of industrial roundwood (without fuel), divided between US and Canada, with 428 million m³ and 203 million m³, respectively (table 4.4.1). Despite the reduced production of forest products, industrial roundwood removals were slightly higher in 2006 than the previous year and 4% higher than five years ago.

TABLE 4.4.1

Roundwood balance in North America, 2005-2006

(1,000 m³)

	2005	2006	Change %
Removals	678 849	678 511	0.0
Imports	10 100	9 675	-4.2
Exports	15 870	14 958	-5.7
Net trade	5 771	5 284	-8.4
Apparent consumption	673 078	673 227	0.0

Source: UNECE/FAO TIMBER database, 2007.

The forest industry in North America was hit by the slump in the US housing market during 2006 and 2007. Demand for most wood products fell, many sawmills and panel producers in both the US and Canada were forced to cut production levels, and a number of mills closed. In addition, Canadian exporters lost market shares as they became less competitive due to a strengthening domestic currency. The Canadian dollar was up from Can$0.86 per US dollar in January 2006 to a record Can$0.95 per US dollar in July 2007, a 10.4% rise. These two major events resulted in reduced consumption of roundwood in Canada.

In 2006, the mountain pine beetle epidemic in western Canada expanded eastward from the province of British Columbia (BC) to Alberta, and it is estimated that there are dead or dying trees covering over 17 million hectares in BC alone and that 580 million m³ of timber has been damaged. Harvest levels have gone up substantially there in the past few years, from 74 million m³ in 2002 to 82 million m³ in 2006. Although the sawmilling industry has taken advantage of the increased timber supply from the affected areas, many sawmills will have to cut back production in the coming years since the quality of the timber is deteriorating (see also chapter 5 on sawn softwood chapter).

The pulp sector in North America is more dependent on residual chips from sawmilling than mills in any other part of the world. Typically, between 90-100% of the total fibre need is supplied by local sawmills. Since sawmills reduced production in late 2006 due to declining sawnwood demand in the export market, the pulp sector was increasingly forced to use more roundwood, thus increasing the costs of wood fibre.

In 2006, roundwood consumption in North America was estimated at 673 million m³, of which 74% was softwood species mainly consumed by the sawnwood and pulp industries. The subregion continues to be a net exporter of softwood logs, exporting 4.9 million m³ from the west coast of the US and Canada to Japan, China and the Republic of Korea. Canada reduced exports to the US as the domestic industry, particularly in the eastern provinces, was experiencing tighter log supply.

Source: AHEC. 2007.

4.5 Raw material prices

In 2006 and 2007, global sawn softwood markets have been fairly strong with high demand in Europe, Asia and Canada. The US market is the only major world market that has experienced a downturn: housing starts have fallen from approximately 2.1 million (annually adjusted) in 2005 to just over 1.5 million starts in May 2007. These market developments have impacted sawlog prices. Prices are higher in Europe and Oceania, while log costs have been stable or declining in North and Latin America.

The *Wood Resource Quarterly* (WRQ) Global Conifer Sawlog Price, which is based on domestic species typically processed into construction and higher grades in 18 key areas around the world, reached a record high of $82/m³ in the first quarter of 2006. This was because log costs in Europe in particular increased drastically with respect to the US dollar. The global average price has been fluctuating between $53/m³ and $78/m³ over the past 12 years. Much of the increase can be contributed to the weakening of the US dollar, but costs have also gone up in the local currencies in Europe, as log supply has tightened over the past two years. In the mid-1990s, the difference between the lowest cost WRQ regions (Latin America at $40/m³) and highest cost WRQ region (Central Europe at $115/m³) was $75/m³, while in 2007 the disparity between the lowest and highest cost region had increased to almost $100/m³. The average European prices are currently all above the global average; the other regions tracked are below the WRQ average.

In early 2007, sawlog prices were rising in both Europe and Russia, but falling in North America. The biggest price changes in the UNECE region in the past year were in Russia, as delivered prices rose substantially last winter when the mild weather created major problems for loggers and truck haulers resulting in tight log supply and low log inventories (graphs 4.5.1 and 4.5.2). In just 12 months, there were also substantial upward price adjustments in central Europe, where sawlog prices in Germany and Austria increased by 55 and 27%, respectively (with respect to the US dollar). In the Nordic countries and eastern Europe, average sawlog prices were up 27% and 36% respectively over the same period.

GRAPH 4.5.1

Global softwood sawlog prices, 1995-2007

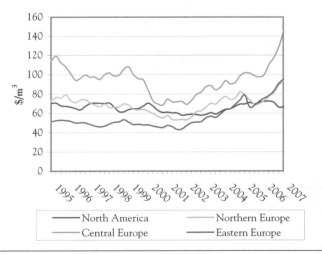

Source: Wood Resource Quarterly, Wood Resources International, 2007.

GRAPH 4.5.2

Delivered softwood sawlog prices in Europe and Russia, 2003-2007

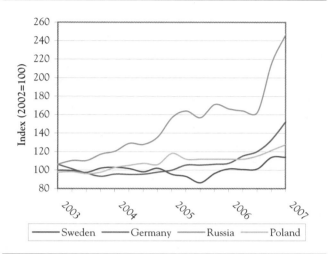

Source: Wood Resource Quarterly, Wood Resources International, 2007.

It is interesting to note that average prices in the Nordic countries, the Baltic States and eastern Europe have steadily converged in the past 12 years, and have become practically identical over the past 18 months. The countries around the Baltic Sea have clearly become one common market for wood raw material.

In North America, softwood sawlog costs have declined as the sawnwood market weakened in 2006 (graph 4.5.3). However, in the western US, prices rose in early 2007, influenced by a more active log export market. Both the Republic of Korea and Japan were increasing sawlog purchases from the US. With the higher export tariffs for Russian logs in the coming years, it is plausible that log importers in Asia will be more active in the US and Canada, thus affecting the costs for domestic sawmills in North America.

Source: Finnish Forest Institute, 2007.

GRAPH 4.5.3

Delivered softwood sawlog prices in North America, 2003-2007

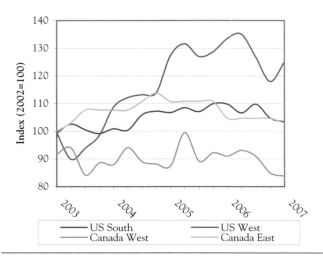

Source: Wood Resource Quarterly, Wood Resources International, 2007.

Prices for oak sawlogs in Germany have trended upward for almost five years, reaching a record level in the first quarter of 2007 (graph 4.5.4). The price increases have mainly been the result of higher demand for sawn hardwood, parquet flooring and wood furniture from the export market. Beech sawlog prices in Germany have fallen in the past two years as demand, particularly in the US and Europe, declined in late 2006 and during the first few months of 2007.

GRAPH 4.5.4

Delivered hardwood sawlog prices, 2003-2007

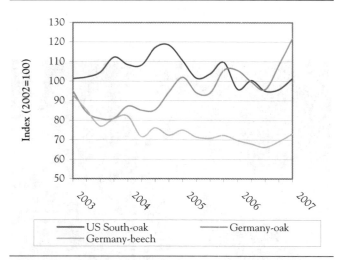

Source: Wood Resource Quarterly, Wood Resources International, 2007.

Oak sawlog prices in the US south reached a five-year low of $55/ton last summer, with the slowing housing starts having an impact on the demand for flooring, cabinets and furniture. With a moderately tighter supply, average prices have gone up slightly to $60/ton in 2007.

The average global wood fibre prices (based on wood prices in countries accounting for 85-90% of the world's wood-based pulp production capacity) reached the highest level in 12 years in the first quarter of 2007 when softwood fibre averaged $102/oven-dry metric ton (odmt) and hardwood fibre reached $91/odmt. The rise in wood fibre costs worldwide has been the result of strong pulp and paper markets, and a number of events affecting the supply, including: higher energy costs, increased competition for raw material from the energy sector (Europe), weak sawnwood markets (North America) and unfavourable weather conditions (Russia). In 2006 and 2007, both softwood and hardwood pulpwood prices have gone up substantially in the UNECE region, with the biggest price increases in western US, Russia, Finland and France (graphs 4.5.5 and 4.5.6).

GRAPH 4.5.5

Delivered softwood pulp log prices in Europe, 2003-2007

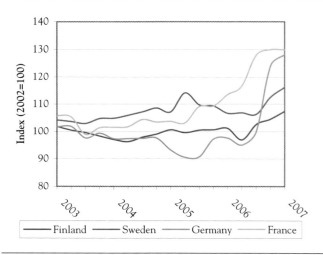

Source: Wood Resource Quarterly, Wood Resources International, 2007.

In 2006 and 2007, wood raw material costs for the manufacturing of sawnwood and pulp have gone up in many regions around the world, with the exception of the US and Canada. Prices for sawlog and pulpwood are likely to stabilize worldwide later in 2007 and 2008 as the demand and pricing structure of manufactured products level off.

GRAPH 4.5.6

Delivered softwood pulp log prices in North America, 2003-2007

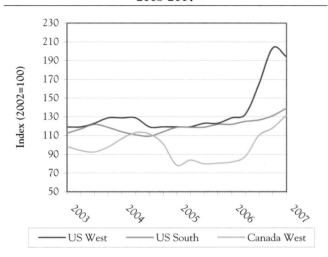

Source: *Wood Resource Quarterly*, Wood Resources International, 2007.

4.6   References

Confederation of European Paper Industries (CEPI). 2007. Available at: www.cepi.org

Europäischer Wirtschaftsdienst (EUWID). 2007. Available at: www.euwid-wood-products.com

Timber Mart-South. 2007. Available at: www.tmart-south.com

UN COMTRADE/EFI. 2007. UN Comtrade database validated by European Forest Institute. Comtrade available at: http://comtrade.un.org/ and EFI available at: www.efi.fi

UNECE/FAO TIMBER Database. 2007. Available at: www.unece.org/trade/timber

Wood Resources International LLC and Seneca Creek Associates. 2004. *Illegal Logging and Global Wood Markets: The Competitive Impacts on the U.S. Wood Products Industry.* Available at: www.afandpa.org

Wood Resources International, LLC. 2007. *North American Wood Fiber Review.* Available at: www.woodprices.com

Wood Resources International, LLC. 2007. *Wood Resource Quarterly.* Available at: www.woodprices.com

Zentrale Markt- und Preisberichtstelle für Erzeugnisse der Land-, Forst- und Ernährungswirtschaft. 2006. Available at: www.zmp.de

Chapter 5

Europe and Russia soar as North America retreats: Sawn softwood markets, 2006-2007[40]

Highlights

- In Europe, strong growth in both production and consumption of sawn softwood occurred in 2006 and continued through mid-2007; however, in the same period North American markets fell.

- German sawmillers continued to significantly increase their production for the third consecutive year, and with more large mills coming in Europe, there is concern over sawlog availability.

- Japan, North Africa and Middle East markets gained importance over the previously attractive United States market for European exporters.

- European sawn softwood prices increased significantly from strong demand – a development that continued into early 2007.

- The production and exports of sawn softwood in the Russian Federation increased again in 2006 – both trends are expected to continue in 2007.

- US housing starts plunged in 2006 by 13% and are forecast to drop below 1.5 million units in 2007, an 18% reduction compared with 2006, causing US sawn softwood demand and production to plummet and prices to dive below break-even levels.

- North American exports to Europe escalated as a weak US dollar and soaring prices in the UK and Germany attracted exporters, a reversal of trends with respect to recent years.

- European exporters to the US in 2006 abandoned the market due to collapsing prices – exports to the US declined by one third in 2006 compared with 2005 and by two thirds in the first quarter of 2007 compared with the same period in 2006.

- Sawlog supply volatility occurred throughout the UNECE region: decreases in Russia and the Baltic States due to a mild winter; increases in western Europe due to the January 2007 windstorms; increases in British Columbia, Canada, due to the mountain pine beetle; and decreases in Quebec, Canada, due to harvesting cutbacks.

---

[40] By Dr. Nikolai Burdin, OAO NIPIEIlesprom, Russian Federation, Mr. Jarno Seppälä, Pöyry Forest Industry Consulting, Finland and Mr. Russell E. Taylor, International WOOD MARKETS Group Inc., Canada.

Secretariat introduction

We are pleased to welcome our returning analysts to the production of the sawn softwood chapter. We wish to thank the authors of this chapter (in alphabetical order) and their associates.

As in previous years, Dr. Nikolai Burdin,[41] Director, OAO NIPIEIlesprom, Moscow, our statistical correspondent for Russia, wrote the analysis for the Russian Federation. Dr. Burdin was formerly Chairman of the UNECE Timber Committee and the FAO/UNECE Working Party on Forest Economics and Statistics. He is a member of the UNECE/FAO Team of Specialists on Forest Products Markets and Marketing.

Mr. Jarno Seppälä,[42] Senior Consultant, Pöyry Forest Industry Consulting, wrote the Europe subregion analysis. His work in the solid wood products business area has been in international trade, market development and strategies. He worked on the *Review* as a marketing assistant while attending the University of Helsinki and has contributed to this chapter since 2006. He is scheduled to present this chapter at the 2007 joint Timber Committee and International Softwood Conference Market Discussions. He is also a member of the UNECE/FAO Team of Specialists on Forest Products Markets and Marketing.

Mr. Russell E. Taylor,[43] President, International WOOD MARKETS Group Inc., again acted as this year's sawn softwood chapter coordinator and analysed the North American markets. Mr. Taylor is also a member of the UNECE/FAO Team of Specialists on Forest Products Markets and Marketing, and presented forest products market and policy developments at the 2004 and 2006 Timber Committee Market Discussions. He is scheduled to present this chapter at the 2007 joint Timber Committee and International Softwood Conference Market Discussions.

---

[41] Dr. Nikolai Burdin, Director, OAO NIPIEIlesprom, Klinskaya ul. 8, Moscow, Russian Federation, RU-125889, tel: +7 095 456 1303, fax: +7 095 456 5390, e-mail: nipi@dialup.ptt.ru

[42] Mr. Jarno Seppälä, Senior Consultant, Pöyry Forest Industry Consulting, P.O. Box 4, Jaakonkatu 3, FIN-01621Vantaa, Finland, tel: +358 10 332 2078, fax: +358 10332 2881, e-mail: jarno.seppala@poyry.com and website: www. poyry.com

[43] Mr. Russell E. Taylor, President, International WOOD MARKETS Group Inc., Forest Industry Strategic Services, Ste. 501, 570 Granville Street, V6C 3P1 Vancouver, British Columbia, Canada, tel: +1 604 801 5996, fax: +1 604-801-5997, e-mail: retaylor@woodmarkets.com and website: www.woodmarkets.com

5.1 Introduction

In 2006, overall consumption of sawn softwood in the UNECE region declined slightly, by 1.6%, to 231.2 million m^3 (graph 5.1.1). There were great differences in the trends, however, with stronger consumption gains in Europe and Canada that were more than offset by declines in the US and the derived figures in the CIS subregion.

GRAPH 5.1.1

Consumption of sawn softwood in the UNECE region, 2002-2006

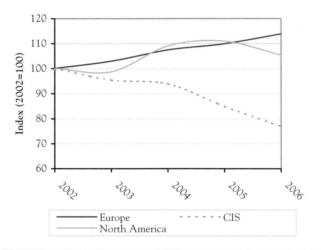

Note: Although the official statistics show CIS apparent consumption declining, the authors believe it is increasing. See section 5.2.

Source: UNECE/FAO TIMBER database, 2007.

In 2006, production in the UNECE region remained steady from 2005, reaching 256.8 million m^3. Notably, the year was characterized by further winter storms, continuing development in German sawnwood capacity and contrasting price trends in Europe, with spectacular price increases, vs. North America, with prices falling to cost levels.

Sawnwood trade flows deviated from previous trends in 2005, in large part due to the oversupply of sawlogs in Europe from the January 2005 storms, which was then processed into sawnwood (graph 5.1.2). Intra-European sawnwood trade accelerated, as did exports from Europe. Russian exports to Europe were constrained by the oversupply during this period. Again, in January 2007, storms damaged forests around the Baltic Sea region; however, the overall damage was less in area and in volume than in 2005 but still significant.

GRAPH 5.1.2

Sawn softwood trade flows, 2001-2005

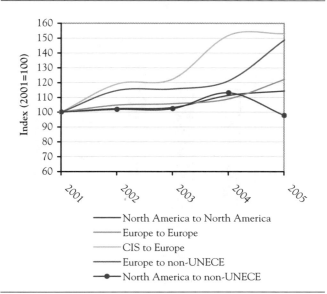

——— North America to North America
——— Europe to Europe
——— CIS to Europe
——— Europe to non-UNECE
—●— North America to non-UNECE

Note: Corresponding trade flow table in the electronic annex.
Source: UN Comtrade/EFI, 2007.

5.2   Europe subregion

In 2006, Europe as a whole showed a growth in sawn softwood production of almost 4.9 million m³ (4.7%), totalling about 110.5 million m³ (table 5.2.1). EU25 sawn softwood production greatly increased yet again, by 4.2 million m³ to 98.3 million m³ (4.5%): these countries represented approximately 85% of the whole European growth, with Germany leading the way. German sawmillers were able to increase their production by almost 2.5 million m³ (11.8%), resulting in a growth of over 5 million m³ during the last two years. Aggressive expansion strategies by German companies have been based on the construction of large, world-class mills, which has increased demand for sawlogs and decreased sawlog exports, especially to Austria. In addition to Germany, the Czech Republic showed an increase of over one million m³, largely as a result of one new mill processing up to 1.0 million m³ of sawlogs. This caused the Czech Republic to record Europe's largest single country growth rate (29.5%). Sweden was third with a major boost (400,000 m³) in 2006. Out of the largest producers, Finland and Austria faced consecutive production declines from tight log supplies, by 45,000 m³ and 620,000 m³, respectively.

At the same time, European consumption totalled 102.1 million m³, showing a total growth of 3.9 million m³, of which 2.8 million m³ (approximately 70%) occurred in EU25 countries. Followed by remarkable production growths, Germany and the Czech Republic also showed strong growth in consumption in line with other strengthened economies, with increases of over 1.5 million

m³ and almost 850,000 m³, respectively. In addition, sawn softwood consumption increased a significant 720,000 m³ in Turkey. In 2006, there were two countries with major consumption decreases: Sweden (almost 900,000 m³) and Slovakia (approximately 600,000 m³).

TABLE 5.2.1

Sawn softwood balance in Europe, 2005-2006

(1,000 m³)

	2005	2006	Change %
Production	105 608	110 545	4.7
Imports	40 199	40 669	1.2
Exports	47 676	49 159	3.1
Net trade	7 476	8 490	13.6
Apparent consumption	98 132	102 055	4.0
Of which: EU-25			
Production	94 095	98 307	4.5
Imports	37 343	37 409	0.2
Exports	44 396	45 925	3.4
Net trade	7 053	8 517	20.8
Apparent consumption	87 042	89 791	3.2

Source: UNECE/FAO TIMBER database, 2007.

Europe as a whole was a net exporter of sawn softwood in 2006 with a net trade volume of 8.5 million m³. Exports grew by approximately 1.5 million m³ in comparison with the previous year while imports gained about 470,000 m³. EU25 represented basically all of Europe's net export increase, but very little of overall import growth.

Sweden held its leading position as Europe's largest exporter (approximately 13.2 million m³), showing a growth of 1.3 million m³. German export volume also grew, increasing by 660,000 m³ (10.0%). These countries were followed by Slovakia with over 400,000 m³ growth. Of the traditional exporters, Finland saw only a modest growth of 64,000 m³, while Austria faced a notable drop of over 400,000 m³. Another major decline occurred in the Baltic countries – the combined export volume from Estonia, Latvia and Lithuania dropped by about 653,000 m³ (13.4%) in comparison with the previous year. The Baltic countries are exporting less sawnwood, since they are consuming more of their production, converting more into value-added softwood products, and exporting them more profitably than commodity sawnwood.

Regarding sawn softwood imports, volume in Italy increased, by approximately 230,000 m³, whereas volumes in the UK and France dropped significantly, by approximately 370,000 m³ (5.0%) and 200,000 m³ (6.0%) respectively. Interestingly, Austria's imports jumped up by over 350,000 m³ (27.6%) after a stable period during the beginning of the decade.

After two consecutive years with over 1 million m³ of annual growth in exports to the US, European shipments reversed the trend, with a decline of over 800,000 m³ in comparison with the record year 2005 (graph 5.2.1). This was due to the unfavourable price developments in the US that created an unprofitable business situation with respect to strong demand and rising price levels in Europe. However, with strong export networks and promotion, German exporters kept their US volumes above 2 million m³, while Austria (with reduced production levels in 2006) lost market share, with exports of almost 380,000 m³, or a 50.4% drop.

GRAPH 5.2.1

Sawn softwood exports to the US from selected European countries, 2002-2006

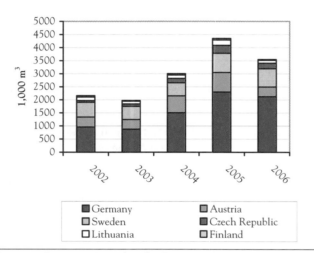

Source: Foreign Agricultural Service, US Department of Agriculture, 2007.

In Japan, European shippers returned to a growth trend, breaking the 3 million m³ level for the first time (graph 5.2.2). Nordic exporters faced a contrasting development: Finland's volume increased by 9%, or approximately 110,000 m³, to reach over 1.0 million m³, while Sweden's volume decreased by 2%, totalling about 825,000 m³. After experiencing eroding prices in the US, Central European countries turned their attention to Asia. Austria exported 400,000 m³ and Germany, 100,000 m³, showing by far the largest relative growth (35.3%) in 2006. Romania has emerged as a leading eastern European supplier to Asia with a volume of around 200,000 m³ due in part to a new, large, export-oriented, Austrian-owned sawmill. Furthermore, the country is expected to strengthen its position in the near future.

GRAPH 5.2.2

European and Russian sawn softwood exports to Japan, 2002-2006

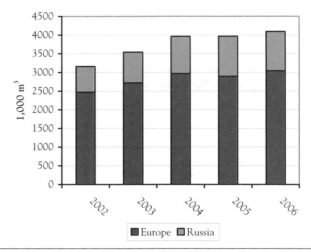

Source: Japan Ministry of Finance, 2007.

There was also positive development in other major non-European markets. In North Africa, Europeans were able to increase their volumes and were led by Finland and Sweden (combined over 200,000 m³ growth), whereas Russia had similar volumes to 2005. This was partly a result of import duties on Russian products in Algeria, Morocco and Tunisia, leaving Egypt as a major target, accounting for over 90% of the African volume. Again, central Europeans also gained a stronger foothold in the market with Austria, Czech Republic and Romania emerging as significant suppliers.

Source: H. Bagley, 2007.

In Middle East markets, Romania has become a major European supplier together with Sweden and Finland, although the market is still dominated by the Russian supply. In addition, sawnwood volumes from North America have started to return to the area – a phenomenon also seen in North Africa as well as in some main western European importing countries, especially in the UK.

Europe has witnessed an extremely strong price development. For example, between December 2005 and March 2007, average export prices for rough sawn softwood from Finland and Sweden increased by approximately 30% and 25%, respectively. Sawmillers have not been able to gain all the advantage, however, as roundwood prices have followed a similar development throughout Europe. A scarce supply situation has aggravated this even further. January 2007 storms in central Europe and in Sweden, causing total damages exceeding over 60 million m³, allowed the earlier log shortage to ease to some extent.

Planned capacity expansion and greenfield start-ups totalling 3 to 4 million m³ of sawnwood in Germany, but also in Switzerland and Austria, are expected to tighten the roundwood supply situation towards the end of 2007.

Sluggish demand and depressed prices in the US have forced European exporters to look for alternative destinations with higher returns Russian sawnwood exporters should be in an improved export position as Russian export duty on sawn softwood was removed in June 2007, and the softwood roundwood export tax increased from a minimum of €4 ($5.50) per m³ to a minimum of €10 ($14) per m³ on 1 July 2007.

5.3 CIS subregion, focusing on Russia

In 2006, sawn softwood production and exports rose for the CIS as a whole (table 5.3.1). Although apparent consumption shows a continued decline, part of the reason is the multitude of smaller mills selling sawnwood to local markets, as explained below.

TABLE 5.3.1

Sawn softwood balance in CIS, 2005-2006

(1,000 m³)

	2005	2006	Change %
Production	23 365	23 618	1.1
Imports	1 660	1 673	0.8
Exports	16 528	17 564	6.3
Net trade	14 868	15 890	6.9
Apparent consumption	8 497	7 728	-9.1

Source: UNECE/FAO TIMBER database, 2007.

The sawmilling industry traditionally occupies an important place in the forest sector of the Russian Federation. In 2006, the share of the sawmilling industry accounted for 12.0% of the forestry sector value. According to the data of the Federal Service of State

Statistics of Russia (Rosstat), the total sawnwood output amounted to 22.5 million m³ in 2006. The major share in the total Russian sawnwood output falls on sawn softwood – 88.1%, or 19.8 million m³ (or 84% of CIS production).

Sawnwood is widely used in industrial and housing construction, repair of buildings and structures, furniture production and machine building, among others.

At present, over 10,000 enterprises are engaged in sawnwood production, of which only 400 are medium- and large-sized. Over the transition period towards a market economy, Russian production of sawn softwood has eroded to one third of its USSR peak. In recent years, however, sawn softwood production and exports have been growing steadily (table 5.3.2 and graph 5.3.1).

TABLE 5.3.2

Production, consumption, export and import of sawn softwood in the Russian Federation for 2000, 2005 and 2006

(1,000 m³)

	2000	2005	2006	2006-2000 Change %	2006-2005 Change %
Production	17 600	19 390	19 800	12.5	2.1
Export	7 332	14 312	15 391	109.9	7.5
Import	4	17	3	-25.0	-82.4
Consumption	10 272	5 095	4 415	-57.0	-13.4

Source: Federal Service of State Statistics of Russia (Rosstat), 2007.

GRAPH 5.3.1

Russian sawn softwood production and exports, 2000-2006

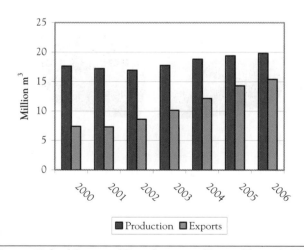

Source: Federal Service of State Statistics of Russia (Rosstat), 2007.

Over the 2000-2006 period, production of sawn softwood increased by 12.5% to 19.8 million m³. Over these six years, exports of sawn softwood have more than doubled, reaching 15.4 million m³ in 2006. This same year, the production of sawn softwood increased by 2.1% against 2005, exports increased by 7.6%, and derived domestic consumption appears to be more than 13% lower.

With regard to derived domestic consumption of sawn softwood during the 2000-2006 period, the trends in the recorded data must be considered against various anecdotal evidence. While apparent consumption appears to be declining, it is estimated by the authors and some industry experts that the actual volume of sawn softwood consumption is most likely rising and would be considerably higher than is reflected in the State statistics. About three-quarters of Russia's sawnwood production is produced by many small mills that cut between 1,000 and 5,000 m³ of sawnwood per year. These small sawmilling enterprises use simplified accounting systems and may not record actual production information on actual volumes of production of sawnwood; tax avoidance could be one reason. These wood volumes may not be recorded, and when sold in local markets for use in the construction and repair of wooden houses and structures in rural areas, under-reporting of consumption occurs.

In 2006, 15.4 million m³ of sawn softwood was exported from Russia (graph 5.3.2).

GRAPH 5.3.2

Russian sawn softwood export markets, 2006

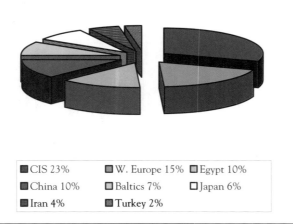

■ CIS 23%	■ W. Europe 15%	▢ Egypt 10%
■ China 10%	▢ Baltics 7%	▢ Japan 6%
■ Iran 4%	■ Turkey 2%	

Notes: For this graph, "CIS" is only Azerbaijan (5.4%), Kazakhstan (6.5%) and Uzbekistan (6.5%). "Baltics" include Estonia (3.9%) and Latvia (2.8%). "Western Europe" includes Finland (2.8%), France (2.3%), Germany (5.4%) and Great Britain (4.2%).
Source: OAO NIPIEIlesprom, 2007.

Sawnwood prices for Russian exporters have improved at an even faster pace than for European exporters. This development has stimulated exports, which are forecast to increase by over 10 % this year. Since early 2006, higher prices received for exported sawnwood have significantly improved sawmill profitability and have further increased the interests of Russian sawmill owners in further capital investments in expansions and even greenfield mills to pursue export markets (and their higher prices). Recently, new sawmilling capacities have been commissioned in Leningrad, Novgorod and Vologda regions, the Republic of Karelia, as well as in Siberia.

The trend of growing sawn softwood production and export is forecast to continue in 2007. At the same time, growth of derived domestic consumption is projected to increase.

The main factors that will have a positive effect on Russian production, consumption and export of sawn softwood are:

- Adoption of a new Forest Code in December 2006.
- Abolition of customs duties on exported sawnwood of all species starting from 15 May 2007.
- Imposition of increasing customs duties on exported roundwood, including sawlogs of softwood species for sawmilling.
- Development of wooden houses construction in Russia, which is the cause for considerable increase in the demand for sawn softwood.

Regarding the last factor, the Government of Russia is enacting a new policy of "affordable and comfortable housing for the citizens of Russia". Due to the acute shortage of housing, Russia will build wooden, low-rise, single-family houses.

5.4   North America subregion

North American sawn softwood consumption eased and in 2006 amounted to 122.6 million m³ following a collapse in housing starts beginning in the third quarter of the same year. This represented a decrease of 5.0 million m³ (3.9%) from 2005 (table 5.4.1). The US accounts for more than 85% of all North American sawn softwood consumption and 28.4% of the UNECE region total. Its demand is driven primarily by new residential construction – as determined by housing starts and interest rates – as well as repair and remodelling activity. US consumption was 102.5 million m³ in 2006 – a decline of 6.9 million m³ from its all-time record high in 2005, while Canada consumption was more stable at 19.7 million m³ (an increase of 2.1%).

Housing starts are a key demand driver and account for over 40% of North American sawnwood consumption. Following an annual increase of 5% (or an extraordinary 100,000 units per year) since 2000, US housing starts started to plunge in the second half of 2006 from an oversupply of new homes that were essentially bought by speculators. This resulted in lower 2006 housing starts of 1.81 million units, down 13%, compared with 2.07 million units in 2005 (see the Housing Start graph in chapter 3). Less than 1.5 million units are expected for 2007, a further 18% drop from 2006).

TABLE 5.4.1

Sawn softwood balance in North America, 2005-2006

	2005	2006	Change %
Production	127 656	122 616	-3.9
Imports	42 259	39 010	-7.7
Exports	41 207	39 398	-4.4
Net trade	-1 051	388	...
Apparent consumption	128 708	122 228	-5.0

Source: UNECE/FAO TIMBER database, 2007.

Between mid-2006 and mid-2007, demand levels for sawnwood in the US have been dropping at their fastest rate since the late 1980s, causing prices to plunge to below break-even levels for sawmills. Sawnwood consumption will continue to be negatively impacted for the rest of 2007 with little chance of a significant rebound until the second half of 2008 or possibly even later. Soft demand and weak prices remain a significant concern for sawnwood producers in North America as well as exporters in Europe and from around the world. The US has only had two minor housing corrections since 1991. As forecast in last year's chapter, the current downturn was caused by overbuilding.

Following stellar sawnwood prices in 2004 and 2005, North American markets became oversupplied starting in mid-2006 and prices moved to cost levels by late in the year where they have stabilized (graph 5.4.2).

Declining prices meant lower production in North America and consumption slumped by 5.0% to 122.2 million m³ in 2006, a decline of 6.5 million m³ compared with 2005. Further reductions have already occurred in the first half of 2007 where output is substantially lower.

In British Columbia (B.C.), Canada, the mountain pine beetle infestation is close to reaching the peak rate of its spread and the Provincial Government continues to step up its annual allowable cut to allow for increases in the roundwood harvest and sawnwood production to salvage the timber. This epidemic is expected to kill almost one billion m³ or 90%, of all mature pine trees in the province. The "shelf life" of dead standing timber is causing considerable debate as some timber deteriorates in just a few years to become uneconomic for processing into sawnwood, while other areas can last well over ten

years. B.C. sawnwood production is comprised of a heavier mix of dead wood, which limits marketing efforts in Japan (blue stain) and to a lesser degree in the important US market (excessive checking, i.e. small cracks from drying too quickly). Output from B.C. Interior sawmills has already increased by 40% since 2001 and is still expected to peak with the timber salvage programme between 2010 and 2012 at slightly higher levels than those achieved in 2006. The outcome will depend on the shelf-life of the timber and the economics of converting dead trees into sawnwood or energy wood. Two of the product adjustments have been increased machine stress rated (MSR) sawnwood and decreased output of appearance or non-blue stained wood to Japan, and, to some extent, to US do-it-yourself (DIY) stores.

GRAPH 5.4.2

Sawn softwood price trends in US, Europe and Japan, 2004-2007

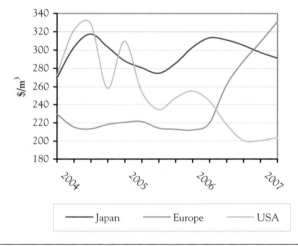

Note: Exporters prices are for structural sawnwood (net sizes) in key markets: 2x4, J-Grade, FOB Japan; 47x100, carcassing, FOB Europe; and 2x4, #2, & Better, delivered to Chicago.

Source: WOOD MARKETS Monthly Newsletter, 2007.

Roundwood supply reductions of 23% imposed by the Government of Quebec have already caused timber harvests and sawnwood output to drop by about 20% since 2004, although some of this decrease is also market-related. Tight roundwood supplies were also evident in the US West where a new ownership regime – increasingly more timberland investment management organizations (TIMOs) – has managed to keep "floor prices" at stronger levels relative to sawnwood prices.

North American exports to Europe, which had declined steadily since the early 1990s, escalated from very low volume levels as a weak US dollar and soaring prices in the UK and Germany attracted exporters (graph 5.4.3). Exports to Japan, on the other hand, stalled against European competition and from limited amounts of non-blue stained spruce-pine-fir (SPF). Canadian exports to Japan were 3.62 million m³ in 2006, a decline of 367,000 (9%) from 2005. By contrast, US exports to Japan in 2006 were essentially unchanged at 122,000 m³ and actually increased in value by 56% in the first four months of 2007, compared with a drop in Canadian exports in the same period.

In contrast, exporters to the US in 2006 diverted sawnwood to alternative destinations due to collapsing prices in the second half of the year. Canada remains the major US sawn softwood supplier, but shipments declined by 6.2%. European exports to the US slowed quickly as prices in Europe soared and US prices plummeted – exports to the US were declined by one-third in 2006 against 2005 and declined by two thirds in the first quarter of 2007 against the same period in 2006.

GRAPH 5.4.3

North American exports to Europe and Japan, 2005-2007

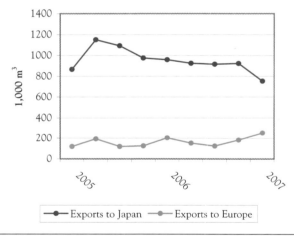

Sources: US Department of Agriculture and Council of Forest Industries, Canada, 2007.

The bulk of remaining European shipments to the US were tied to contract volume sales in the DIY sector. The perceived quality of European sawnwood allowed for much higher premiums than in previous years from the large DIY stores for "square-edged" sawnwood, which encouraged mills to continue with some US business.

Canada and the US started the fourth quarter of 2006 with a new seven-year "softwood deal" following four years of litigation. The previous agreement involved countervailing and anti-dumping duties on Canadian sawnwood that started out at 27.2% and finished up at 10.8% as a result of various US reviews and rulings. Under the new agreement, export taxes are based on a sliding scale that initiates taxes when sawnwood prices reach preset thresholds and/or quota volumes. The

maximum export taxes are 15% for "Option A" mills (Western provinces) and 5% plus volume quotas for "Option B" mills (east of Alberta). As prices decreased, maximum export taxes were triggered in the early third quarter of 2006 on Canadian sawnwood shipments to the US and were also in effect for the first six months of 2007. Due to the complexity of the new agreement, disputes have already arisen that require interpretation of the "surge mechanism" or excess shipments in a month that would trigger a 50% increase in tariffs, and consultation on funding procedures of federal and provincial forestry programmes.

Source: H. Bagley, 2007.

The outlook for North American sawnwood consumption in the mid-2007 to mid-2008 period is flat, but at levels that are significantly lower than in 2006 (by 10 to 12%) as a result of depressed housing starts. An excess of domestic sawnwood capacity is expected to maintain very low prices that may force many high-cost mills to close. Offshore imports in 2007 are expected to be one half of their 2005 levels with Europeans accounting for a greater proportion of this decline. A market turnaround is not expected until the second half of 2008, indicating hard times ahead.

5.5 References

Baltic Business Weekly, 25 June 2007.

British Columbia Ministry of Forests. 2007. *Mountain Pine Beetle Action Plan Update, 2007*. Available at: www.for.gov.bc.ca

EUWID Wood Products and Panels. 2007. Various issues. Available at: www.euwid-holz.de/holzspecial

Japan Lumber Reports. 2007. No. 475. Available at: www.n-mokuzai.com/english.htm

International Wood Markets Group – Global Database. 2007. Available at: www.woodmarkets.com

Kauppalehti. 2007. 25 June edition. Available at: www.kauppalehti.fi

OAO NIPIEIlesprom. 2007. Joint Stock Company Research and Design Institute on Economics, Production Management and Information of Forestry, Pulp & Paper and Woodworking Industry, Moscow.

Pöyry Forest Industry Consulting databases. 2007. Available at: www.poyry.com

Random Lengths International. 2007. Issues 6 and 11. Available at: www.randomlengths.com/base.asp?s1= Newsletters&s2=Random_Lengths_International

The Global Wood Book – Trends & Statistics (Country Profiles of Softwood & Hardwood Wood Product Industries). 2007. Available at: www.woodmarkets.com

Timber Trade Journal. 2007. Issues17/24 February 2007 and 9/16 June 2007. Available at: www.ttjonline.com

UNECE/FAO TIMBER database. 2007. Available at: www.unece.org/trade/timber

Wood Focus. 2006 and 2007. Various issues. Available at: www.woodfocus.fi

Wood Markets. 2006. The Solid Wood Products Outlook: 2006 to 2010. Available at: www.woodmarkets.com

Wood Markets International Monthly Report, volume 12, No. 5 June 2007. Global Housing Trends, 2007. Available at: www.woodmarkets.com

Wood Markets Monthly International Report, volume 12, No. 4 May 2007. US Imports of Wood Products - 2006. Available at: www.woodmarkets.com

Wood Markets Monthly International Report, volume 12, No. 4 May 2007. US & Canadian Exports Move up in '06. Available at: www.woodmarkets.com

Wood Markets Monthly International Report, volume 12, No. 3 April 2007. US Housing Market Slump. Available at: www.woodmarkets.com

Wood Markets Monthly International Report, volume 12, No. 2 March 2007. Canada & US Top Lumber Producers. Available at: www.woodmarkets.com

Wood Markets Monthly International Report, volume 12, No. 2 March 2007. Japan Market Dynamics. Available at: www.woodmarkets.com

Wood Markets Monthly International Report, volume 12, No. 1 February 2007. US Homebuilders Facing Hard Times. Available at: www.woodmarkets.com

Wood Markets Monthly International Report, volume 11, No. 10 December 2006. Global Lumber Outlook 2007. Available at: www.woodmarkets.com

Wood Markets Monthly International Report, volume 11, No. 9 November 2006. MSR Lumber Output Increasing. Available at: www.woodmarkets.com

Wood Markets Monthly International Report, volume 11, No. 8 October 2006. BC Exports. Available at: www.woodmarkets.com

Chapter 6
Russia makes a bid to boost production, while China turns up the pressure:
Sawn hardwood markets, 2006-2007[44]

Highlights

- In a reversal from the previous year, in 2006 sawn hardwood production across the entire UNECE region grew by 0.2% to 49.1 million m^3 due to increased production in Europe.

- Consumption of sawn hardwood in the UNECE region decreased by 2.7% in 2006, principally due to the continuing eastward shift in secondary processing.

- Overall European production increased in 2006 and was partly accounted for by a recovery in production levels in Romania, but also due to the growth in hardwood flooring production and interest in European species in export markets.

- Oak continued to dominate hardwood market consumption, with increasing demand across Europe and Asia.

- Production of sawn hardwood in North America decreased by 1.5% in 2006 due to lower domestic demand and the resultant continuing recession in the sawmilling industry.

- China's shift from consumer to competitor is likely to influence all aspects of the global trade in sawn hardwoods through 2007 and beyond, which will increase the pressure on roundwood supplies and raise sawn hardwood prices across the region.

- Exports of sawn hardwood from the United States recovered in 2006, rising by 3.8%, especially to Asia, as the relative importance of export markets increased considerably to 11.4% of all US sawn hardwood produced.

- In a move to boost domestic sawnwood production, Russia introduced a higher export tax on logs and plans further major increases over the next two years.

- The availability of certified European hardwood logs has started to increase and hardwood trading companies are offering more certified wood products to their customers.

- The US may soon adopt a regulatory approach to tackle the international trade in illegal wood and is about to undertake a risk assessment of its own hardwood resources.

_____

[44] By Mr. Roderick Wiles, Broadleaf Consulting, UK.

Secretariat introduction

The *Review* is fortunate to collaborate with the European Office of the American Hardwood Export Council (AHEC) and be able to engage hardwood specialists to perform this analysis for the needs of our organisations. Mr. Roderick Wiles[45], Broadleaf Consulting, was again the author of this chapter. He was assisted by Mr. Rupert Oliver[46], Forest Industries Intelligence Limited. They have previously been authors and contributors, have spoken at the Timber Committee Market Discussions, and they are again scheduled to present this chapter at the 2007 joint Timber Committee and International Softwood Conference. They are also members of the UNECE/FAO Team of Specialists on Forest Products Markets and Marketing.

Engaging hardwood experts is possible thanks to the continued support of Mr. David Venables,[47] European Director, American Hardwood Export Council (AHEC), London, UK. This collaboration between AHEC and the secretariat is mutually rewarding, as shown by, *inter alia*, this chapter's analysis, which is also useful for AHEC. Mr. Venables is also a member of the Team of Specialists and of the UNECE/FAO Forest Communicators Network. He has also spoken at the Timber Committee Market Discussions. Our sincere appreciation goes to Mr. Venables and AHEC.

Readers' attention is drawn to a more detailed analysis of tropical hardwoods in chapter 12.

6.1   Introduction

In line with developments of the past few years, 2006 continued to see the effects of increased globalization across all sectors of the world's hardwood trade and industry. The Chinese impact on every aspect of the global hardwood trade continued to be felt and the steady upward movement of fuel, transport and energy costs throughout the world have contributed to rising prices in all wood products. Additionally, hardwood secondary processors continued to pursue cheap labour around the world, while investment and trading in the sector have become increasingly geographically flexible.

---

[45] Mr. Roderick Wiles, Broadleaf Consulting, Milehouse Cottage, Chittlehampton, Umberleigh, Devon, EX37 9RD, UK, tel. and fax: +44 · 1769 540 092, e-mail: rod@broadleafconsulting.com, www.broadleafconsulting.com

[46] Mr. Rupert Oliver, Forest Industries Intelligence Limited, 19 Raikeswood Drive, Skipton, North Yorkshire, BD23 1NA, UK, tel. and fax: +44 1756 796 992, e-mail: Rupert@sustainablewood.com, www.sustainablewood.com

[47] Mr. David Venables, European Director, American Hardwood Export Council, 3 St. Michael's Alley, London, UK EC3V 9DS, tel. +44 20 7626 4111, fax +44 20 7626 4222, e-mail: David.Venables@ahec.co.uk, www.ahec-europe.org

China and neighbouring Southeast Asian countries, such as Viet Nam, also continued to expand their production and exports of hardwood products other than furniture. This has created a significant diversion of hardwood raw materials (both saw and veneer logs) away from traditional processors, as well as increased competition in export markets for traditional sawn hardwood suppliers. In fact, the latest figures show that China exported approximately 470,000 m³ of sawn hardwood in 2006, which marks a 36.1% increase over the previous year (graph 6.1.1). Furthermore, China's imports of hardwood logs (both temperate and tropical) in 2006 reached a volume of 12.4 million m³, signalling a 12.2% increase over 2005 (graph 6.1.2).

GRAPH 6.1.1

Chinese exports of sawn hardwood, 2003-2006

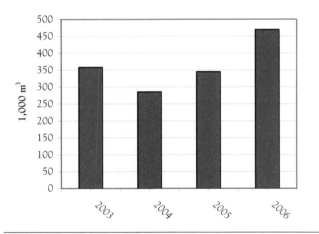

Source: Sustainablewood,com, 2007.

GRAPH 6.1.2

Chinese imports of hardwood logs, 2003-2006

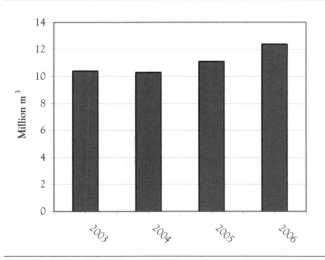

Source: Sustainablewood.com, 2007.

Sawn hardwood production in 2006 across all three UNECE subregions totalled 49.1 million m³, a 0.2% increase over the previous year. This marginal increase was accounted for entirely by a 3.2% rise in sawn hardwood production in Europe, which just managed to offset reductions in the US, Canada and the CIS. This increase in European production helps to underline how important the European hardwood resource is becoming to the world's marketplace, with temperate hardwood species remaining in high demand throughout the UNECE region. The trend for oak (European and, to a lesser extent, American white) remains dominant throughout the region. This is proven by the latest figures for European wood flooring production, showing that 55.1% of all wood flooring was made from oak during 2006, an increase of 5.0% on the previous year (graph 6.1.3). Demand for beech – Europe's main hardwood species – remains weak compared with oak, but exports of beech logs to China have increased dramatically in recent months. Further, there has also been a marginal increase in the use of beech for hardwood flooring.

GRAPH 6.1.3

European hardwood flooring species, 2005-2006

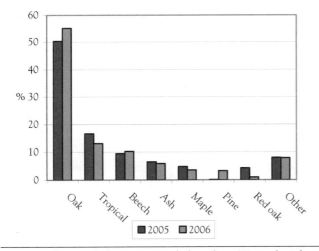

Note: "Other" includes species with less than 3% market share: cherry, birch, eucalyptus, acacia and chestnut.
Source: European Federation of the Parquet Industry, 2006.

Apparent consumption of sawn hardwood in all three subregions fell during 2006, dropping by 2.7% from the previous year to a total of 48.8 million m³ (graph 6.1.4). However, the slight drop in consumption in the Europe subregion accounted for only a small portion of the decrease in the UNECE region as a whole, which perhaps underlines how important sawn hardwood is becoming to the building sector in Europe despite a loss of consumption in the region's furniture industries. There is no doubt that architects and other specifiers are turning towards hardwood as a fashionable and sustainable building and interior finishing material. Furthermore, hardwood flooring production in Europe continues to increase year on year, helping to take up a certain amount of the slack in furniture production. The same cannot be said for North America, where the significant contraction of the furniture sector, coupled with a downturn in housing construction, have been detrimental in both sawn hardwood production and imports.

GRAPH 6.1.4

Consumption of sawn hardwood in the UNECE region, 2002-2006

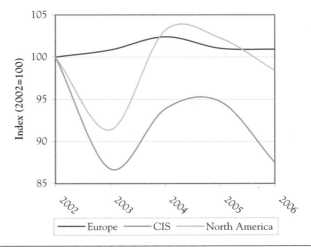

Source: UNECE/FAO TIMBER database, 2007.

6.2 Europe subregion

European production of sawn hardwood saw an overall increase of 3.2% in 2006, which takes production back to the 2004 level, after a decrease in 2005 (table 6.2.1). Turkey maintained its position as the number one producer in the region, with production reaching over 2.7 million m³. While this volume is significant, however, the reality is that much of the sawn hardwood produced in Turkey is from low-grade domestic forests, and small dimension plantation logs, with only a fractional percentage of output earmarked for export.

Production of sawn hardwood in France maintained its slow decline in 2006, with demand and supply gradually evening out after the storms of December 1999. At the same time, Romanian production regained momentum after a significant decrease in 2005, which resulted from severe flooding and reduced access to large areas of commercial forest.

TABLE 6.2.1

Production of sawn hardwood in Europe, 2002-2006

(1,000 m³)

| | 2002 | 2003 | 2004 | 2005 | 2006 | Change 2005 to 2006 | |
						Volume	%
Europe	15 173	15 351	15 862	15 490	15 986	495	3.2
of which:							
Turkey	2 564	2 629	2 590	2 658	2 756	98	3.7
France	2 329	2 099	2 057	1 967	1 950	-17	-0.9
Romania	1 432	1 550	1 780	1 737	1 850	113	6.5
Germany	1 140	1 071	1 089	1 128	1 178	50	4.4
Latvia	848	868	1 108	1 002	1 024	22	2.2
Spain	843	920	1 000	910	946	36	4.0
EU25	9 815	9 737	9 593	9 197	9 423	226	2.5

Source: UNECE TIMBER database, 2007.

Meanwhile, in Germany, production rose for the third consecutive year and reached a total of just under 1.2 million m³. Despite a significant and growing trade in hardwood logs from Germany to China (approximately 470,000 m³ in 2006, of which 285,000 m³ were beech) and the resultant shortfall in supply to the domestic sawmilling sector, Germany has been able to maintain and increase sawn hardwood production levels. In particular, new mills have opened in order to supply the growing demand for sawn beech (especially steamed) in the US, China and many other markets outside Europe. This increasing demand for beech has meant that European beech prices have started to climb significantly after a number of years of steady decline (graph 6.2.1).

In line with production, European sawn hardwood exports also rose by 3.6% during 2006 to reach a volume of 5.6 million m³ (table 6.2.2). In particular, demand for sawn beech in markets outside Europe helped to boost exports, while healthy intra-European demand for oak was maintained. As a result, increases in exports were seen from all the major European sawn hardwood producers, including Romania, Germany, France and Croatia.

TABLE 6.2.2

Sawn hardwood balance in Europe, 2005-2006

(1,000 m³)

	2005	2006	Change %
Production	15 490	15 986	3.2
Imports	8 277	7 959	-3.9
Exports	5 414	5 610	3.6
Net trade	-2 863	-2 349	…
Apparent consumption	18 354	18 334	-0.1
of which: EU25			
Production	9 197	9 423	2.5
Imports	7 746	7 373	-4.8
Exports	3 544	3 660	3.3
Net trade	-4 201	-3 713	…
Apparent consumption	13 398	13 136	-2.0

Source: UNECE/FAO TIMBER database, 2007.

GRAPH 6.2.1

German and French beech sawnwood prices, 2003-2007

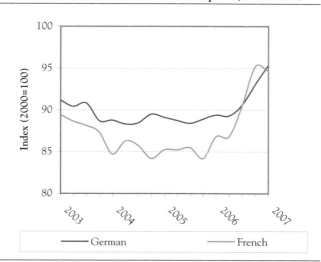

Sources: Centre d'Economie du bois and Statistischen Bundensamt Preise, 2007.

For the fifth consecutive year, total apparent consumption of sawn hardwood in Europe remained reasonably steady in 2006, at 18.3 million m³, a decrease of just 0.1% over 2005. However, in the former EU25, there has been a gradually falling trend in consumption, which continued in 2006, dropping by 2.0%. This has been due principally to the transfer of processing eastwards as imports of semi-finished and component products into the EU have increased. This trend has, however, been tempered to some extent by two key sectors in the EU, where sawn hardwood consumption has been rising. One of the major market drivers in Europe has been hardwood flooring production, which grew substantially in 2006 (graph 6.2.2). Another has been the relative strength of the European construction sector, which, together with a rising interest in specifying hardwood as a building and interior finishing material, has offset some of the decline in the need for hardwood by the shrinking furniture sector.

GRAPH 6.2.2

European hardwood flooring production, 1997-2006

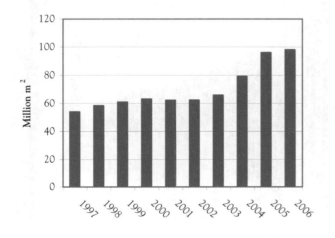

Source: European Federation of the Parquet Industry, 2007.

6.3   North America subregion

Total North American sawn hardwood production reached a volume of 29.1 million m³ in 2006, down by 1.5% on 2005 (table 6.3.1). While there was a decrease of 4.4% in Canadian production, the overall decrease was largely accounted for by the US, which made up approximately 94% of all North American production (and about 56% of total UNECE production). While reduced demand for sawn hardwood in the US domestic furniture and flooring sectors has been a major influencing factor, lowered production has also been affected by continued and significant restructuring of several hardwood production and sales organizations, as well as numerous sawmill closures, and increased importing of components and finished goods by domestic end-users.

TABLE 6.3.1

Sawn hardwood balance in North America, 2005-2006

(1,000 m³)

	2005	2006	Change %
Production	29 550	29 109	-1.5
Imports	3 472	2 683	-22.7
Exports	4 358	4 205	-3.5
Net trade	885	1 522	71.9
Apparent consumption	28 665	27 587	-3.8

Source: UNECE/FAO TIMBER database.

Source: S. Bratkovich, 2007.

Until recently, one of the remarkable things about the recession in the US hardwood industry has been the continuing strength of log prices, which has added to the squeeze on profitability in the sawmilling sector. Many mills are now concentrating on the production of higher grade sawnwood rather than industrial products, e.g. pallet stock and crossties, which are seen as less profitable. This focus has meant that demand for higher grade logs has increased compared with lower grade logs. Because mills are now more efficient and their production costs lower, and due to the competitive nature of the hardwood market, mills had been willing to pay higher prices for the better logs. In addition, most hardwood forest owners are individuals who have the luxury of not having to sell their timber during periods of low demand. Therefore, short-term falls in sawnwood prices did not necessarily filter through to falls in stumpage prices, and previous high prices caused forest owners to hold out until the price rose again. This situation is now changing, however, as sawmills have become far more resilient in their demands and have refused to allow forest owners to control log prices to such an extent. The result has been that prices for certain species in lower demand have actually been falling. White oak sawnwood prices continued to climb in 2006 and 2007, while prices for red oak and maple fell significantly in the face of weaker demand (graph 6.3.1). Another factor reducing the availability of logs to mills in recent years has been the increased export of US hardwood logs to China, which reached 384,600 m³ in 2006, up by 38.3% on 2005.

Despite a decrease in shipments to Canada in 2006, overall exports of sawn hardwood from the US rose by 3.8% in 2006 to 3.1 million m³. All of the US traditional major markets increased their purchases of US sawn hardwood in 2006, with China (including Hong Kong SAR and Taiwan Province of China) up by 13.0% to 751,014 m³, EU25 up by 7.7% to 723,124 m³, Mexico up by 6.7% to 291,563 m³, and Southeast Asia up by 28.5% to 233,036 m³. The increase in exports, coupled with lower production, has meant that the relative importance of export markets for US sawn hardwood producers has grown significantly. In 2006, 11.4% of production was exported, rising from 10.8% in the previous year and from an estimated 7.5% in 1998. The reduction in domestic demand has forced US hardwood mills to focus more on exports in recent years and, in the main, export markets have been ready to accept increased volumes of US sawn hardwood.

GRAPH 6.3.1

US sawn hardwood prices, 2003-2007

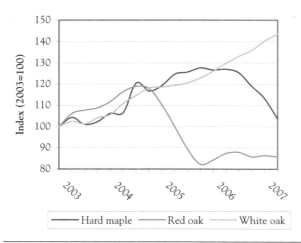

Source: Weekly Harwood Review, 2007.

While China is the most significant export market for US sawn hardwood (excluding Canada) in terms of volume, the EU remains the highest value export market for the US. The difference in the value of these two major markets for US sawn hardwood can partly be accounted for by the difference in how the wood is being used. While the emphasis in Europe is moving away from furniture and into the higher value interior joinery sector, the emphasis in China is still on furniture, flooring and components. This situation is also changing, however, as the Chinese domestic market for wood products is also developing and the higher value interiors sector is gaining in importance. In 2006, for example, the value of US

sawn hardwood shipments to the EU25 reached $503.5 million, which accounted for 31.1% of all US sawn hardwood exports and marked an increase of 6.5% increase over the previous year. However, the value of Chinese purchases of US sawn hardwoods also increased considerably, rising to $327.9 million from $261.2 million in the previous year. This increase can also partially be accounted for by the overall increase in US hardwood prices.

Source: AHEC, 2007.

While production of sawn hardwood in North America fell in 2006, imports also dropped by 22.7%, having peaked in 2004. However, much of this fall was accounted for by Canada. Furthermore, if the US imports of sawn hardwood from Canada are also excluded from the equation, US imports of sawn hardwood actually increased by 3.0% last year, instead of falling by the reported 14.2%. US imports of sawn hardwood from Brazil, Peru and Indonesia did fall last year compared with 2005, but were more than offset by rising imports from Malaysia, China and Germany, as well as from a number of Latin American producer countries. In fact, Germany was the fourth most important US supplier of sawn hardwood in 2006 (excluding Canada), with exports to the market rising by 49.8% to 63,141 m³ from the previous year, and mainly accounted for by steamed beech. At the same time, China jumped from the 13th to the 7th most important supplier, with exports of sawn hardwood, reaching 43,000 m³ and rising by 117.2% from 2005. The rise in imports can be explained in part by the remodelling and renovation sector, which continues to be buoyant despite the end to the housing boom.

6.4 CIS subregion

During 2006, total sawn hardwood production in the CIS subregion reached 3.98 million m³, amounting to just 8.1% of production in the UNECE region as a whole (table 6.4.1). It must be stated, however, that the production figure is far from accurate due to inadequacies in the data available for major producers, such as Belarus and Ukraine. The Russian Federation accounted for approximately 2.7 million m³ of this total production and reported an increase in production of 2.0% over 2005. At the same time, Ukraine and Belarus probably accounted for approximately 550,000 m³ to 650,000 m³ each, with production marginally down or stable in comparison with the previous year.

TABLE 6.4.1

Sawn hardwood balance in CIS, 2005-2006

(1,000 m³)

	2005	2006	Change %
Production	3 989	3 982	-0.2
Imports	188	174	-7.8
Exports	1 083	1 299	20.0
Net trade	894	1 125	25.8
Apparent consumption	3 095	2 857	-7.7

Source: UNECE/FAO TIMBER database, 2007.

Despite definite increases in sawn hardwood production in the Russian Federation, the development of sawn hardwood processing has been slow to take hold. Efforts have been made in Russia to boost wood processing, with President Putin himself asking for the introduction of far-reaching measures to improve the sector. In 2005, for example, tax cuts were granted for imports of woodworking machinery, while an export tariff of 6.5% on all logs was also introduced. These measures have been moderately effective in boosting domestic log conversion, but Russia's exports of hardwood logs are continuing to increase, with rising demand from China and other markets. In fact, official statistics report that China imported approximately 3.7 million m³ of hardwood logs from Russia in 2006, accounting for 29.8% of all Chinese hardwood log imports. It is likely that the actual volume of Russian hardwood logs shipped to China was far greater, possibly as much as double the official statistics.

In view of this increased trade and its resultant disincentive to the development of Russian sawn hardwood processing, the Russian Government has decided to phase in further export taxes on logs over the next two years, with President Vladimir Putin arguing, "our neighbours continue to make billions of dollars out of Russia's forests. We, meanwhile, are doing little to develop our own wood products and timber processing industry" (President Vladimir Putin, 2006). The first was introduced on 1 July 2007 and will constitute a 20% levy, but no less than €10.00 ($14) per m³. The second will come into effect on 1 April 2008 and will comprise a 25% tariff, but no less than €15.00 ($20) per m³, and the third, which will involve a massive 80% tax, with no less than €50.00 ($68) per m³, will be introduced on 1 January 2009. The impact of this effective ban on Russian log exports is likely to be felt first in China, Japan and Finland, where dependence on Russian logs (both hardwood and softwood) is highest. While many analysts argue that it is the correct thing for Russia to do, others wonder if it will lead to increased illegal harvesting and exports. It could also lead to a welcome reduction in competition for other hardwood log exporting countries, such as the US.

While the development of Russia's domestic hardwood-processing sector has been slow until now, the latest statistics show a significant increase in its exports of sawn hardwood. Exports rose to a volume of 700,000 m³ in 2006, marking an increase of 50.2% on the previous year. Once again, there is some uncertainty over the accuracy of these figures, but little doubt that the trade in sawn hardwoods leaving Russia is increasing, driven by a continued and rising demand for temperate hardwoods both in Europe and Asia.

Imports of sawn hardwood into the CIS subregion were low again in 2006, amounting to only 177,000 m³. Overseas demand for sawn hardwood from Russia and other CIS countries shows little consistency, as they have limited secondary processing capacity and poorly organized end-user sectors.

6.5 The 2007 sawn hardwood market

The UNECE market for sawn hardwoods in 2007 has so far proved to be similar to 2006, with globalization being the key influencing factor. China's role in the global sawn hardwood market is becoming ever more significant, with rising domestic consumption and re-export production creating an insatiable need for hardwood logs and sawnwood. China has quickly turned from consumer to competitor in terms of sawn hardwoods, and it will be interesting to see in which direction China's wood product exports are headed over the coming years. Clearly, new wood products and markets need to be developed quickly if China is to maintain its export levels, especially given the slowdown in the US market. Together with production for re-export, the need for wood in the Chinese market has forced sawn hardwood and hardwood log prices upwards across the globe, as supplies have been put under increased pressure. This is particularly relevant for European and American white oak, which have seen 3-

5% annual price increases for the past four years or so and could increase by as much as 10% through 2007 (graph 6.5.1). This has given a much needed boost to European and American sawn hardwood producers, but has also created a shortfall in oak log supply to European and American sawmills, as well as traditional oak-consuming markets. Together with rising demand, rising fuel costs, and therefore production and shipping costs have also contributed to the overall price increases seen in sawn hardwoods.

GRAPH 6.5.1

European and American white oak sawnwood prices, 2003-2007

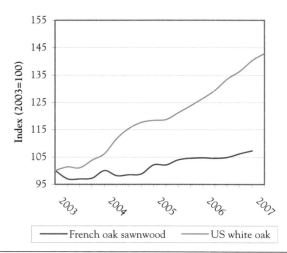

Sources: Centre d'Economie du bois and *Weekly Hardwood Review*, 2007.

The situation for red oak, although still uncertain, seemed to be showing signs of improvement through the latter stages of 2006 and the first half of this year. Sawn red oak production in the US has decreased steadily over the past three years or more, falling by 500,000 m³ since 2004. Sawmills have consistently cut back output in order to correct the oversupply situation in view of reduced demand from the domestic market, and many have switched to white oak and other profitable species. At the same time, exports of sawn red oak have also decreased, falling from just under 600,000 m³ in 2004 to just under 490,000 m³ last year. However, during the first few months of 2007, both market commentators and statistics seem to show that red oak demand in export markets is picking up. The American Hardwood Export Council (AHEC) has mounted an aggressive campaign to improve demand in Europe, while it appears that some manufacturers have been forced to turn to red oak as a result of the high price and limited availability of European and American white oak. In fact, exports of sawn red oak to the EU have more than doubled during

the first four months of 2007, compared with the same period in 2006.

Similarly, demand for European beech in export markets started to improve through 2006, a situation that is likely to develop further during this year. Chinese demand for beech is certainly on the rise, with imports of beech logs from Germany alone reaching 340,700 m³ during the first four months of 2007, up by 23.9% on the same period in 2006. In addition, Germany exported approximately 385,000 m³ of sawn beech in 2006, which marked a 10.8% increase over the previous year, while Poland's exports of sawn beech rose by 101.1% to 143,000 m³. Just as in China, US demand for European beech has been gaining momentum in recent years, with about 57,000 m³ of sawn beech imported from Germany in 2006, a rise of 43.0% on the previous year.

Other significant factors influencing the UNECE region's sawn hardwood market in 2007 include the status of the US housing market. Through 2004 and much of 2005, demand for sawn hardwood – both domestically produced and imported – rose considerably, driven by unprecedented growth in the housing and general construction sectors. With 95% of new homes in the US being constructed out of wood, any change in this sector has a profound impact on overall demand for wood products. The situation in 2006 and this year, however, is that US housing starts have levelled off or even fallen, while interest rates have begun to rise in earnest. In fact, US private housing starts for May 2007 were recorded as being 24.2% below the same month in 2006. The US housing boom is now most definitely at an end, which means that US sawn hardwood suppliers will be forced to rely more heavily on export markets, although remodelling and renovation within the sector may help to give a much needed boost to domestic demand.

One other major factor that could influence the UNECE region's sawn hardwood market in 2007 and beyond is the recent and planned increase in export tariffs on Russian logs. This is likely to help boost Russian sawn hardwood production over time and will add to the competition by other traditional suppliers for the sawn hardwood market share. Furthermore, it is likely that much of the sawn hardwood eventually produced in Russia will be through foreign investment or foreign operators. With China's great dependence on imports of Russian hardwoods, Chinese wood processors are being urged by their Government to look at the possibility of moving wood processing to Russia. These taxes will also serve to improve global market conditions for other hardwood log exporters.

Data for sawn hardwood trade flows in the UNECE region are not yet available for 2006, but some of the trends shown above are expected to have continued (graph 6.5.2). The most positive trend was in non-UNECE to non-UNECE markets, which was dominated by tropical sawn hardwood suppliers shipping to markets such as China. It seems likely that in 2006 this curve will have started to level off, since tropical hardwood supplies became increasingly limited and as China started to import far greater volumes of sawn hardwood from Russia.

GRAPH 6.5.2

Sawn hardwood trade flows, 2001-2005

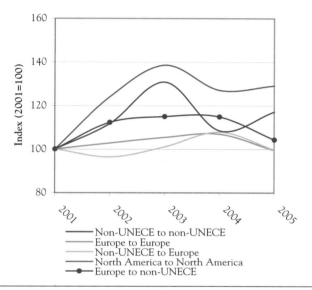

Note: Corresponding trade flow table in electronic annex.
Source: UN Comtrade/EFI, 2007.

The continued development of environmental procurement policies and forest certification are also factors influencing the UNECE sawn hardwood market in 2007. Until recently, the direct impact of these issues was fairly limited for temperate sawn hardwoods, with most consumers focusing their environmental concerns more on tropical species. With little interest from final consumers and a lack of any real price premium, the incentive for temperate hardwood producers to shift to certification has generally been limited. Furthermore, barriers to entry into the certified wood products market tend to be high for temperate hardwoods, as a significant proportion derives from smaller non-industrial forest owners in North America and Europe. Thus, chain of custody is relatively complex and unit costs of certification tend to be far higher than for large industrial and State forest owners.

However, the market situation has been changing in recent years for a variety of reasons. The significant increase in the area of FSC-certified State forests in eastern Europe and of PEFC-certified forests in France and Germany in the last six years has finally begun to filter through to the sawn hardwood market. As

availability of certified logs has increased, European hardwood trading companies have been pursuing chain-of-custody certification and have begun to actively market certified wood products to their customers. Many suppliers of European sawn hardwood are now able to offer these products as standard without requiring a price premium. This is giving rise to more market interest.

International concern about illegal logging is also now encouraging implementation of demand-side measures by timber-consuming countries. Far-reaching commitments to sourcing "legal and sustainable" timber in the public sector have been made by Governments in the UK, France, Netherlands, Denmark, Germany, Belgium and Japan. These Governments are now developing technical standards and procedures to ensure more effective implementation. Other countries are likely to follow.

Meanwhile, there are signs that the US may adopt a regulatory approach to tackle international trade in illegal wood. The Hardwood Federation, which is the largest forest products industry association in the US, representing over 14,000 businesses, has been working closely with environmental groups and legislators to encourage an amendment to the US Lacey Act. This Act makes it illegal to import, sell or process fish or wildlife produced illegally in foreign countries. The amendment would extend the scope of the Act to cover timber products and effectively create a requirement for due diligence by wood importers to ensure that the products that they handle are legally sourced.

As these procedures have yet to be fully implemented in most countries, their real market impact is still uncertain. But it seems certain that temperate hardwood supplies will come under increasing pressure to provide reliable assurances of sustainable management.

While European hardwood producers are responding to these measures by adopting forest certification, American hardwood producers are pioneering a different approach. AHEC has acquired funding from the US Government for a study to assess the risks that American hardwoods may derive from illegal sources. The study will be undertaken in the second half of 2007 by an independent consultant and the results will be subject to peer review by an independent third-party auditing company. AHEC representatives have been involved in direct discussions with procurement officials in Europe and representatives of certification schemes to ensure that the project meets with their requirements for verified legal timber.

Source: AHEC, 2007.

6.6 References

American Forest & Paper Association.2007. Available at: www.afandpa.org

American Hardwood Export Council. 2007. Available at: www.ahec-europe.org

Centre d'Etudes de l'Economie du Bois. 2007. Paris.

EUWID Wood and Panel Products. 2007. Available at: www.euwid-wood-products.com

Federation of the European Parquet Industry. 2007. Available at: www.parquet.net

Fédération Nationale du Bois. 2007. Available at: www.fnbois.com

Forest Industries Intelligence Limited. Available at: www.sustainablewood.com

French Timber. Available at: www.frenchtimber.com

Gesamtverband Deutscher Holzhandel. Available at: www.holzhandel.de

Hardwood Markets. Available at: www.hardwoodmarkets.com

Hardwood Review Export. Available at: www.hardwoodreview.com

President Vladimir Putin. 2006. Opening remarks on Forestry Sector and Timber Industry Development. Syktyvkar, Komi Republic, Russian Federation. Available at: www.kremlin.ru/eng/text/speeches/2006/04/06/2344_type82913_104294.shtml

Sustainable Forestry Initiative. Available at: www.afandpa.org/Content/NavigationMenu/Environment_and_Recycling/SFI/SFI.htm

UN Comtrade/EFI. 2007. UN Comtrade database validated by European Forest Institute. Comtrade available at: http://comtrade.un.org/ and EFI available at: www.efi.fi

UNECE/FAO TIMBER database. Available at: www.unece.org/trade/timber/mis/fp-stats.htm

UNECE Timber Committee market forecasts. Available at: www.unece.org/trade/timber/mis/forecasts.htm

US Bureau of the Census. Available at: www.census.gov

US Department of Agriculture, Foreign Agriculture Service. Available at: www.fas.usda.gov

US Department of Agriculture, Forest Service. Available at: www.fs.fed.us

Chapter 7

Panel industry squeezed by energy costs, fibre supply and globalization: Wood-based panels markets, 2006-2007[48]

Highlights

- Panel markets strengthened in Europe due to enhanced construction activity and revival of the furniture sector, and Russian panel markets continued strong growth, but North American markets stagnated in 2006.

- Panel manufacturers faced increased costs for wood, resins and energy, although buffered by higher prices in Europe; however, in North America profitability shrank, with lower prices.

- In the light of new EU renewable energy targets, competition for wood raw material with the biomass industry remains tight in Europe despite the mild 2006/2007 winter.

- European producers dependent on imported wood are concerned about rising Russian roundwood export taxes.

- Plywood producers in the United States and Europe continue to be confronted with rising imports, especially from China; however, imports from Brazil fell.

- Regulatory constraints on formaldehyde emissions have been increased in California and will significantly impact the US MDF and particle board industry.

- Maximum achievable control technology regulations to control emissions in the wood-based panel industry will be enforced beginning in October 2007 in the US, which will add additional business costs.

- Because of the decline in furniture manufacturing demand, North American MDF and particle board manufacturers rely on residential construction-related demand for cabinets and mouldings.

- Weak US housing starts and large North American capacity increases in OSB have drastically reduced prices of OSB.

- CIS panel production continued escalating, by 7.8% in 2006, with the additional volume consumed domestically, as consumption jumped by 14.8%.

---

[48] By Dr. Ivan Eastin, University of Washington, US, Ms. Bénédicte Hendrickx, European Panel Federation, Belgium and Dr. Nikolai Burdin, OAO NIPIEIlesprom, Russian Federation.

Secretariat introduction

The secretariat sincerely appreciates the continued collaboration with three regional experts in the panel sector and their contributors listed in the references. Dr. Ivan Eastin,[49] Director, Center for International Trade in Forest Products, University of Washington, once again coordinated the production of this chapter and produced the North American analysis. He is a member of the UNECE/FAO Team of Specialists on Forest Products Markets and Marketing.

Ms. Bénédicte Hendrickx,[50] Economic Advisor, European Panel Federation (EPF), conducted the European analysis. Her analysis is based on the recently published EPF *Annual Report 2007*. She is also a member of the UNECE/FAO Team of Specialists on Forest Products Markets and Marketing. Ms. Hendrickx is scheduled to present this chapter at the October 2007 joint Timber Committee and International Softwood Conference Market Discussions.

We would like to thank Dr. Nikolai Burdin,[51] Director, OAO NIPIEIlesprom, Moscow, who wrote the section on Russian panel markets. Dr. Burdin is the former Chairman of both the Timber Committee and the FAO/UNECE Working Party on Forest Economics and Statistics, and a member of the Team of Specialists. He is also the statistical correspondent for Russia. We look forward to continued cooperative efforts with all of these authors and their institutions.

7.1 Introduction

In 2006, consumption rose in each of the UNECE subregions for wood-based panels (graph 7.1.1). Demand for panels continued rising in the CIS subregion, although total panel consumption jumped by over 14%, reaching 12 million m³. This was lower than consumption in Europe and North America, however, which was over 68 million m³ in each subregion. Nevertheless, each subregion posted record high consumption in 2006.

[49] Dr. Ivan Eastin, Professor and Director, Center for International Trade in Forest Products, University of Washington, US, tel: +1 306 543 1918, fax: +1 206 685 3091, e-mail: eastin@u.washington.edu, www.cintrafor.org

[50] Ms. Bénédicte Hendrickx, Economic Adviser, European Panel Federation, 24 Rue Montoyer boite 20; 1000 Bruxelles, Belgium, tel: +32 2 556 25 89, fax: +32 2 287 08 75, e-mail: benedicte.hendrickx@europanels.org, www.europanels.org

[51] Dr. Nikolai Burdin, Director, OAO NIPIEIlesprom, Klinskaya ul. 8, RU-125889 Moscow, Russian Federation, tel: +7 095 456 1303, fax: +7 095 456 5390, e-mail: nipi@dialup.ptt.ru

GRAPH 7.1.1

Consumption of wood based panels in the UNECE region, 2002-2006

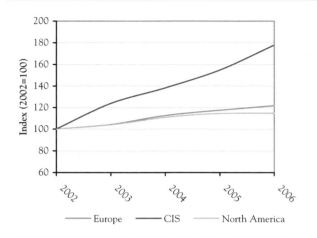

Source: UNECE/FAO TIMBER database, 2007

Panel products trade was active in the UNECE region, with exports exceeding imports. North America, and particularly the US, saw imports decline for the first time since 2000 in response to sharp declines in plywood imports from Brazil and Canada (graph 7.1.2). In 2006, European exports, including trade within the subregion, were at record levels of 32.6 million m³. In North America, Canada's exports fell after 15 years of volume growth owing to the downturn in the US residential construction demand, while US exports declined from their peak in 1992, a trend similar to other US primary wood products.

GRAPH 7.1.2

Wood-based panels trade flows, 2001-2005

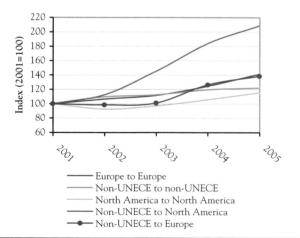

Note: Corresponding trade flow table in electronic annex.
Source: UN COMTRADE/EFI, 2007

7.2 Europe subregion

The European wood-based panel industry had a good year in 2006. Production growth has accompanied increased consumption owing to the improved macro-economic situation and increased construction activity (table 7.2.1).

TABLE 7.2.1

Wood-based panel balance in Europe, 2005-2006

(1,000 m³)

	2005	2006	Change %
Production	69 671	71 802	3.1
Imports	29 908	30 776	2.9
Exports	31 839	32 777	2.9
Net trade	1 931	2 001	3.6
Apparent consumption	67 740	69 801	3.0
of which: EU25			
Production	61 550	63 114	2.5
Imports	25 758	26 511	2.9
Exports	28 863	29 487	2.2
Net trade	3 105	2 976	-4.2
Apparent consumption	58 445	60 138	2.9

Source: UNECE/ FAO TIMBER database, 2007.

Particle board production increased by 2.2% to 45.5 million m³, while demand accelerated by 1.0% to reach 41.8 million m³. Enhanced activity in the furniture industry underpinned MDF demand, gaining 12.3% and reaching a record 11.7 million m³. Production rose by 6.8%, reaching 14.7 million m³. OSB capacity rose to 3.4 million m³, and demand also increased. For each of these products, Europe is a clear net exporter. However, Chinese panel producers are expanding their sales volumes in all continents, especially for MDF.

Plywood production in 2006 remained fairly stable, compared to 2005, amounting to 4.6 million m³, although the situation differed significantly on the country level. European plywood demand continued to grow, gaining 0.7%, to reach 7.6 million m³. Imports underpinned consumption growth. Contrary to other wood-based panels, plywood is Europe is a net importer, with the steadily growing Chinese market share. In particular, imports from China to the EU soared, gaining another 46%. Russia became the largest supplier to the EU, as imports from Brazil decreased by 17% due to a lower domestic production and enhanced competition from other South American and Asian countries. European plywood producers are trying to stay ahead of the competition of low-cost producers in the commodity plywood markets through innovation and technical improvements.

The good market situation is overshadowed by exceptionally high cost increases for nearly all cost factors, but in particular for glues and wood raw material (graph 7.2.1). Wood and glue prices soared by more than 20% in 2006, thereby confirming the 2005 trend. Wood costs suffered from tight competition with the biomass industry for raw materials. Costs for petroleum-based glues followed the strong upward trend of oil prices in 2005 through mid-2007. However, whereas oil prices decreased from the second half of 2006, resin prices in general did not. Moreover, costs for energy and transport continuously increased. This scenario clearly presents a challenge for all companies to safeguard their competitiveness now and in the future.

Obviously the rising production costs are a concern for profitability of panel manufacturers. During 2006, panel prices also rose (graph 7.2.2).

GRAPH 7.2.1

European panel manufacturers wood and resin costs, 2002-2007

Source: European Panel Federation, 2007.

GRAPH 7.2.2

European panel prices, 2002-2007

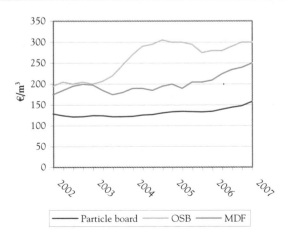

Sources: EUWID and Erzeugpreisse Index-VHI, 2007.

Source: EPF, 2007.

Wood availability is the biggest concern for wood-based panel producers. The mild 2006/2007 winter restricted harvesting in the northern regions. Russia, the Baltic States and the Nordic countries suffered the greatest harvesting problems, and some plywood producers were forced to reduce production. On the other hand, the exceptionally warm winter tempered demand for woodfuels, especially for pellets. Therefore, demand eased for wood energy.

In January 2007, the storm Kyrill temporarily increased wood availability around the Baltic Sea, although it increased risks in harvesting and endangered future harvests. However, it is difficult for the woodworking industries to take advantage of this situation, as these quick changes in raw material are a cause for uneasiness. European panel producers are worried about the announced Russian export duties on roundwood and the lack of clarity on this issue. Moreover, plywood producers suffer from dubious increasing tropical and poplar log exports to China. Okoumé Chinese plywood exports are still subject to EU anti-dumping measures of 66.7%.

These developments together caused uncertainty, which makes long-term planning difficult for panel producers. After the summer of 2007, wood supply shortages are expected. The European Panel Federation (EPF) and the Federation of the European Plywood Industry (FEIC) are thus co-operating with Governments via the UNECE/FAO Timber Section and the European Commission in a study to determine and predict current and future wood availability and demand, which will be presented to the Policy Forum[52] in conjunction with the Timber Committee session in October 2007.

---

[52] *Opportunities and Impacts of Bioenergy Policies and Targets on the Forest and Other Sectors.* Available at: www.unece.org/trade/timber/docs/tc-sessions/tc-65/policyforum/welcome.htm.

7.3 CIS subregion (focusing on Russia)

For the panels sector in the CIS, the particle board industry has the highest growth rates for production, consumption and trade (table 7.3.1). Over the 2002-2006 period in Russia, production of particle board increased by 67.8%, exports grew by 94.5% on smaller volumes, imports shot up by 230.7% and consumption grew by 88.1% to reach 5.6 million m³. Particle board is used for furniture production, construction and machine building. Different pieces of household furniture are produced from particle board, e.g. cabinets, tables and bedroom furniture. Particle board is imported by the Russian Federation from Poland, Germany, Belarus, Finland, Ukraine and Italy. The Russian Federation, in turn, exports particle board mainly to CIS countries of Kazakhstan, Uzbekistan and Azerbaijan. According to forecasts by OAO NIPIEIlesprom, production and consumption of particle board will increase in Russia in 2007. Production will increase by 17.5% over 2006, exports by 11.5%, imports by 18.0% and consumption by 18.0%.

TABLE 7.3.1

Wood-based panel balance in the CIS, 2005-2006

(1,000 m³)

	2005	2006	Change %
Production	10 472	11 298	7.9
Imports	2 880	3 852	33.8
Exports	2 873	3 124	8.7
Net trade	-7	-728	...
Apparent consumption	10 479	12 025	14.8

Source: UNECE/FAO TIMBER database, 2007.

The Russian Federation produces and exports more plywood than any other European country. In 2006 its output of plywood was 2.6 million m³, of which 1.6 million m³, or 60.5%, was exported to the US, Egypt, Germany, Italy, Denmark, Finland, the UK and the Baltic countries. In 2006, plywood production had increased by 75.1% over 2000, export by 61.2% and consumption by 64.0%. Compared with 2005, plywood production grew by 1.6% and exports by 2.8%. However, in 2006, consumption fell by 2% from 2005, which is attributable mainly to reduction in import volumes. In 2007, plywood production is forecast by OAO NIPIEIlesprom to grow by 3.1%. With slight increases of only 0.6% forecast in plywood exports, Russian consumption is expected to grow.

In recent years, the fibreboard sector has developed dynamically in the Russian Federation. Production of fibreboard increased 1.4 times over the 2000-2006 period. Trade and domestic consumption have also increased rapidly. Increasing fibreboard production is assured by new capacities in administrative regions such as the Central, Northwestern, Privolzhskiy and Southern Regions. In the Far Eastern Federal District, production of fibreboard has halved in recent years. In 2006 major changes occurred in the locations of the largest fibreboard enterprises. High demand for fibreboard in Russia and high prices for these types of wood-based panels attracted the largest European fibreboard producers to invest in Russia. In 2006, the world's largest fibreboard plant was commissioned in the Kostroma Region.

Over the 2000-2006 period, fibreboard exports increased 1.7 times, imports by 5 times, and domestic consumption by 1.9 times. The major share of fibreboard export, 72.3%, goes to CIS countries: Uzbekistan, Kazakhstan, Azerbaijan, Ukraine, Tajikistan and Kyrgyzstan. The remaining 27.3% of fibreboard exports are shipped to countries such as Poland, Turkey, Syria and Morocco. In 2005 and 2006, prices for exported fibreboard increased. In 2006, there were considerable volumes of fibreboard export, 668,000 m³. Fibreboard is imported by the Russian Federation from such countries as Germany, Poland, China, Ireland and Thailand. In 2006 domestic consumption of fibreboard increased 1.9 times over 2000. The most important use of fibreboard is in the construction sector. Fibreboard is mainly used in the construction of housing and dachas and social and cultural projects. It is used for insulation, exterior siding and interior panelling instead of traditionally used materials, such as sawnwood, plywood and plaster.

Fibreboard is widely used in furniture production, since its smooth surface allows different textures and surface materials. This makes application of fibreboard in furniture production considerably wider and provides still more promising markets for fibreboard producers. Fibreboard is also used in other spheres, such as machine building, production of containers and packaging, decoration of exhibitions, trade and advertising. It is estimated that in 2007 production of fibreboard in the Russian Federation will increase by 13.5% over 2006, which would translate into 1.5 million m³: export will grow by 13%; import will remain practically unchanged (growth by only 0.3%); and domestic consumption will grow by 7.9%.

7.4 North America subregion

Wood-based panel markets continued to stagnate in 2006 with production increasing by just 0.2% and imports declining by almost 1% (table 7.4.1). As a result, panel consumption remained relatively flat, increasing only slightly, from 69.7 to 70 million m³. Most of the production decline can be attributed to a 5.8% decline in the production of plywood.

TABLE 7.4.1

Wood-based panel balance in North America, 2005-2006

(1,000 m³)

	2005	2006	Change %
Production	62 370	62 501	0.2%
Imports	22 902	22 701	-0.9%
Exports	15 549	15 167	-2.5%
Net trade	-7 353	-7 534	-2.5%
Apparent consumption	69 723	70 036	0.4%

Source: UNECE/FAO TIMBER database, 2007.

Particle board prices, which rallied in the first half of 2006 in response to the closure of several mills in the US and Canada, dropped substantially in the second half of the year (graph 7.4.1). Structural panel demand is closely tied to housing starts, which are highly seasonal. In contrast, particle board is an industrial raw material and its demand is not seasonal. The crash in structural board prices is thus directly related to the severe downturn of the US housing market, which dramatically reduced demand for OSB.

US particle board production increased from 7.2 to 7.4 million m³ between 2005 and 2006, while Canadian particle board production declined from 2.6 to 2.4 million m³ over the same period. However, with the re-opening of one mill in Canada and improved production efficiency in the US, North American particle board production increased by 1.3% in 2006 to reach almost 10 million m³. Concerns about future raw material shortages, particularly given the strong competition with biomass energy generation in Canada and the strengthening Canadian dollar, further fuelled the price surge during the first half of 2006. As in Europe, there is competition for wood among the panel and the energy producers, mainly in Canada, but also in the US. It is certainly of concern to the particle board and MDF industries, and less so to the plywood and OSB industries.

One trend of concern is the increasing reliance of the particle board and MDF industries on the residential construction sector. The closure of many furniture mills in the eastern US has dramatically reduced demand for particle board and MDF in this sector. Manufacturers are scrambling to adjust to the new market situation by operating on smaller margins and trying to reduce their operating costs.

North American imports of particle board jumped by 17.3% in 2006. While US imports were down by 7.2%, Canadian imports jumped by 107%. The jump in Canadian imports was a reflection of both a drop in production capacity and the strength of the Canadian dollar against the US dollar.

GRAPH 7.4.1

US particle board, OSB and structural panel prices, 2002-2007

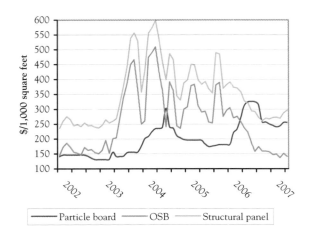

Source: Random Lengths, 2007.

MDF prices in North America strengthened throughout much of 2006, with eastern MDF prices increasing about 11%, while western MDF prices rose by about 3.7%. Between 2005 and 2006, North American production of MDF dropped slightly to 4.8 million m³. US production of MDF dropped from 3.9 to 3.4 million m³, while Canadian production increased slightly, from 1.35 to 1.4 million m³. Increasing imports of furniture from China and Viet Nam have undermined the demand for domestically produced MDF within the furniture industry. While the number of MDF mills has been stable, three new plants are under construction in the US southeast that are planned to come on-line in 2008 and 2009, increasing North American production capacity by 7 to 8%. With the decline in demand from the furniture sector, this increased production capacity will mean that some smaller, less efficient mills will likely close and prices will weaken.

North American imports of MDF totalled 1.6 million m³ in 2006, approximately 31% of the volume of domestic MDF production. MDF imports into North America were down by 5.7% in 2006, with almost the entire decline occurring in the US. The US is by far the dominant importer of MDF in North America, with imports of 1,408,000 m³, compared with Canada's 219,000 m³. The biggest suppliers of MDF to the US are Canada, Chile and Spain, which accounted for 53.8% of US MDF imports in 2006.

OSB prices plunged throughout 2006 as housing starts dropped from 2.1 million in 2005 to just 1.8 million in 2006. OSB production in the US decreased slightly down to 1.5 million m³ in 2006, while Canadian OSB production increased from 11.2 million m³ to 11.5 million m³. However, the decline in housing starts will have serious implications for the structural panel industry, particularly

OSB, especially since North American production capacity is forecast to increase from 28.1 million m³ in 2006 to 36 million m³ in 2012 according to the APA – The Engineered Wood Association (2007a) (graph 7.4.2). This large capacity increase represents a serious concern for the OSB industry, since North American OSB production capacity will increase by 28%, whereas housing starts might only increase by 5% during the same period.

While North American OSB production capacity is scheduled to increase by 28% by 2012, demand for structural panels in North America is only projected to increase by 8.3% across all end-use markets. As a result, capacity utilization rates in the North American OSB industry are expected to drop from 94% in 2006 to 85% by 2012. Imports of OSB, which totalled 9.1 million m³ in 2006, are expected to decline in 2007 and 2008 as a result of both the strong Canadian dollar and the euro. The combination of an increased supply, lower capacity utilization rates and soft demand should work to keep OSB prices low for the next few years.

GRAPH 7.4.2

OSB capacity additions in North America, 2004-2011

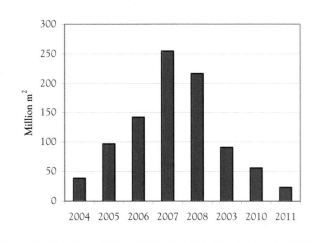

Note: m² on a 3/8-inch basis (9.525 mm).
Source: APA – The Engineered Wood Association, 2007a.

While North American OSB production capacity is scheduled to increase by 28% by 2012, demand for structural panels in North America is only projected to increase by 8.3% across all end-use markets. As a result, capacity utilization rates in the North American OSB industry are expected to drop from 94% in 2006 to 85% by 2012. Imports of OSB, which totalled 9.1 million m³ in 2006, are expected to decline in 2007 and 2008 as a result of both the strong Canadian dollar and the euro. The combination of an increased supply, lower capacity utilization rates and soft demand should work to keep OSB prices low for the next few years.

Demand for structural softwood plywood, which had been increasing in recent years, is expected to resume its slow decline as housing starts continue dropping. North American softwood plywood production, which decreased from 16.8 million m³ in 2005 to 15.9 million m³ in 2006, is expected to drop below 15 million m³ in 2007. As a result, capacity utilization in the North American softwood plywood industry will drop from 92% in 2006 to 87% in 2012. A higher capacity utilization rate has been maintained by shutting down mills that are less efficient, both technically and economically.

Source: The Engineered Wood Product Association, 2007.

Softwood plywood production in the US dropped from 14.4 million m³ in 2005 to 13.7 million m³ in 2006, while Canadian softwood plywood production was relatively stable at 2.2 million m³. US softwood plywood production fell across the southern (by 2.2%), western (by 1.8%) and inland regions, i.e. east of the Rocky Mountains (by 3.8%).

North American softwood plywood imports declined to 1.6 million m³ in 2006. An 8% import tariff was applied by the US to Brazilian softwood plywood imports in mid-2005. Softwood plywood imports from Brazil dropped from 1.4 million m³ in 2005 to 940,000 m³ in 2006 for some of the same reasons as stated above for European imports (see section 7.2). As a result, Brazil's market share declined from 65.5% in 2005 to 57.7% in 2006. This suggests that the import tariff has not been particularly effective in moderating Brazilian exports of softwood plywood into the US. Imports of softwood plywood from China remained stable in 2006 at 41,000 m³.

7.5   References

APA – The Engineered Wood Association. 2007a. *Regional Production and Market Outlook, 2007-2012*. Available at: www.apawood.org

APA – The Engineered Wood Association. 2007b. *Structural Panel and Engineered Wood Yearbook, 2007*. Available at: www.apawood.org

Composite Panel Association. 2007. Available at: www.pbmdf.com

European Federation of the Plywood Industry (FEIC). 2006. *Annual Report 2005/2006*. Available at: www.europlywood.com

European Panel Federation. 2006. *Annual Report 2005/2006*. Available at: www.europanels.org

EUWID. 2006. *Wood Products and Panels* (various issues). Available at: www.euwid-wood-products.com

OAO NIPIEIlesprom. 2006. Joint Stock Company Research and Design Institute on Economics, Production Management and Information of Forestry, Pulp & Paper and Woodworking Industry, Moscow.

Random Lengths. 2007a. As mill capacity grows, 2007 output projected to slip. OSB Survey, Part 1. *Random Lengths*. V(63)N(24). Available at: www.randomlengths.com

Random Lengths. 2007b. Co-ops, producer-owner DCs increase their share of the market. *Random Lengths*. V(63)N(25). Available at: www.randomlengths.com

Random Lengths, 2007c. Forest *Product Market Prices and Statistics, 2006 Yearbook*. Available at: www.randomlengths.com

Random Lengths. 2007d. Structural panel production lags year-ago record. *Random Lengths*. V(63)N(19). Available at: www.randomlengths.com

UN Comtrade/EFI. 2007. UN Comtrade database validated by European Forest Institute. Comtrade available at: http://comtrade.un.org/ and EFI available at: www.efi.fi

UNECE/FAO TIMBER database. 2007. Available at: www.unece.org/trade/timber

US Department of Agriculture (USDA), Foreign Agricultural Service. 2006. Online Trade Database. Available at: www.fas.usda.gov/ustrade/USTExBICO.asp?QI=

Chapter 8

Paper and pulp output continues to climb in Europe and Russia, but falls in North America: Markets for paper, paperboard and woodpulp, 2006-2007[53]

Highlights

- Overall in the UNECE region in 2006, paper and paperboard consumption, production and trade continued growing, with gains in Europe and the CIS, but a downturn in North America.

- North American pulp and paper production and consumption decreased slightly in 2006 and early 2007, in part due to the slowdown in United States housing construction and its subsequent economic impacts.

- Russia's exports of paper, paperboard and woodpulp fell slightly in 2006, while domestic consumption accelerated by 11%.

- North American prices of many major pulp, paper and paperboard commodities were approaching ten-year highs by early 2007 due to a weaker US dollar and declining capacity; prices also rose in Europe.

- Projects to produce cellulosic fuel ethanol from biomass are underway in North America, and although wood energy use is low, paper companies are supporting efforts to develop integrated biorefineries to complement existing pulping facilities and produce bioenergy and biofuels.

- Fuel prices rocketed, raising concerns about energy security and climate change, which resulted in widespread discussions on renewable energy sources, with the pulp and paper industry on centre stage, since it is the foremost industrial producer and user of renewable energy in Europe.

- Initiatives such as the Forest-based Sector Technology Platform play a key role in helping the European pulp and paper industry develop sustainable, effective bio-solutions to alleviate climate change and find solutions to greater wood mobilization.

- The new EU chemicals directive, REACH, with the objective of safe use of man-made products from the chemical industry, was essential in ensuring that both pulp and recovered paper were treated in a manner that did not constrain the paper industry's competitive wood procurement.

---

[53] By Prof. Eduard Akim, PhD, the St. Petersburg State Technological University of Plant Polymers and the All-Russian Research Institute of Pulp and Paper Industry, Dr. Peter J. Ince, USDA Forest Service, Mr. Bernard Lombard, Confederation of European Paper Industries, Belgium, and Mr. Tomás Parik, Wood and Paper, A.S., Czech Republic.

Secretariat introduction

The UNECE/FAO Timber Section expresses its appreciation once again to the four authors of this chapter (in alphabetical order): Professor Eduard Akim, PhD,[54] The St. Petersburg State Technological University of Plant Polymers and The All-Russian Research Institute of Pulp and Paper Industry, who analysed the Russian pulp and paper sector; Dr. Peter Ince,[55] Research Forester, USDA Forest Service, who produced the North American section; Mr. Bernard Lombard,[56] Trade and Competitiveness Director, Confederation of European Paper Industries (CEPI), who described trends in CEPI member countries in Europe; and Mr. Tomás Parik,[57] Director, Wood and Paper, A.S., who analysed developments in central and eastern Europe.

Mr. Eric Kilby, Statistics Manager, and Ms. Ariane Crevecoeur, Statistics Assistant, once again provided the European data from CEPI member associations, which is the basis for the European analysis. Please note the different European country groupings: CEPI's group of 20 countries, the EU25 countries in 2006, and the UNECE European group of 41 countries. Due to some discrepancies between CEPI and UNECE/FAO definitions, the figures may vary slightly, but the trends remain the same. Thanks to these regular contributors, the *Review* has an overview of paper, paperboard and woodpulp market and policy developments across the UNECE region.

8.1 Introduction

The countries of the UNECE region consume over 55% of the world's paper and paperboard, and consume over 70% of the world's pulp in order to make that paper. After its primary use, a growing percentage of this paper and paperboard is recovered and recycled. For example, CEPI raised its recycling target to 66% in 2010. Increasing volumes of the recovered paper are exported to China and other Asian countries – 5 million tons from Europe and over 9 million tons from North America to China in 2006.

[54] Prof. Eduard Akim, PhD, The St. Petersburg State Technological University of Plant Polymers, The All-Russian Research Institute of Pulp and Paper Industry, 4, Ivana Chernykh Str., St. Petersburg, RF-198095 Russia, tel: +7812 53 213, fax: +7812 786 5266, e-mail: akim-ed@mail.ru and inna@home.ru.

[55] Dr. Peter J. Ince, Research Forester, USDA Forest Service, Forest Products Laboratory, One Gifford Pinchot Drive, Madison, Wisconsin, US, 53726-2398, tel: +1 608 231 9364, fax: +1 608 231 9592, e-mail: pince@fs.fed.us.

[56] Mr. Bernard Lombard, Confederation of European Paper Industries, 250 avenue Louise, B-1050 Brussels, Belgium, tel: +32 2 627 49 11, fax: +32 2 646 81 37, e-mail: b.lombard@cepi.org.

[57] Mr. Tomás Parik, Director, Wood & Paper a.s., Hlina 18, CZ-66491 Ivancice, Czech Republic, tel: +420 546 41 82 11, fax: +420-546 41 82 14, e-mail: t.parik@wood-paper.cz.

In 2005, paper and paperboard production and consumption was rising throughout the UNECE region, but this trend changed in 2006 with a downturn in North America, which continued into 2007 (graph 8.1.1). European production and consumption improved by 2 to 3% in 2006, and Russian consumption increased by 11.1% per capita, but on lower volumes. However, for the first time since 2002, North America production and consumption dropped, and trade, both imports and exports, has continued its decline since the recent peaks in 2004. The sharp drop in US housing construction in 2006 and 2007 is having multiple impacts on forest products markets and the overall economies of Canada and the US, which in turn constrains the paper and pulp sector.

GRAPH 8.1.1

Consumption of paper and paperboard in the UNECE region, 2002-2006

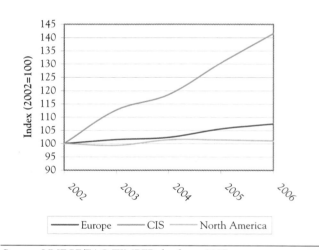

Source: UNECE/FAO TIMBER database, 2007.

European pulp and paper production were at record levels in 2006, driven by countries such as Finland, whose production level was also at record levels. Russia's production and consumption of pulp and paper continued to rise from the low point in 1996-1997, but is still not back to the late 1980s levels before the economic and political transition period. Exports within and from the UNECE region increased overall in 2006; however, again, the slight drop in North America was compensated by gains in the CIS and Europe. In 2006, CIS exports fell for the first time in ten years; the small drop in exports, plus the increase in production, went to higher domestic consumption.

The paper and paperboard trade continued its previous trends of slight increases year after year, with the exception of exports from Europe to countries outside the UNECE region (graph 8.1.2). Previously in 2004, Europe had exported more paper products than in 2005, to destinations such as China, Hong Kong SAR, Japan,

Mexico, Australia, Malaysia and India. In 2005, there was a slight decline in the exports outside of the UNECE region, which were previously the fastest growing exports, primarily to China and India.

Woodpulp trade showed different trends than paper, with the fastest growing trade from North America to China, Japan, Republic of Korea and Mexico (in descending order); however, the trend stopped rising in 2005 (graph 8.1.3).

GRAPH 8.1.2

Major paper and paperboard trade flows in the UNECE region, 2001-2005

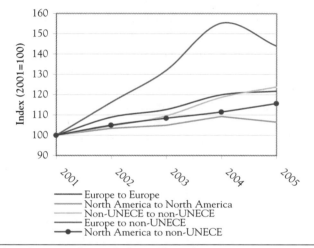

Note: Corresponding trade flow table in electronic annex.
Source: UN Comtrade/EFI, 2007.

GRAPH 8.1.3

Major woodpulp trade flows in the UNECE region, 2001-2005

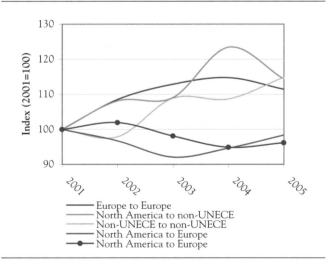

Note: Corresponding trade flow table in electronic annex.
Source: UN Comtrade/EFI, 2007.

8.2 Europe subregion

8.2.1 Market developments

In 2006, the European paper industry's production increased by 3.0% over the previous year, and was 3.4% higher in the EU25[58] and 3.3% higher in the CEPI countries.[59] Consumption also rose in Europe, by 1.8% (table 8.2.1), and even a little higher, by 2.6% in the CEPI countries. Shipments of paper to countries outside of Europe increased by 6.8%, while imports from countries outside of Europe fell by 10.1%.

TABLE 8.2.1

Pulp, paper and paperboard balance in Europe, 2005-2006
(1,000 m.t.)

	2005	2006	Change %
Paper and paperboard			
Production	104 516	107 634	3.0
Imports	56 119	58 490	4.2
Exports	66 043	69 852	5.8
Net trade	9 924	11 361	14.5
Apparent consumption	94 592	96 272	1.8
of which: EU25			
Production	97 096	100 400	3.4
Imports	50 547	52 920	4.7
Exports	62 058	66 027	6.4
Net trade	11 512	13 108	13.9
Apparent consumption	85 585	87 292	2.0
Woodpulp			
Production	41 919	43 788	4.5
Imports	19 940	19 194	-3.7
Exports	11 518	12 398	7.6
Net trade	-8 421	-6 796	…
Apparent consumption	50 340	50 584	0.5
of which: EU25			
Production	38 534	40 597	5.4
Imports	18 645	17 895	-4.0
Exports	10 617	11 548	8.8
Net trade	-8 028	-6 347	…
Apparent consumption	46 562	46 945	0.8

Source: UNECE/FAO TIMBER database, 2007.

---

[58] See map in annex. The main differences from CEPI countries are that the EU25 includes Cyprus, Estonia, Latvia, Lithuania, Luxembourg, Malta, Slovenia and excludes Norway and Switzerland. In 2006, the year of the most recent statistics, the EU included 25 countries, i.e. without Bulgaria and Romania, which became members in May 2007.

[59] CEPI countries include: Austria, Belgium, Czech Republic, Finland, France, Germany, Hungary, Italy, Norway, Poland, Portugal, Slovakia, Spain, Sweden, Switzerland, Netherlands and UK.

Source: Finnish Forest Industries, 2007.

The paper and paperboard final output for 2006 was 107.6 million tons for all of Europe (102.2 million tons for CEPI countries, a rise of 3.3 million tons). This represents another record level of annual production by CEPI countries and is the first time that their final annual total has exceeded 100 million tons. The paper production capacity in CEPI countries standing at 110 million tons, indicates that the calculated operating rate for 2006 was 93.0%, 3.2 points higher than in 2005, which was affected by the paper and pulp mill labour dispute in Finland.

Production across the grades in 2006 generally showed an increase over the previous year. Overall output of graphic grades rose by approximately 2.8%. The output of coated graphics increased by 1.4% and the output of uncoated graphic grades increased by 4.8% over 2005. For the packaging sector, production increased by 3.5 to 4.0%. Most of this increase was in case material grades, where production rose by 4.3%. Output of paperboard rose by 4.7%, while production of wrapping paper increased by 5.7%. Hygienic paper manufacturers increased their output by 1.5%. In addition, production of industrial and speciality grades rose by 5.0%.

The overall consumption of paper and board rose in Europe in 2006 in line with the real growth in GDP of 2.8%. For CEPI countries, consumption of graphic grades increased by 2.6%. Imports of graphic grades from outside CEPI countries fell by 16.1%. Exports to countries outside

CEPI increased by 6.2%. Exports of newsprint fell slightly for the second consecutive year and imports from outside the CEPI area fell by 4.5%.

Corresponding to the increase in paper production, the output of pulp also increased, by 4.5% in all of Europe and by 5.9% in CEPI countries. In 2006, market pulp production, i.e. the pulp produced for sale on the open market as opposed to that used for companies' paper production, rose by 5.9% over 2005. Pulp production capacity decreased slightly, resulting in an operating rate of 93.0%, 4.6 points higher than in 2005, which was also affected by the paper and pulp mill labour dispute in Finland.

Overall consumption of pulp progressed by 2.1% in CEPI countries, although consumption remained steady in all of Europe. For CEPI countries, consumption of mechanical and semi-chemical pulp increased by 2.4% and consumption of chemical pulp increased by 1.6%.

In 2006 exports to non-CEPI countries accounted for 17.3% of total paper deliveries by CEPI countries and recovered after the decline in 2005. Exports to outside the CEPI area increased by 6.8%. Shipments to Asian markets accounted for 26.5% of exports. Imports into the CEPI countries contributed 5.2% of total European paper consumption in 2006. Total imports from non-CEPI countries fell by 10.1%. Imports from North America accounted for 34.3% of all imports and decreased by 17.8%. CEPI countries had an overall positive trade balance (exports exceeding imports) in paper of 13.3 million tons.

In 2006 consumption of recovered paper continued to increase. Utilization was up by 3.9%, reaching 48.9 million tons. Apparent collection increased by 3.8%, reaching 55.6 million tons. Exports of recovered paper to countries outside Europe reached 8.2 million tons, of which 93.4% was sent to Asian markets. Woodpulp and recovered paper both represent 42% of the fibre used in papermaking in CEPI countries. CEPI launched a new target for the recycling rate to be achieved by 2010: 66% of the paper volumes put on the market, including traded volumes.

8.2.2   Policy issues

Energy and climate change proved to be some of the hottest topics on Europe's political agenda in 2006. Fuel prices rocketed, concerns were raised about energy security in the region, and the debate on climate change gained momentum. This prompted widespread discussions on renewable energy sources (RES), where the pulp and paper industry was placed on centre stage, being the foremost industrial generator and user of RES in Europe. With the increasing competition in Europe for wood fibre from the paper and pulp sector, the panel sector and the energy sector, CEPI is concerned about market distortions caused by subsidies and the need for greater wood mobilization.

Central and eastern European countries are fully integrated with the EU in tackling key issues. For example, they participate with the EU's clear commitment to increase production of energy from renewable sources. Their forest and forest industry sector produce wood and paper products, as well as biofuels for domestic use. These rapidly developing economies must find their own way to increase their sustainability and decrease their ecological footprint.

The EU has shown some progress in its energy market liberalization. More transparency and efficient price-setting mechanisms in the sector should benefit energy-intensive sectors in the long term, such as the pulp and paper industry. The energy question is clearly an area where continued efforts and investment in R&D are vital if the industry is to fulfil its potential as part of the bio-solution to climate change. Initiatives such as the Forest-based Sector Technology Platform will play an important role in helping the European pulp and paper industry to develop increasingly interesting solutions in the future. New concepts would help exploit the full potential of bio-energy, especially for wood mobilization, and contribute to creating a sustainable, effective bio-solution that would help alleviate the effects of CO_2 emissions on climate change. A 2007 CEPI study, *The European Paper Industry. A Bio-Solution to Climate Change*, showed that conversion of forest resources to wood and paper products creates four times the added value of simply burning wood fibre for energy, in addition to six times more jobs.

These results support the theory that using renewable raw materials first for wood and paper products, then recycling them into new products, and only afterwards burning them for energy, optimizes added economic value and environmental benefits such as CO_2 capture and storage, and helps to preserve employment in EU manufacturing industries.

Close cooperation between all subregions, as well as good coordination of all supportive measures in developing policy on the local or global level are absolutely necessary to support the belief in highest value use. In 2006, coordination started at the EU level with the main goal of supporting bioenergy production efficiently while avoiding major market disturbances. Stakeholder associations play a key role in this process.

One of the most important issues is wood mobilization with respect to the growing wood industry and the role of wood in bioenergy in connection with climate change. One of the consequences of climate change on European forests is increased damage by windstorms, drought, insect outbreaks, and various combinations thereof. In central

Europe, softwood timber volumes are growing on non-native sites, and have sustained storm damage. The issue of how to sustainably produce wood when confronted with the risk of devastating windstorms, e.g. Lothar (2005) and Kyrill and Per (2007), must therefore be tackled.

Transportation limitations were mentioned in the past *Reviews* in relation to salvaging storm-damaged timber. In many countries, transport capacities are becoming a limiting condition for wood utilization for a number of reasons: local situation, infrastructure, public policy and capacity availability, etc. R&D activity must be focused on this area as on many others.

The new EU chemicals directive for Registration, Evaluation and Authorisation and Restrictions of Chemicals (REACH) was one of the most important issues of the year. REACH concerns producers and importers of chemical substances, and its requirements also affect downstream users. The pulp and paper industry will be affected in several ways: as a user, an importer and a producer. REACH has been developed with the main objective of guaranteeing the safe use of man-made products from the chemical industry. It was essential in ensuring that both pulp and recovered paper were treated in a manner that did not constrain the paper industry's competitive raw material procurement. CEPI estimates that REACH could: (a) increase chemical prices from 2 to 5%; (b) result in processing changes if some chemicals are withdrawn from market; and (c) require greater reporting.

Source: Finnish Forest Industries, 2007.

The third CEO Roundtable of the International Council of Forest and Paper Associations (ICFPA)[60] was held in Shanghai, China in June 2007. CEOs and association leaders addressed issues of sustainability, climate change and energy. The wood and paper sector affirmed its vital and constructive role in combating climate change and confirmed its intention to further reduce its greenhouse gas emissions and thereby mitigate climate change by:

- Committing to sustainable forest management.

- Recycling paper and wood.

- Committing to innovative energy solutions that increase efficiency, reduce reliance on fossil fuels and expand the use of renewable energy sources.

On the occasion of the G8 Summit in Berlin in June 2007, ICFPA launched its first *Sustainability Progress Update*.[61] According to the *Update*, the industry has:

- Continuously improved its sustainability performance.

- Invested in certification systems ensuring that sustainable forest management standards are met.

- Participated in initiatives to protect forests from illegal logging.

- Adopted paper recovery goals.

8.3 CIS subregion, focusing on Russia

In 2006 and the first part of 2007, Russia continued to experience robust economic growth, reflected by continued growth in Russian pulp and paper output (graph 8.3.1). The growth in Russia's paper and paperboard output was 2.8% in 2006, compared with 1.7% in 2005 and 6.8% in 2004.

The important forest-sector policy developments of 2004-2007 in Russia were:

- The Kyoto Protocol ratification by Russia (and its coming into effect in the spring of 2005 with new efforts to monitor carbon emissions).

- A new alliance formed between International Paper and Ilim Pulp Enterprise.

- A new Forest Code adopted.

- The use of space satellites to monitor and prevent illegal timber harvests.

- Increased export taxes on roundwood in 2007 and beyond.

- Investment in Giprobum-Engineering (the major Russian design and engineering company) by Pöyry Forest Industries Consulting, Finland.

[60] www.icfpa.org

[61] www.icfpa.org/media_center/publications/index.php

GRAPH 8.3.1

Production of pulp, paper and paperboard in the Russian Federation, 1995-2006

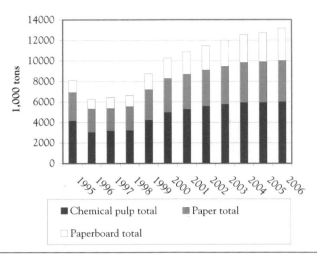

Sources: Goscomstat of the Russian Federation, PPB-express, and author's data interpretation, 2007.

From 2005 to 2006, both demand and output of pulp and paper products in the CIS increased and rose again in the first half of 2007 (table 8.3.1). In Russia, owing to relative economic and political stability established in the country since the major currency revaluation of 1998 and more expansionary macro-economic policy under President Vladimir Putin since 1999, there has been a continuous increase in output of pulp, paper and paperboard, more than doubling since 1996. Despite this, output has yet to reach previous record levels of the 1988-1989 pre-transition period (i.e. the late Soviet era).

TABLE 8.3.1

Paper and paperboard and woodpulp balance in the CIS, 2005-2006

(1,000 m.t.)

	2005	2006	Change %
Paper and paperboard			
Production	8 281	8 630	4.2
Imports	2 157	2 429	12.6
Exports	2 994	2 984	-0.3
Net trade	837	555	-33.7
Apparent consumption	7 444	8 075	8.5
Woodpulp			
Production	7 114	7 117	0.0
Imports	158	158	-0.1
Exports	1 947	1 909	-2.0
Net trade	1 789	1 751	-2.1
Apparent consumption	5 325	5 366	0.8

Note: Updated paper and pulp statistics were received only from two of the 12 CIS countries, Russia and Ukraine.

Source: UNECE/FAO TIMBER database, 2007.

In 2005-2006, the Russian pulp and paper sector continued to expand production of pulp, paper and paperboard, particularly output of paperboard for packaging. During 2006, Russia's total output of pulp (both pulp for paper and paperboard and market pulp) increased by 0.1%; the output of market pulp increased by 0.4%; and the output of paper and paperboard increased by 2.7%, including a 4.2% increase in output of paperboard.

An important development is increasing consumption of paper and paperboard in Russia. In 2006, the per capita consumption jumped by 11.1%, from 41.3 kg per person in 2005 to 46.0 kg in 2006. Although production increased in the country by 4.6% in 2006, this greater domestic demand resulted in lower exports of pulp and paper.

Exports of pulp and paper products hold a dominant position in the total Russian exports of forest-based products, and the overall structure of forest product exports still has a pronounced raw material character. In 2005, in terms of roundwood equivalents, roundwood timber exports and sawnwood exports accounted for 82% of Russia's exports, which is up from 77% in 2000 (graph 8.3.2). Pulp and paper accounted for only 19% of exports in 2006, down from 23% in 2000 (graph 8.3.3).

GRAPH 8.3.2

Export share of Russian forest products, 2000

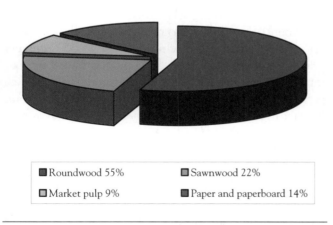

| ■ Roundwood 55% | ■ Sawnwood 22% |
| ■ Market pulp 9% | ■ Paper and paperboard 14% |

Sources: Goscomstat of the Russian Federation, PPB-express and author's data interpretation, 2007.

GRAPH 8.3.3

Export share of Russian forest products, 2006

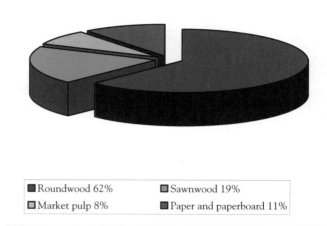

| ■ Roundwood 62% | ■ Sawnwood 19% |
| ■ Market pulp 8% | ■ Paper and paperboard 11% |

Sources: Goscomstat of the Russian Federation, PPB-express, UNECE/FAO TIMBER database, and author's data interpretation, 2007.

Exports of pulp and paper products have been increasing since 1990 and peaked in 2005 (graph 8.3.4). In 2006, the increased production was consumed domestically. However, since 1996, Russian exports have remained largely unchanged as a percentage of production, with exports comprising about 80% of output for market pulp and around 40% for paper and paperboard (graph 8.3.4). Major export destinations for these Russian products are China (market pulp, kraft linerboard), Ireland (market pulp, kraft linerboard), India (newsprint) and Turkey (newsprint).

GRAPH 8.3.4

Exports of market pulp, paper and paperboard from the USSR (1987-1990) and from Russia (1992-2006)

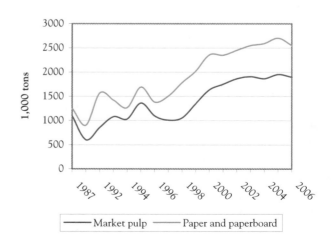

Sources: Goscomstat of the Russian Federation, PPB-express, and author's data interpretation, 2007.

GRAPH 8.3.5

Share exported of paper, paperboard and woodpulp from Russia and the USSR, 1988-2006

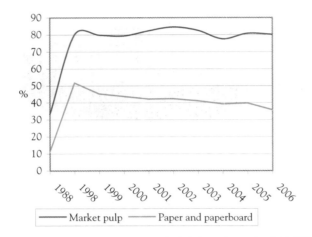

Sources: Goscomstat of the Russian Federation, PPB-express, and author's data interpretation, 2007.

GRAPH 8.3.6

Russian trade balance of paper and paperboard, 2000-2006

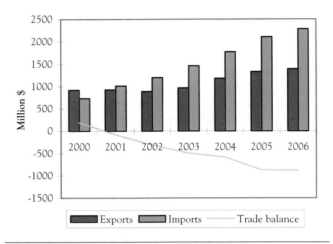

Sources: State Customs Committee, Pulp. Paper. Board Magazine, PPB-express, PPB Exports, PPB Imports, author's data handling, 2007.

In February 2007, the Russian Government signed into law Resolution 75 with a new level of export tax on roundwood in 2007-2011. The export tariff on sawlogs is expected to increase from €4 ($5.40) per m³ in 2006 to the prohibitive level of €50 ($68) per m³ in 2009. In 2011 this level of export taxes, i.e. €50 per m³, is also expected to be applied to birch pulpwood. Significant quantities of birch pulpwood are currently exported to Finland, and these future export tariffs, if enacted, will undoubtedly disrupt the trade.

Although the tonnage of Russian paper and paperboard exports exceeds that of imports, the trade balance in value has continued to deteriorate as Russia has expanded imports of higher-value paper products. Since 2001, the annual trade deficit in paper and paperboard has been negative, amounting to over $870 million in 2005 (graph 8.3.6). The higher value of imports of paper and paperboard compared with exports is mainly due to the fact that Russia is importing expensive products such as high quality materials for container and packaging, coated paper and tissue, whereas less expensive commodity products such as newsprint and kraft linerboard are being exported.

Currently, the largest Russian enterprise produced 75% of market pulp, 80% of paper and 50% of paperboard. A new alliance was announced in October 2006 between International Paper and Ilim Pulp Enterprise, which constitutes 40% of the national capacity of pulp, paper and paperboard combined.

Reconstruction and restructuring of the Russian pulp and paper industry is continuing, with some progress being made towards higher value products with better processing of wood raw material. As an example, International Paper Company recently announced plans to add capacity to an uncoated free-sheet machine and add 50,000 tons per year of production capacity at the paper mill in Svetogorsk (about 140 km from St. Petersburg). The mill is also reportedly installing a coater on a liquid packaging machine to add 15,000 tons per year of capacity. More than $200 million have been put into reconstruction of the mill in recent years. Office paper produced by the mill currently supplies more than 60% of the Russian market demand. In addition, a new 200,000 tons per year aspen-based BCTMP pulp line is planned in 2007, according to International Paper, which will supply pulp to paper mills in Europe and elsewhere.

The future development of Russia's pulp and paper sector is linked to expanded production of more technologically advanced products (such as coated printing and writing paper rather than newsprint), and also more integrated utilization of forest resources.

Implementation of important environmental projects provides examples of steps being taken towards applying the new Russian environmental laws adopted in late 2002 (based on a comparison of environmental indices of individual mills and those of "best available technology" BAT). Furthermore, in connection with ratification of the Kyoto Protocol, a number of mills (e.g. the Arkhangelsky Pulp and Paper Mill) initiated inventory work on greenhouse gas emissions. This inventorying of carbon and greenhouse gas emissions is being carried out at the Arkhangelsky and other mills to prepare for limits on emissions and perhaps trading in carbon emissions.

8.4 North America subregion

In North America, output of paper and paperboard decreased by 0.7% in 2006 to 102.5 million m.t., while apparent consumption of paper and paperboard decreased by 0.3% to 98.3 million m.t. (table 8.4.1). Canadian production and exports declined, but US production and consumption increased modestly. Slower overall economic growth in 2007, partly attributable to a slowdown in the US housing market, appears to be resulting in lower consumption and production of paper and paperboard (based on US data for the first quarter 2007).

TABLE 8.4.1

Paper and paperboard and woodpulp balance in North America, 2005-2006

(1,000 m.t.)

	2005	2006	Change %
Paper and paperboard			
Production	103 195	102 493	-0.7
Imports	20 501	19 710	-3.9
Exports	25 094	23 904	-4.7
Net trade	4 593	4 195	-8.7
Apparent consumption	98 603	98 298	-0.3
Woodpulp			
Production	80 259	79 226	-1.3
Imports	6 454	6 608	2.4
Exports	16 428	16 842	2.5
Net trade	9 975	10 234	2.6
Apparent consumption	70 284	68 993	-1.8

Source: UNECE/FAO TIMBER database, 2007.

Despite lacklustre growth in overall product demand, North American prices of many major pulp, paper and paperboard commodities were approaching ten-year highs by early 2007 (graph 8.4.1). The market situation with relatively high prices resulted from the influence of a weaker US dollar (generally declining in value since 2002) and negative industry capacity growth. Producers also generally experienced high prices for chemicals and energy inputs in 2006.

Canadian producers had to cope with a strong Canadian dollar in 2006, which weakened their competitiveness in North American and global markets, and resulted in a downturn in Canadian industry profitability and output. The Canadian dollar remained historically high compared with the US dollar into early 2007.

GRAPH 8.4.1

US monthly price indexes for woodpulp, paper, and paperboard, 2000-2007

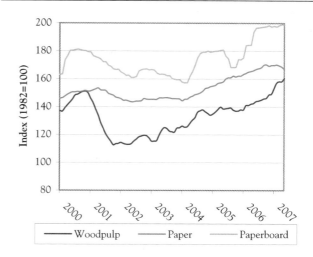

Source: US Department of Labor, Bureau of Labor Statistics, Producer Price Indexes, 2007.

Commercial biofuel production in North America consists primarily of fuel ethanol made from corn, and to a lesser extent, biodiesel made primarily from soybeans, but interest is expanding in use of cellulosic biomass. The US Department of Energy (DOE) recently made a commitment to provide partial funding for the construction of six biorefinery projects over the next four years. When fully operational, the six plants are expected to produce more than 490 million litres of cellulosic ethanol per year (DOE, 2007). At expected yields, this amount of ethanol output would correspond to biomass inputs of 1.5 to 2 million dry m.t. per year (or the equivalent of a little more than 1% of current North American pulpwood consumption). Only three of the plants are expected to use wood as input, however, and most are expected to use other cellulosic materials such as agricultural residues. Potential market implications are obvious, including the possibility of competition for wood between bioenergy and conventional products. Nevertheless, it remains to be seen how successful the cellulosic ethanol technology will be and whether it will have noticeable impacts on pulpwood supply and demand in North America.

8.5 References

American Forest & Paper Association. 2007. *Paper, Paperboard & Wood Pulp* (monthly statistical summary). Vol. 85, No. 05 (and earlier issues).

Confederation of European Paper Industries (CEPI). Available at: www.cepi.org

Paperonline. 2007. CEPI. Available at: www.paperonline.org

PPB-Express. 2007. Moscow.

Pulp and Paper Products Council. 2006. Canadian Pulp and Paper Industry Key Statistics. Available at: www.pppc.org/en/1_0/index.html.

RAO Bumprom. 2007. Available at: www.bumprom.ru

UN Comtrade/EFI. 2007. UN Comtrade database validated by European Forest Institute. Comtrade available at: http://comtrade.un.org/ and EFI available at: www.efi.fi

US Department of Energy. 2007. DOE Selects Six Cellulosic Ethanol Plants for Up to $385 Million in Federal Funding. Press release 28 February. Available at: www.energy.gov/news/4827.htm

Chapter 9

Energy policies reshaping forest sector: Wood energy development in the UNECE region, 2006-2007[62]

Highlights

- Climate change awareness has increased political and public interest in wood energy, and government and market policies are reshaping the entire forest sector in the UNECE region.

- In 2007, the EU launched an ambitious energy policy, with a target of 20% renewable energy by 2020, in which wood, currently the largest component of bioenergy, will play a major part.

- The sustainability of bioenergy is increasingly being put under scrutiny especially in the wake of the controversies surrounding non-sustainable production of palm oil for energy purposes.

- Wood pellet markets are growing rapidly in Europe, pushed by escalating fossil fuel prices and government policies, resulting in shortages and increasing prices.

- With the large increase in western European demand for wood pellets, Russia could become a major supplier of wood energy to Europe.

- Russia has tremendous potentials for increased use of wood energy, but up until now, low cost fossil fuels and low harvests have been obstacles to their development of wood energy.

- In Canada, high fossil fuel prices have led to wood energy development picking up pace, both in the form of increased self-generation in forest industry as well as rapid increase in wood pellet production, of which 90% is aimed at export markets.

- In the Canadian province of British Columbia, large amounts of beetle-damaged wood are to become raw material for wood pellet production.

- The United States has set a number of goals aiming to reduce its dependence on imported fossil fuels, among these are targets to reduce gasoline use by 20% by 2017 and to make cellulosic ethanol cost competitive with corn ethanol by 2012.

- US forest products companies are supporting efforts to develop integrated forest biorefineries that would complement existing pulping plants and produce bioenergy and biofuels.

- Wood-based electric power production has received support in some of the 24 US states with Renewable Portfolio Standards (RPS), where wood power is seen as competitive with other renewable power technologies in meeting RPS requirements.

- Concern has been expressed about emissions of pollutants, notably particles and persistent organics, from wood-burning installations, especially households.

---

[62] By Dr. Bengt Hillring, Swedish University of Agricultural Sciences (SLU), Mr. Olle Olsson, SLU, Dr. Christopher Gaston, FPInnovations-Forintek Division, Canada, Dr. Warren Mabee, University of British Columbia, Dr. Kenneth Skog, USDA Forest Service, Dr. Tatiana Stern, SLU.

Secretariat introduction

Driven by government policies to reduce climate change, improve energy security and achieve a more sustainable energy sector, wood-based energy has accelerated rapidly in the UNECE region. The developments in Europe are led by ambitious European Union (EU) targets and Member States in early 2007 were establishing their corresponding targets and policies to achieve those targets. In North America the federal Governments, states and provinces are promoting alternative energy sources, such as wood. However, similar government policies in the Commonwealth of Independent States (CIS) are lacking, but industry associations are making strides towards domestic and export wood energy market development.

The explosion in wood energy demand has created new market options for forest owners, often paying for timber stand improvement, which previously was unprofitable. Sawmills have new outlets for their by-products of barks and chips, while their small-log raw material choices continue to be indistinguishable between sawlogs, pulplogs and energy logs. In Europe, panel and pulp producers are caught between the rising demand for energy wood and associated raw material prices for assortments of roundwood, chips, residues and recovered wood.

The need to mobilize more wood for energy and rising wood processing needs was the basis of two meetings in the past year. In October 2006 an "International Seminar on Energy and the Forest Products Industry"[63] was held in Rome, organized by FAO, UNECE/FAO, International Energy Agency, International Council of Forest Products Associations, International Tropical Timber Organization and the World Business Council for Sustainable Development. In January 2007, a "Mobilizing Wood Resources" workshop[64] was held in Geneva. It was organized by UNECE/FAO, FAO, Confederation of European Paper Industries, Ministerial Conference for the Protection of Forests in Europe and the European Forest Institute. Outcomes of the two meetings were presented at another venue, the "International Conference on Wood-based Bioenergy"[65] organized by ITTO and FAO at the Ligna trade fair in Hannover, Germany, in May 2007. Results of the Rome and Geneva meetings were covered in the earlier policy chapter. All of these meetings will be built upon by the October 2007 Policy Forum: "Opportunities and Impacts of Bio-Energy Policies and Targets on the Forest and Other Sectors", to

be held in conjunction with the UNECE Timber Committee session.

This chapter is new in the *Forest Products Annual Market Review*, having started last year with an analysis of Sweden's wood energy markets. The secretariat expresses its appreciation for coordinating this chapter to Dr. Bengt Hillring,[66] Associate Professor, Swedish University of Agricultural Sciences, who brings a wealth of experience in this field. Dr. Hillring has been a frequent collaborator in UNECE/FAO energy market work, and previously led the Team of Specialists on Recycling, Energy and Market Interactions. We thank Mr. Olle Olsson,[67] Ph.D. student, Swedish University of Agricultural Sciences who contributed again to this chapter, specifically as the main author of the European and Russian sections. Dr. Hillring and Mr. Olsson are members of the UNECE/FAO Team of Specialists on Forest Products Markets and Marketing.

The secretariat expresses its gratitude to the Swedish Ministry of Industry, Employment and Communications, which provided the necessary financial support for this chapter, and especially to Mr. Peter Blombäck, Head, International Division, Swedish Forest Agency, and Ms. Birgitta Naumburg, Ministry of Industry, Employment and Communications, who facilitated this critical support. Mr. Blombäck is a Vice-Chairman of the FAO European Forestry Commission.

A major difference from last year's chapter is the addition of an analytical review of North American and Russian wood energy policy and market developments. The chapter benefits from the Canadian analysis by Drs. Warren Mabee,[68] Research Associate, Forest Products Biotechnology, University of British Columbia, and Christopher Gaston,[69] National Group Leader, Markets & Economics, FPInnovations-Forintek Division, with both experts based in Vancouver, British Columbia, Canada.

---

[63] www.fao.org/forestry/site/energy/en/

[64] www.unece.org/trade/timber/mis/energy/welcome.htm

[65] www.itto.or.jp/live/PageDisplayHandler?pageId=223&id=3292

---

[66] Dr. Bengt Hillring, Associate Professor, Department of Bioenergy, Swedish University of Agricultural Sciences (SLU), P.O. Box 7061, SE-75007 Uppsala, Sweden, tel: +46 1867 3548, fax: +46 1867 3800, e-mail: Bengt.Hillring@bioenergi.slu.se, www2.bioenergi.slu.se

[67] Mr. Olle Olsson, M.Sc., Department of Bioenergy, Swedish University of Agricultural Sciences (SLU), P.O. Box 7061, SE-75007 Uppsala, Sweden, tel: +46 1867 3809, fax: +46 1867 3800, e-mail: Olle.Olsson@bioenergi.slu.se, www2.bioenergi.slu.se

[68] Dr. Warren Mabee, Research Associate, Forest Products Biotechnology, University of British Columbia (UBC), 4043-2424 Main Mall, Vancouver, British Columbia, Canada V6T 1Z4, tel. +1 604 822 2434, fax +1 604 822 9104, email warren.mabee@ubc.ca, www.ubc.ca

[69] Dr. Christopher Gaston, National Group Leader, Markets & Economics, FPInnovations-Forintek Division, 2665 East Mall, V6T 1W5 vancouver, Canada, tel. +1 604 222 5722, fax +1 604 222 5690, e-mail gaston@van.forintek.ca, www.forintek.ca

We thank Dr. Kenneth Skog,[70] Project Leader, Economics and Statistics Research, USDA Forest Service, Forest Products Laboratory, who wrote the US report. And we also thank Dr. Tatjana Stern,[71] Associate Professor, Swedish University of Agricultural Sciences, who contributed information for the Russian section.

9.1 Introduction

The year 2006 saw climate change move to the top of the political agenda in national and international politics alike. Although global warming and the greenhouse effect have been discussed for a long time, the past year was marked by several major events, notably the issue of the Intergovernmental Panel on Climate Change reports, the start of negotiations for the second commitment period under the Kyoto Protocol and the declaration of the G8 leaders in June 2007. There was also strong media attention. With events such as the release of former US Vice President Al Gore's climate change film "An Inconvenient Truth" and the release of the Stern report (Stern, 2006), the issue of global warming became truly a mainstream topic.

This chapter has been enlarged from its initial appearance in last year's *Review* and now encompasses wood energy policy and market developments in Europe, Russia and North America. It benefits from international experts in these other subregions, with their knowledge of the statistics and other developments. Since last year's chapter, the UNECE/FAO, with partners, issued a report in February 2007, on "Wood energy in Europe and North America: A new estimate of volumes and flows."[72] Since the above mentioned meetings, the UNECE/FAO, along with partners, are working to improve the statistics on wood energy, as the report in early 2007 showed that the statistics in the UNECE/FAO TIMBER Database seriously underestimate the volumes of wood used for energy. Therefore, much of this chapter is based on the UNECE/FAO report, which is the most recent, comprehensive and official source of data on wood energy.

---

[70] Dr. Kenneth Skog, Project Leader, Economics and Statistics Research, USDA Forest Service, Forest Products Laboratory, One Gifford Pinchot Drive, Madison, Wisconsin 53726-2398, USA, tel. +1 608 231 9360, fax +1 608 231 9508, email: kskog@fs.fed.us, www.fpl.fs.fed.us/econ

[71] Dr. Tatiana Stern, Associate Professor, Department of Bioenergy, Swedish University of Agricultural Sciences (SLU), P.O. Box 7061, SE-75007 Uppsala, Sweden, tel: +46 18 67 1922, fax: +46 1867 3800, e-mail: Tatiana.Stern@bioenergi.slu.se, www2.bioenergi.slu.se.

[72] http://www.unece.org/trade/timber/docs/stats-sessions/stats-29/english/report-conclusions-2007-03.pdf

9.2 Europe

9.2.1 New EU energy policy

In the wake of the increased awareness of the dangers of climate change, of the need for energy security, and in view of rising prices for fossil fuels, the EU has presented several new policy measures that are to work against climate change and for the promotion of renewable energy in Europe. In January 2007, the European Commission (EC) released a proposal for a "Renewable Energy Roadmap" (EC, 2007). The document concludes that the EU will not meet its previous target of a 12% share of renewable energy by 2010. The Commission recognizes that the failure to meet the "12% by 2010" goal is largely a consequence of the absence of willingness to, "back political declarations by political and economic incentives" (EC, 2007). Despite this lack of success, the EU is now to set a new, perhaps even more ambitious target. The roadmap, "proposes that the EU establish a mandatory (legally binding) target of 20% for renewable energy's share of energy consumption in the EU by 2020" (EC, 2007).

Wood energy is expected to contribute to the fulfilment of these targets in all three energy sectors:

- Electricity from the biomass sector "can grow significantly using wood, energy crops and bio-waste in power stations" (EC, 2007)

- The share of renewables in heating and cooling "could more than double [...]. Most of this growth could come from biomass" (ibid.)

- While sugar cane and agriculture is expected to contribute the most when it comes to transportation biofuels, these will be "later complemented by cellulosic ethanol" (ibid.).

Source: Stora Enso, 2006.

9.2.2 *Amounts and utilization of wood energy in Europe*

As the interest in wood energy is growing, so is the demand for more and better information about how much wood energy is used. At present the information situation is profoundly unsatisfactory and an obstacle to rational policy-making. A recent report[73] by Steierer et al., (2007) presents the results of an enquiry that was conducted in order to obtain a better overview of wood energy volumes and flows in Europe and North America. The authors have received satisfactory information from 12 European countries[74] on national production and consumption of woodfuels (graphs 9.2.1, 9.2.2 and 9.2.3). The total amount of wood used for energy generation in the 12 European countries was roughly 185 million m³ or about half of all the roundwood consumed in the countries.[75] In energy terms, this corresponds to 39.6 million tons of oil equivalent (Mtoe) (equal to approximately 1658 petajoules (PJ)) or about 3.4 % the total primary energy supply in the 12 countries.

GRAPH 9.2.1

Sources of woodfuel in 12 European countries, 2005

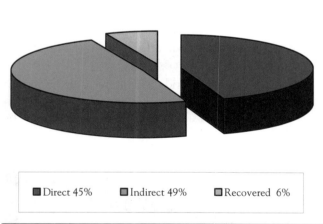

■ Direct 45% ■ Indirect 49% ■ Recovered 6%

Notes: 185 million m³ in total. Direct is wood from forests. Indirect is processed and unprocessed by-products from wood processing industries. Recovered wood is post consumer after serving one lifecycle.
Source: Steierer et al., 2007.

---

[73] www.unece.org/trade/timber/docs/stats-sessions/stats-29/english/report-conclusions-2007-03.pdf

[74] Austria, Czech Republic, Finland, France, Germany, Lithuania, Netherlands, Norway, Slovenia, Sweden, Switzerland and the United Kingdom. Together they account for almost 50% of European forest area.

[75] It is not self-evident to express the amounts of wood fuel in roundwood equivalents. Large shares of the wood energy used are in fact logging residues, black liquor, etc., i.e. assortments that cannot be accurately converted to roundwood cubic metres.

GRAPH 9.2.2

Usage of woodfuel in 12 European countries, 2005

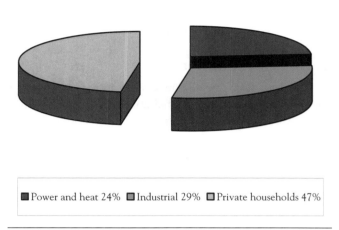

■ Power and heat 24% ■ Industrial 29% ■ Private households 47%

Source: Steierer et al., 2007.

GRAPH 9.2.3

Wood energy share of countries' primary energy usage, 2005

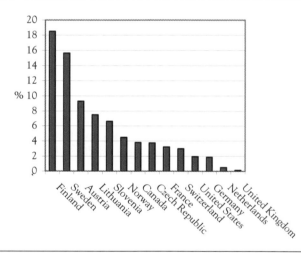

Source: Steierer et al., 2007.

The sources and usage sectors of wood energy reflect the specific conditions in the different countries. In countries with large forest industries, such as Finland and Sweden, "industry" is the dominating user, whereas the "power and heat" category is the dominating one in Germany, Switzerland and the Netherlands. Wood for domestic use in small houses or apartments is a traditional use of wood for energy. The sector has been growing in the past years and while some of the wood for this sector is purchased on an open market, the main bulk is cut by small wood lot owners on their own land, cut by relatives and friends or handled in the grey or black market. As a result of this, official statistics are not precise, but according to the survey, almost half (47.4%) of wood energy use in Europe is utilized in private households. In France, Slovenia and the Czech Republic the private sector is by far the largest user category with e.g. 89.5% of French wood energy use. On an overall note, the authors comment that "harvested wood volumes, in particular wood for energy generation, seem to be significantly higher than reported by official international statistics" (Steierer at al., 2007).

Another recently published study focuses on recovered (post-consumer) wood, which is increasingly being seen as an interestingly valuable resource. The amounts of recovered wood in Europe were estimated to be around 30 million tons or 65 kg per capita in 2006 (Merl, A. et al., 2007). Results show that recovered wood is mainly used for energy production, particularly in some Nordic countries (e.g. Sweden) and as raw material for the panel industry, for instance in the Mediterranean countries (e.g. Spain). There is in many countries clear competition between the two types of utilization of recovered wood (Hillring et al., 2007).

9.2.3 *Sustainability and greenhouse gas neutrality of bioenergy production*[76]

The demand for renewable energy is continuously increasing. Compared with many other renewable forms of energy, bioenergy is relatively easy to integrate into existing energy systems, e.g. by co-firing wood residues and woodfuel pellets, with coal in power stations which reduces sulphur and other harmful emissions, as well as CO_2 emissions. This means that the demand for biofuels in general and woodfuels in particular has increased severely and will continue to do so in the coming years. However, another important property of bioenergy is that it is a renewable and sustainable form of energy only under certain conditions. Firstly, to maintain the CO_2 balance between what is emitted during combustion and what is absorbed during photosynthesis, biomass harvest must not exceed biomass increment (also taking account of carbon emissions during the process, for instance during stand establishment, when large quantities may be released e.g. if there is ploughing of peat land. Secondly, the greenhouse gas (GHG) emissions from production and transportation must be minimized. Thirdly, land use changes should be monitored closely, e.g. to prevent deforestation, which in itself is a climate change issue.

While bioenergy certainly can contribute significantly to mitigate climate change, the drive for new sources of supply can have undesired consequences which undermine the positive environmental effects of the biofuel. These problems were the focus of a recent UN

Energy report (UN Energy, 2007) and have also received increased interest in several European countries recently. One example is the 2006 controversy in the Netherlands surrounding the use of palm oil as a biofuel.

Source: FAO, 2007.

9.2.3.1 *Palm oil*

Palm oil has been increasingly used for energy purposes in recent years. One of the main reasons for its popularity is that it can easily be used in existing facilities as a substitute for fossil oil. However, there are many environmentally questionable aspects of the production of palm oil.

Large areas of rainforest are cleared to make room for the oil palm plantations. Not only has this increased the threat to several endangered species, such as the orangutan and the Sumatran tiger, but the production of palm oil has also caused large emissions of carbon into the atmosphere. The latter is especially true when oil palm plantations are located on drained peat lands, which 27% of oil palm plantations are, according to a study by Hooijer at al., (2006). The authors have studied CO_2 emissions from tropical peat lands and conclude that 2,000 mega tons of CO_2 per annum are released from drained peat lands in Indonesia, 1,400 mega tons from peat land fires and 600 mega tons from decomposition of drained peat lands. The authors note that this "equals almost 8% of global emissions from fossil fuel burning" and that this will help put Indonesia "in third place (after the US and China) in the global CO_2 ranking" (Hooijer et al., 2006). After reports such as the one by Hooijer et al., and severe criticism from NGOs and others, the Government of the Netherlands has cut all subsidies for palm oil as a biofuel.

---

[76] This section draws heavily from the report "Biofuels and climate neutrality" (Holmgren at al., 2007, to be released)

9.2.3.2 Certification – a way to monitor GHG neutrality in biofuel production?

The palm oil controversy is one example of how the sustainability and environmental impacts of biofuels are increasingly being put under scrutiny and the complexities and interactions (e.g. between palm oil production and deforestation) recognized and introduced into policy. Currently there is an international discussion on how to properly deal with sustainability of biofuel production. One option that is being discussed is to introduce certification schemes for biofuels, similar to forestry certification schemes like the Forest Stewardship Council (FSC) and Programme for the Endorsement of Forest Certification (PEFC) schemes. A fundamental criterion for any biofuel production chain to be worthy of the term "GHG-neutral" is that the production of biomass is conducted in a sustainable manner and that harvest does not exceed increment. This is especially important for biofuels produced from forests. Both FSC[77] and PEFC[78] regulations have sections that focus on the importance of sustainable yield. Thus, it could be argued that FSC and PEFC certified forestry is carbon neutral in the sense that biomass removal does not exceed increment. However, from studies that have been made, it seems that neither PEFC, FSC, nor any other certification organization has put much work into examining the GHG balance of the production chains. [79]

9.2.4 European wood pellet market development

In 2006, thanks to government incentives and the highest oil prices in 25 years, the European pellet market has grown substantially, as evidenced by the record numbers of pellet combustion units having been installed (graph 9.2.4).

This has naturally led to an increase in the demand for pellets, which in turn has led to higher prices. Another interesting development is that the different national pellet markets in Europe are becoming more and more integrated. According to Rakos (2007), the Austrian pellet price rise in the second half of 2006 was to a large degree a consequence of an increase in pellet demand from outside Austria. About 100,000 pellet stoves were installed in Italy in 2006, which makes the

Italian pellet stove market the largest in Europe (Rakos, 2007). The boom in Italian pellet stove sales has contributed to the price increase along with higher demand in the Netherlands where several large power plants co-fire wood pellets with coal.

GRAPH 9.2.4

Pellet combustion unit sales in selected European countries, 2003-2006

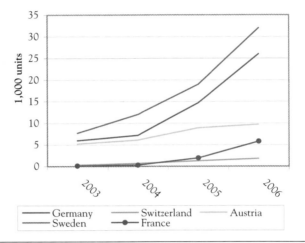

Note: Combustion units include stoves, burners and boilers.
Sources: Davidsson, 2007; Rakos, 2007; Ortner, 2006.

In the early months of 2007 pellet prices fell considerably (graph 9.2.5). This can largely be attributed to the mild winter of 2006/2007 which, according to the US National Oceanic and Atmospheric Administration (NOAA), was the warmest that the world has experienced since record-keeping began in 1880 (Reuters website, 18 April 2007).

GRAPH 9.2.5

Pellet prices in Europe, 2006-2007

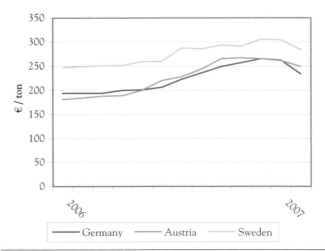

Sources: ÄFAB, ProPellets, DEPV, 2007.

---

[77] Paragraph 5.6 of the FSC criteria states that "the rate of harvest of forest products shall not exceed levels which can be permanently sustained." http://www.metafore.org/downloads/fscprinciplescriteria.pdf

[78] PEFC criteria are based on the Montreal Process Working Group Criteria for Sustainable Forestry, which demands that "timber and other forest resources are not being harvested unsustainably from a given forest area." http://silvae.cfr.washington.edu/ecosystem-management/Montreal.html

[79] For example, the World Wide Fund For Nature (WWF) has published a report in which sustainability standards of bioenergy production are discussed (WWF, 2006).

Strong growth can also be seen in the number of European pellet production facilities, which may have also influenced the pellet price. The periodical *Bioenergy International* has compiled a list of European pellet production facilities with a production capacity of more than 5,000 tons/annum. The 2007 list includes 285 plants compared with 236 the year before, a 20% increase. The increase seems particularly to be a consequence of the strong development in the Alpine countries (*Bioenergy International*, 2007).

9.2.4.1 Obstacles to further pellet market development

There is strong consensus within the biofuel community that several problems still need to be solved if biofuel trade is to develop into a real commodity market. Standards for pellet properties (ash content, moisture content, etc.) have been developed but not yet properly implemented universally and there is also demand for standard contracts for biomass trade.

Another important factor is the lack of market information, especially price information. However, there are now indications that a proper biomass price index, based on prices in the Port of Rotterdam, Netherlands, is to be developed. The idea is to publish the prices at which different assortments of biofuels (pellets, chips, etc.) are traded in the Port of Rotterdam and that this will increase market transparency and stimulate international biofuel trade (Van Essen, 2007).

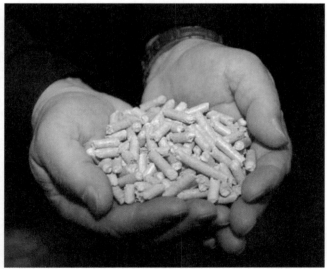

Source: VAPO Oy, 2007.

9.2.4.2 Biocombinates and biorefineries – bioenergy production of the future?

In order to optimize the way input resources are utilized in the production of pellets and other forms of bioenergy, many projects are under way in which production of woodfuels is integrated with a combined heat and power (CHP) plant. This approach is called "biocombinate" and the idea is to minimize the energy losses by using excess heat and steam from the CHP as process heat in the pellet production. Furthermore, CHP plants can usually only produce electricity during winter since the demand for district heating is small in summer. But by using the steam as process heat in pellet production during the summer months, electricity can be generated all the year around without energy losses. At several sites in Finland and Sweden biocombinates are in operation or in planning. Included in many of the planned projects is the future prospect of producing ethanol from cellulose, thereby enabling the biocombinate to produce transportation fuel in addition to heat, electricity and solid woodfuels.

Another interesting concept that is under discussion is "biorefineries", which can be described as an extension of the biocombinate to include not only production of heat, electricity and fuels but of industrial products as well. Modern day pulp mills, which in some cases are net producers of heat and electricity, can be described as prototypes of biorefineries. Large-scale pilot projects on black liquor gasification, a process which can be used to produce transportation fuel from pulp mill residues, are under way. Black liquor gasification can be used to produce a number of different biofuels (e.g. dimethyl ether, methanol and biodiesel) and the production process is efficient compared with, for example ethanol from corn or wheat. The vision is that pulp mills will go from being large energy consumers and producers of just pulp and paper, to being producers of heat, electricity, pulp, paper, transportation fuels and speciality chemicals. Furthermore, they will be able to adjust the product mix depending on the market situation, thus optimizing the profit made from a certain amount of wood. At the May 2007 International Conference on Wood-based Bioenergy, Dr. Manual Sobral, Executive Director, ITTO, stated that in 20 years, pulp and paper companies might produce more value in energy than in pulp and paper. A major element of the European Forest-Based Sector Technology Platform is R&D on biorefineries.

9.2.4.3 Air pollution from burning wood

Although wood from sustainably managed forests may be considered carbon neutral when used as a source of energy, there is concern about the possible increase in air pollution and its ecological and health impacts if wood combustion expands (World Health Organization, 2006). In particular, wood combustion in installations without sufficient filters or with incomplete combustion, releases fine particulate matter (technically called $PM_{2.5}$). These are an acknowledged health hazard. Fine particles arise from many other sources than wood combustion, e.g. diesel motors. An increase in biomass combustion, especially in households with inefficient fireplaces and stoves, would increase particle emissions in Europe, with consequential health risks, including reduced life expectancies.

Some countries have burning device standards, but the best intentions can be compromised by low fuel quality, e.g. wet wood, and ineffective burning techniques.

This air pollution aspect should receive more attention in discussion of wood energy policy. As there are major consequences of increased biomass combustion, many of which are interlinked, a holistic approach is necessary when setting targets and making policies to combat climate change.

9.3 Russian wood energy development

The Russian Federation has the largest forest area of all the world's countries, more than 800 million hectares or more than 20% of the total forest area in the world (FAO, 2007). However, the annual cuttings are only about 120 million m³, which can be compared to around 75 million m³ in Sweden, a country which has only 2-3% of Russia's forest resources. Furthermore, large parts of Russia's forests are made up of mature or over-mature stands. The low harvest level in Russian forests is largely a consequence of underdeveloped infrastructure, lack of qualified personnel and low soil-bearing capacity. This also means that the amounts of forest industry residues which can be used for energy purposes are significantly smaller than the potential (Stern and Kholodkov, 2006). Russia also exports large amounts of unprocessed roundwood to, for instance Finland, China and Sweden, which further diminishes the potential supply of sawdust for pellet production (Yaremchuk, 2006).

Russia is the world's largest producer of natural gas and also has extensive reserves of oil and coal. Hence, fossil energy has been inexpensive in many parts of Russia, . providing little incentive to switch to wood energy for domestic heating. However, Russia is an extremely large country and the fossil energy resources are not evenly distributed. This means that oil, gas and coal have to be transported vast distances (often by train) in order to supply remotely located provinces with little or no fossil fuel reserves of their own. Therefore, private woodfuel removals are an important source of energy in many rural areas with large (but unquantified) amounts of firewood used for domestic heating.

9.3.1 Russian wood pellet market development

Although the Russian wood energy sector is rather underdeveloped compared to neighbouring Finland, for example, things are starting to change. There are signs of quick expansion in the wood pellet industry, which is mostly export-oriented. Russian pellets are priced at approximately €85/ton ($115/ton) FOB Russia in the summer, but were €110/ton ($155/ton) in the winter of 2006/2007 (Ovsyanko, 2007) which can be compared to €250-300/ton ($335-400/ton) in western Europe (as shown in graph 9.2.4 above), which of course provides an incentive for negotiation and is one of the major reasons for Russian pellet industry growth. In the last few years, pellet production in Russia has grown at breakneck speed (graph 9.3.1).

GRAPH 9.3.1

Russian pellet industry development, 2003-2007

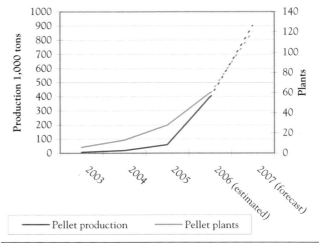

Source: Ovsyanko, 2007.

The development has, however, not been without obstacles. The underdeveloped infrastructure has been a barrier to Russian forestry development in general and this applies to the pellet sector as well, including exports. Quality problems have also been apparent, with a lack of harmonized standards in Russia and consuming countries' standards being an obstacle to the emerging industry (Benin and Klishko, 2006). Additionally, there is a lack of available venture capital needed for investments in the bioenergy industry (Kuchinskiy, 2006).

One issue that is being heavily debated within the forest communities in Sweden and especially Finland[80] is the Russian decision to increase export duties on certain assortments of unprocessed timber. With this new trade policy, Russia aims to stimulate investments in the domestic wood-processing industry, thereby attempting to move the Russian forest industry in a direction more towards being an exporter of processed wood products than of raw materials. As for how this will affect the development of the Russian pellet market, and more

---

[80] Finland imports about 20% of its timber from Russia.http://www.printweek.com/news/660721/Russian-timber-export-hikes-hit-paper-industry/

specifically, the Russian pellet export, the answer seems to be that pellets will not be included in the product portfolio affected by the increased duties. Although the raw material for wood pellets is usually sawmill residues, the pellets are a highly refined product which seems to fit within the "processed wood products" category.

9.4 North American developments

Approximately 260 million m³ of roundwood, or 55.79 million tons of oil equivalent (Mtoe or 2,336 PJ), is used for energy purposes in North America (graphs 9.4.1 and 9.4.2) (Steierer at al., 2007). Wood energy's share of the total primary energy supply is smaller than in Europe, slightly more than 2% in Canada and the US.

9.4.1 Wood energy in Canada

9.4.1.1 Introduction

Canada's forest industry will change the way it does business in the 21st century. Increasing competition from tropical regions of the world (particularly pulp production in Brazil and Indonesia) and the impacts of global environmental change will create challenges that can only be overcome through innovation. One pathway that the industry might follow would lead to bioenergy production.

GRAPH 9.4.1

North American sources of woodfuel, 2005

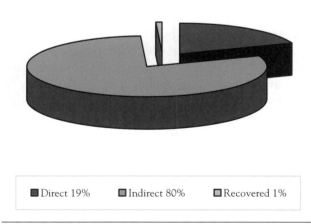

■ Direct 19%　■ Indirect 80%　■ Recovered 1%

Note: 260 million m³ in total.
Source: Steierer et al., 2007.

GRAPH 9.4.2

North American uses of woodfuel, 2005

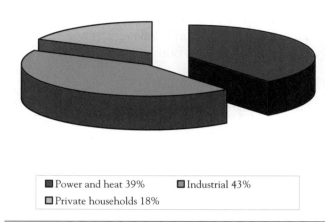

■ Power and heat 39%　■ Industrial 43%
■ Private households 18%

Source: Steierer et al., 2007.

9.4.1.2 Wood pellets

Canada currently has 19 active pellet plants, with a number of new facilities under construction. A large number of planned facilities in Western Canada is part of the response to the Mountain Pine Beetle outbreak in Alberta and British Columbia. Current production of wood pellets in British Columbia is approximately 600,000 tons. Expected capacity by 2009 in British Columbia is 1.35 million tons, growing up to 3 million tons by 2012. Total Canadian production in 2007 is around 1 million tons, which is about 55% of North American capacity. Canadian production is geared towards European markets, with sales in Germany, Sweden, Denmark, and other EU members. Led by the rising consumption in Europe, North American production is forecast to rise by over 70% in 2010 (graph 9.4.3).

One company considering an innovative approach to wood pellet production is TallOil AB, a Swedish company that has four non-replaceable forest licences in British Columbia, totalling 1,050,000 m³ per year of beetle-killed wood. In British Columbia, non-replaceable forest licenses have been issued to clear the accumulated inventory of beetle-killed wood, and thus are not sustainable and are not expected to be re-issued at the end of tenure. Unlike most facilities, which use residues from sawmilling operations, these plants would convert whole logs (compromised in quality by the beetle infestation) into pellets, and then ship these via rail and sea to Europe. TallOil Canada continues to push ahead on plans to build as many as four wood pellet plants in northern British Columbia costing US$30 million each. As of May 2007, these projects had not progressed as fast as originally hoped. The terms of their arrangement with the government of British Columbia dictate that a plant must be completed within two years of the award of timber rights; this places a deadline of autumn 2007 for completion of these projects. TallOil Canada is currently in discussions to extend this deadline. Sites under consideration include land belonging to the Saik'uz First Nation near Vanderhoof, British Columbia.

GRAPH 9.4.3

Production and consumption of wood pellets, 2000-2010

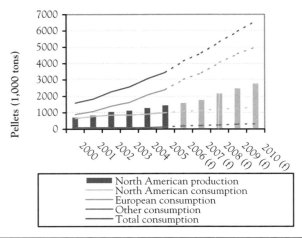

Notes: f=forecast. Other includes Australasia, Russia, Africa and Latin America.

Source: Canadian Wood Pellet Association, as quoted by Swaan, 2006.

9.4.1.3 Bioenergy and cogeneration of heat and electricity

Bioenergy is the single largest source of renewable energy in use in Canada, largely due to the existence of recovery boilers and power boilers used by the forest industry. Figures from Natural Resources Canada show a steady increase in the demand for spent liquor and wood residues for energy production by the pulp and paper industry (graph 9.4.4). A rise in energy costs has provided an incentive for the forest industry to invest in self-generation of heat and power. At the same time, a decline in the number of kraft pulp mills in Canada since 2001 resulted in lower energy demand from wood residues and spent liquors in the years 2001-2005, which means that the latest predictions for future energy demand (light green dotted line) to 2020 are about 150 PJ lower than earlier predictions (dark green dotted line).

GRAPH 9.4.4

Demand for wood residues and spent liquor for energy, 1990-2020

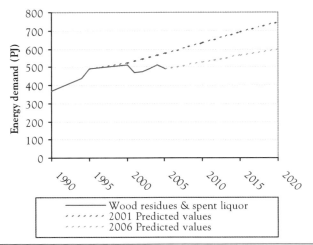

Notes: Historical data from Statistics Canada. Projections from Natural Resources Canada made in 2001 and 2006.

Sources: Statistics Canada, 2006, and Natural Resources Canada, 2006.

The same technology used in pulp and paper mills to generate a combination of heat and power can be used in a stand-alone power plant, given appropriate economic conditions. The largest example of a biomass power facility in Canada is the plant in Williams Lake, British Columbia, a 60 MW electricity generating plant that has been operational since 1993. This facility consumes about 600,000 tons of wood residues, including bark, chips and sawdust annually, and produces electricity as an industrial product (however, process heat is not used downstream by any other users in this example). The wood waste fuel is provided by five surrounding sawmill operations; the electricity generated at the facility is sold under a 25-year electricity purchase agreement to BC Hydro. Construction of the facility was justified by payment of a government-mandated environmental premium for the power cost which recognized benefits that this facility had on local air quality. McCloy reports that the cost of power from this plant has been estimated at 6 cents per kWh, which is high compared to traditional technologies such as coal. The rising cost of natural gas and petroleum, however, means that electricity derived from wood waste could be quite competitive at these prices.

Combined heat and power (CHP) is an up-and-coming segment of the industry; rising energy prices have provided an impetus to expand CHP capacity in Canada. Because historical energy prices were lower, only a few facilities have been built to date; the number of jobs is estimated to be fewer than 200. The potential for growth over the next five years is considerable, given the federal and provincial/territorial support for municipal "green programmes," the financial incentive to reduce energy costs, and the interest in eliminating greenhouse gasses.

Source: J. Bolles, 2007.

9.4.1.4 Biofuels

The 2000 Climate Change Plan for Canada had set the following production objectives: 1.4 billion litres of ethanol by 2010 (compared with 200 million litres in 2001) and 500 million litres of biodiesel by 2010 (compared with practically zero in 2001). In 2005, production of bioethanol from corn and wheat grain had reached around 240 million litres, while installed biodiesel production capacity had reached about 35 million litres. In 2006, bioethanol production capacity had increased to 750 million litres, and biodiesel capacity had risen to 95 million litres. In 2006, two new targets were set by the federal Government. By 2010, ethanol consumption was targeted to be 5% of gasoline usage (energy basis), or approximately 3.1 billion litres. By 2012, biodiesel consumption was targeted to be 2% of diesel usage (energy basis), or approximately 517 million litres. These targets anticipate annual growth in gasoline use to be approximately 0.25% per year, and annual growth in diesel use to be approximately 0.37% per year.

The primary source of federal funding for biofuels has been the Ethanol Expansion Program (EEP), two phases of which were launched in 2003 and 2004. Phase 1 accepted seven proposals for ethanol production facilities, representing a total investment of approximately C$78 million (US$60 million) from the Government of Canada. Phase 2 accepted an additional five proposals for the construction of ethanol production facilities, representing a total investment of C$46 million (US$37 million) from the Government of Canada. Most recently, the 2007 Canadian Federal budget earmarked C$500 million (US$450 million) for the production of next generation renewable fuels.

The introduction of a mandate for renewable fuel content, coupled with funding for new facilities will promote development of the Canadian ethanol and biodiesel industries; a lack of readily, accessible agricultural feedstocks (such as corn or oilseeds) should encourage exploration of wood-based biofuel processes. Two technological platforms are being considered, which could deliver liquid fuels from wood. The thermochemical conversion platform has the potential to liquefy or gasify wood, collect the chemical components which are generated, and ultimately reassemble these components into fuels and possibly industrial chemicals. The bioconversion platform applies biological agents, in the form of enzymes and microorganisms, to carry out a structured deconstruction of wood (lignocellulose) components. This platform combines process elements of pretreatment with enzymatic hydrolysis to release carbohydrates and lignin from the wood, followed by fermentation to create end products including ethanol. A number of Canadian biotechnology companies are pursuing wood-based biofuel and bioenergy technologies, including Iogen, Lignol, SunOpta, Greenfields Ethanol, and Enerkem.

9.4.2 Wood energy trends and selected policy initiatives in the United States

9.4.2.1 Introduction

Aggregate wood use for US energy production has been relatively constant over the last several years, but it has been increasing from modest levels in electric power production. Significant federal goals have been set and new national initiatives undertaken to increase biomass use – including woody biomass use – for liquid fuels production. Renewable fuel portfolio standards (RPS) set by US states have provided some support for increasing power production from wood. A proposed Mandatory Fuels Standard for biofuels may also increase the use of wood for energy. In general, as concerns over fossil-fuel dependency and climate change increase, interest in wood energy, underlying policies, and shifts in production and demands have also increased.

9.4.2.2 Wood energy production

In 2006, wood biomass use for energy in the US was 2,215 petajoules (2.1 quadrillion British thermal units or quads). Aggregate use has been relatively constant since 2001 and short of the recent high of 2,848 petajoules (2.7 quads) in 1985. Wood biomass now accounts for about 3% of US energy production.[81] Other sources of biomass account for an additional 1% of energy production. Since

[81] US Department of Energy EIA. 2007. Monthly Energy Review. April 2007. www.eia.doe.gov/emeu/mer/renew.html

about 2000, wood biomass use for energy is estimated to be relatively constant in residential, commercial and industrial uses, but increasing from a relatively low level in producing electricity. Electric power production has increased from 137 petajoules (0.13 quad) in 1990 to 200 petajoules (0.19 quad) in 2006. A number of government initiatives could increase use of wood energy, including the federal Biofuels Initiative and state-level RPS. A Mandatory Fuels Standard, if enacted, could also have an effect.

9.4.2.3 Federal initiatives to produce biofuels including biofuels from woody biomass

In 2002, fossil fuels (non-renewable) supplied 86% of the energy consumed in the US. In addition, the US imported 62% of its petroleum, and this dependency is increasing. Recognizing this over dependence on non-renewable imported fuel, the President announced in his 2006 State of the Union address an "Advanced Energy Initiative" which included a national goal of replacing more than 75% of US oil imports from the Middle East by 2025. To help attain this goal, the US Department of Energy established the Biofuels Initiative, which includes goals to make cellulosic ethanol cost competitive with gasoline by 2012, and to replace 30% of current levels of gasoline consumption with biofuels by 2030.

In 2007, the President initiated the "20 in 10" effort to reduce US gasoline use by 20% by 2017. The plan calls for increasing renewable and alternative fuels by setting a mandatory fuels standard of 132 billion litres (35 billion gallons) of production annually and by improving gasoline conservation and fuel mileage in cars and light trucks.[82] Currently the US consumes approximately 555 billion litres of gasoline annually.[83]

As a limit is approached in the amount of ethanol that can be produced from corn, it is envisioned that cellulosic feedstocks, which includes wood, could be used to make many billions of litres of ethanol, or other fuel. One oven-dry metric ton (hereafter referred to as "ton(s)") of wood may produce 80-375 litres of ethanol, according to how much of the cellulose is used for energy and the type of conversion process. For example, if hemicellulose is extracted and used for ethanol, then the yield may be 80-145 litres per ton of wood. The remaining cellulose could be used to make paper or composite panels. If all wood material is used, ethanol yield may be 270-400 litres per ton. If, for example, yield is 333 litres per metric ton, 4 billion litres of ethanol would require about 12 million tons of agricultural residues or wood biomass. Four billion litres made from wood biomass would require an amount equal to almost

5% of current US wood harvest. An assessment by the US Department of Agriculture and the Department of Energy suggests 905 million tons of agricultural residue and 334 million tons of wood biomass are expected to be physically available each year by 2030.[84] Wood biomass sources in the estimate include a portion of what are now logging residues, wood from fire hazard reduction thinnings, mill residues, and urban construction and demolition waste. Amounts available at particular prices would vary by type of material and location. Studies to estimate the cost to supply particular amounts are under way in the South and West.

Source: A. Korotkov, 2006.

[82] www.whitehouse.gov/stateoftheunion/2007/initiatives/energy.html

[83] http://auto.howstuffworks.com/question417.htm

[84] Perlack, R.D. and others. 2005. Biomass as feedstock for a bioenergy and bioproducts industry: The technical feasibility of a billion-ton annual supply. Oak Ridge National Laboratory, Oak Ridge, Tennessee. http://www1.eere.energy.gov/biomass/pdfs/final_billionton_vision_report2.pdf

9.4.2.4 *Biofuels pathways, industry focus, and recent federal support*

Two basic technology pathways or platforms are being developed to convert wood to liquid fuels and chemicals: biochemical conversions and thermochemical conversion (gasification or pyrolysis). In biochemical conversion wood is pretreated using enzymes, acids and auto-hydrolysis to release hemicellulose and cellulose as sugars. These sugars are then generally further converted to fuel ethanol or other products. The lignin residue is available for catalytic conversion to other products, gasification, or combustion to provide heat and power for the plant's operation or for sale.[85]

In gasification, wood and bark are heated in the minimum presence of oxygen in a gasifier to produce producer (water) gas, a mixture of carbon monoxide and hydrogen. After clean up, producer (water) gas is called synthesis gas (syngas). Pyrolysis is the process of treating wood with heat, as with gasification, but at a lower temperature in the absence or minimum presence of oxygen to convert wood to char, non-condensable gases and pyrolysis oils. Syngas may be further converted to liquid transportation fuels.[86] Pyrolysis oil may be used directly for fuel or refined into fuel and chemicals.

Currently biochemical conversion technologies require clean wood chips (without bark) while thermochemical conversion can use a mix of wood and bark. Obtaining clean wood chips could draw on the same wood resources as pulp mills. Forest products companies have developed a number of strategies for advancing production of bioenergy and biochemicals from wood.

US forest products companies (the American Forest and Paper Association (AF&PA) Agenda 2020 Alliance) are supporting efforts to develop integrated forest biorefineries that would add to or complement existing pulping plants and would produce renewable bioenergy and bio-products that process both forest and agricultural materials. Their current efforts are in three focus areas. The first focus area – called Value Prior to Pulping (VPP) – seeks cost effective processes to separate and extract selected components from wood prior to pulping, and to process the extracted components to produce liquid fuels and chemicals. Estimates by Princeton University suggest that industry-wide, the fuels and chemicals produced could be at least 2.2 billion barrels of oil equivalent.[87]

The second objective is to use gasification technologies to convert biomass, including forest and agricultural residues and spent pulping liquor (black liquor), into a synthetic gas (syngas), which is subsequently converted into liquid fuels, power, chemicals and other high-value materials.[88] Initial estimates indicate the potential to offset 2.5 billion cubic metres (90 billion cubic feet) of natural gas consumption and 80 gigawatt hours of purchased electric power. The Alliance expresses the view that with sufficient effort and government support, forest products industry facilities could be producing transportation fuels from gasification within five years. The industry-wide potential production volume for renewable fuels using these technologies is 38 billion litres per year.[89]

The third focus is on enhancing forest productivity, including developing fast-growing biomass plantations designed to produce economic, high-quality feedstocks for bioenergy and bio-products.[90] Liquid biofuels/ biochemical projects are being pursued by pulp and paper companies using thermochemical conversion at the Potlatch Corp. for the Cypress Bend mill in McGee, Arkansas and Flambeau River Papers in Park Falls, Wisconsin. Although biomass gasification is relatively new to the pulp and paper industry, there are at least 20 commercial biomass gasifiers operating in North America which serve as a base of experience for further advances.[91]

The US Department of Energy announced in February 2007 that it will invest up to $385 million for six biorefinery projects over the next four years to support the goal of cost-competitive biofuels from cellulosic feedstocks by 2012. One of the projects, by Range Fuels Inc. in Soperton, Georgia, would primarily use wood residues, including logging residues, to eventually produce about 151 million litres of ethanol and 34 million litres of methanol per year. As feedstock, the plant will use 1,089 metric tons of wood residues per day. It will use a

[85] US Department of Energy. Energy Efficiency and Renewable Energy. 2007. Sugar platform. http://www1.eere.energy.gov/biomass/sugar_platform.html

[86] US DOE Energy Efficiency and Renewable Energy. 2007. Thermochemical platform. http://www1.eere.energy.gov/biomass/thermochemical_platform.html

[87] AF&PA Agenda 2020 Technology Alliance. 2007. Statement for the record for US Senate Agriculture, Nutrition, and Forestry Committee hearing on The Role of Rural America in Enhancing National Energy Security, 10 January 2007. http://www.agenda2020.org/PDF/Jan2007_Agenda2020_Senate_Ag_Testimony.pdf

[88] Ibid.

[89] Ibid.

[90] Ibid.

[91] Thorp, Ben. 2007. Paper industry must protect its lead in cellulosic innovation. Pulp and Paper. May 2007. pgs 30-34.

thermoconversion process to convert wood to syngas, then to alcohol and ultimately ethanol.[92]

9.4.2.5 Wood energy power production and renewable portfolio standards

Renewable Portfolio Standards (RPS) are state policies mandating a state to generate a percentage of its electricity from renewable sources. Each state has a choice of how to fulfil this mandate using a combination of renewable energy sources, including wind, solar, biomass, geothermal, or other renewable sources. Some RPSs will specify the technology mix, while others leave it up to the market.[93] Currently 24 states have Renewable Portfolio Standards or goals.

In some states wood-fuelled plants may be a competitive means (compared with other renewable alternatives) of contributing to an RPS and would obtain financial support. However, in other states this may not be true. The competitive position of wood-fuelled plants varies by state. The Massachusetts Division of Energy Resources has selected two wood-fuelled power plants to obtain support to help meet the Massachusetts RPS. They are the 50 MW Shiller station in Portsmouth, New Hampshire, and the 5.5 MW plant in Ellicottville, New York run by Laidlaw Energy & Environmental, Inc.[94] For California, the 2007 report by the public service commission on progress in meeting their RPS indicates that the majority of 2010 RPS generation will likely come from geothermal and wind energy, but solar energy may see a large percentage increase in coming years. Wood-fuelled electric power may play a role but the report cites concern for cases where there are significant distances and costs to transport wood from its source to a power plant.[95] Currently, there are about 139 biomass-fuelled electric power generators in the continental US, based mainly on wood or black liquor fuel (figure 9.4.1).[96]

[92] US Department of Energy. 2007. DOE Selects Six Cellulosic Ethanol Plants for Up to $385 Million in Federal Funding. News release, 28 February 2007. http://www.energy.gov/news/4827.htm

[93] Renewable energy policy project. 2007. Renewable portfolio standards. http://www.crest.org/rps/index.html

[94] Massachusetts Division of Energy Resources. 2007. Renewable portfolio standard. http://www.mass.gov/doer/rps/

[95] California Public Utilities Commission. 2007. Progress toward the California Renewable Fuels Portfolio Standard as Required by the Supplemental Report of the 2006 Budget Act. http://www.cpuc.ca.gov/published/REPORT/66515.htm

[96] US EPA. 2006. National Electric Energy Data System (NEEDS) 2006. http://www.epa.gov/airmarkets/progsregs/epa-ipm/index.html#needs

FIGURE 9.4.1

US wood biomass fuelled electric power plants, 2004

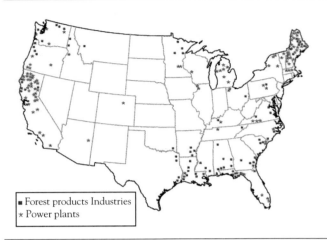

- Forest products Industries
- Power plants

Sources: US Environmental Protection Agency. 2006. National Electric Energy Data System (NEEDS), 2006.

9.5 References

AF&PA. 2007. Agenda 2020 Technology Alliance. 2007. Statement for the record for US Senate Agriculture, Nutrition, and Forestry Committee hearing on The Role of Rural America in Enhancing National Energy Security, 10 January 2007. Available at: http://www.agenda2020.org/PDF/Jan2007_Agenda2020_Senate_Ag_Testimony.pdf

ÄFAB. 2007. Available at: http://www.afabinfo.com/bioguiden/pellets/pelletspris/pelletstermometern.htm

Benin, A. and Klishko, A. 2006. Perspectives of biofuels production in Russia. Presentation at FTP conference in Lahti, 22-23 November 2006. Available at http://www.forestplatform.org/easydata/customers/ftp/files/Lahti_presentations/Benin-Klishko_FTP,_Russia.pdf

Bioenergy International. 2006. The Pellets Map 2006/07. Issue 23, December 2006.

California Public Utilities Commission. 2007. Progress toward the California Renewable Fuels Portfolio Standard as required by the supplemental report of the 2006 Budget Act. Available at: http://www.cpuc.ca.gov/published/REPORT/66515.htm

Database of State Incentives for Renewables & Efficiency (DSIRE). 2007. Available at: http://www.dsireusa.org/index.cfm?&CurrentPageID=10&EE=0&RE=1

Davidsson, M. 2007. Swedish Heating Boilers and Burners Association (SBBA). Presentation at Pellets 07 conference. Available at: http://www.sbba.se/files/000068.pdf

Deutscher Energie Pellet Verband. 2007. Available at: http://www.depv.de/marktdaten/pelletspreise/

Energyshop.com. 2007. Available at: http://www.energyshop.com

European Commission. 2007. "Renewable Energy Road Map – Renewable energies in the 21st century: building a more sustainable future", COM(2006) 848 final, 2007

Hillring, B., Canals, G. and Olsson, O. 2007. *Markets for recovered wood in Europe – an overview*. 3rd European COST E31 Conference. Management of Recovered Wood. Reaching a Higher Technical, Economic and Environmental Standard in Europe. Thessaloniki. 2007. University Studio Press. Conference held in Klagenfurt, Austria. May 2007. ISBN 978-960-12-1596-9

Hooijer, A., Silvius, M., Wösten, H., Page, S. 2006. Assessment of CO2 emissions from drained peatlands in South-east Asia. Delft Hydraulics. Delft Hydraulics report Q3943.

Kuchinskiy, V. 2006. Presentation at EUBIONET II / IEA Bioenergy study tour, October 2006.

Massachusetts Division of Energy Resources. 2007. Renewable portfolio standard. Available at: http://www.mass.gov/doer/rps/

McCloy, B.W. and Associates. 1999. Opportunities for increased woodwaste cogeneration in the Canadian pulp and paper industry.

Merl, A., Humar, M., Okstad, T., Picardo, V., Ribeiro, A. and Steierer, F. 2007. *Amounts of recovered wood in COST E31 countries and Europe*. 3rd European COST E31 Conference. Management of Recovered Wood. Reaching a Higher Technical, Economic and Environmental Standard in Europe. Thessaloniki. University Studio Press. Conference held in Klagenfurt, Austria. May 2007. ISBN 978-960-12-1596-9.

Natural Resource Canada. 2000. Canada's Emissions Outlook Updated 1997-2020.

Natural Resources Canada. 2000. Canada's Emissions Outlook Updated 1997-2020. Ottawa, Ontario: Natural Resources Canada.

Ovsyanko, A. 2007. Presentation at conference in Khaborovsk, Russia, April 2007.

Perlack, R.D. at al., 2005. Biomass as feedstock for a bioenergy and bioproducts industry: The technical feasibility of a billion-ton annual supply. Oak Ridge National Laboratory, Oak Ridge, Tennessee. Available at: http://www1.eere.energy.gov/biomass/pdfs/final_billionton_vision_report2.pdf

Printweek. 2007. Available at: http://www.printweek.com/news/660721/Russian-timber-export-hikes-hit-paper-industry/

ProPellets. 2007. Available at: http://www.propellets.at/images/content/images/1aapelletspreiscentkg_april_bg.jpg

Rakos, C. 2007. ProPellets. Presentation in Rotterdam. Available at: http://www.eubionet.net/ACFiles/Download.asp?recID=4611

Renewable energy policy project. 2007. Renewable portfolio standards. Available at: http://www.crest.org/rps/index.html

Reuters. 2007. Available at: http://www.reuters.com/article/wtMostRead/idUSN1520305020070316

Statistics Canada. 2006. CANSIM Table 128-0006. Ottawa, Ontario. Available at: http://www40.statcan.ca/l01/cst01/prim74.htm

Statistics Canada. 2007. CANSIM 128-0006. Available at: http://www40.statcan.ca/l01/cst01/prim74.htm

Steierer, F. and Fisher-Ankern, A. 2007. *Wood Energy in Europe and North America: A new estimate on volumes and flows*, UNECE/FAO/IEA/EU. Study in progress. Available at: http://www.unece.org/trade/timber/docs/stats-sessions/stats-29/english/report-conclusions-2007-03.pdf

Stern, N. 2007. The Stern Review on the economics of climate change. Available at: http://www.hm-treasury.gov.uk/independent_reviews/stern_review_economics_climate_change/stern_review_report.cfm

Stern, T. and Kholodkov, V.S. 2005. Analysis of bioenergy development in Sweden and northwest Russia – Swedish-Russian cooperation, Proceedings of the conference "Bioenergy 2005", Veliky Novgorod.

Swaan, J. 2006. Biomass: Responsible, sustainable renewable energy option. Wood Pellet Association of Canada, 23 March 2006. Available at: http://www.pollutionprobe.org/Happening/pdfs/gp_march06_van/swaan.pdf

Swedish Energy Agency. 2006. Energy in Sweden 2006. Eskilstuna, Sweden. ET 2006:44.

The Prince George Citizen Review. 10 March 2007. Available at: http://www.princegeorgecitizen.com

Thorp, B. 2007. Paper industry must protect its lead in cellulosic innovation. Pulp and Paper. May 2007. pp. 30-34.

UN-Energy. 2007. *Sustainable Bioenergy: A framework for decision makers*, May 2007. Available at: http://esa.un.org/un-energy/pdf/susdev.Biofuels.FAO.pdf

US Department of Energy EIA. 2007. Monthly Energy Review. April 2007. Available at: http://www.eia.doe.gov/emeu/mer/renew.html

US Department of Energy. 2007. DOE Selects Six Cellulosic Ethanol Plants for Up to $385 Million in Federal Funding. News release, 28 February 2007. Available at: http://www.energy.gov/news/4827.htm

US Department of Energy. Energy Efficiency and Renewable Energy. 2007. Sugar platform. Available at: http://www1.eere.energy.gov/biomass/sugar_platform.html

US Department of Energy. Energy Efficiency and Renewable Energy. 2007. Thermochemical platform. Available at: http://www1.eere.energy.gov/biomass/thermochemical_platform.html

US Environmental Protection Agency. 2006. National Electric Energy Data System (NEEDS) 2006. Available at: http://www.epa.gov/airmarkets/progsregs/epa-ipm/index.html#needs

Van Essen, P. 2007. Port of Rotterdam Authority, presentation in Rotterdam. Available at: http://www.eubionet.net/GetItem.asp?item=file;4619

World Health Organization, Europe. 2006. Health risks of particulate matter from long-range transboundary air pollution.

Yaremchuk, G. 2006. Presentation at EUBIONET II / IEA Bioenergy study tour, October 2006.

Chapter 10

Biomass for energy and plantations – new certification driver: Certified forest products markets, 2006-2007[97]

Highlights

- The area of certified forest grew by 8.3% from 2006 to 2007, reaching 292 million hectares, which is 7.6% of the global forest area; however, the rate of increase is slowing.

- More than 84% of the world's certified forest is located in the northern hemisphere, with more than half (56%) in North America and another 28% in Europe; however, their shares are decreasing with an expected boom in Russia and China.

- The global push to reduce carbon emissions and to produce more forest-based biofuels means woodfuels have to be considered in terms of their sustainable production, which could mean their certification.

- The introduction of new certified species from plantations, such as hybrid poplar, into the solid wood and biomass market sectors is expected to rapidly increase both the volume of certified supply and market demand.

- Half of the world's certified forest area is in plantations, mixed plantations and semi-natural forests, all of which are necessary for forest products.

- Forest certification helps to accelerate access to international voluntary carbon markets, where regional climate registries acknowledge qualified certification systems as a baseline for forest-based offset verification.

- Certification of the same forests and products by multiple schemes is a trend originating from the desire of industry and consumers for mutual recognition by the major certification schemes.

- Paper purchasers are driving increased demand for certified wood, with impacts felt across major geographic regions and pulp and paper distribution channels.

- Due to low consumer awareness, and therefore demand, as well as the lack of incentive for the producer, the majority of certified forest products are marketed without any reference to certification.

- Non-wood forest-products are being certified for sustainable production, including cork, essential oils, chestnuts, honey, berries, truffles and mushrooms.

---

[97] By Mr. Florian Kraxner, International Institute for Applied Systems Analysis, Austria, Dr. Catherine Mater, Mater Engineering, US, and Dr. Toshiaki Owari, University of Tokyo, Japan.

Secretariat introduction

This chapter provides an update on certified forest products (CFPs) and the certification of forests for sustainable forest management. The mandate to analyse and report on developments comes from the UNECE Timber Committee and the FAO European Forestry Commission. When certification of forest management began in 1995, the Committee and the Commission established a Team of Specialists to predict how certification would affect the forest sector. It was an overly challenging task at that time, but the Team produced various scenarios. As certification grew, the Committee and the Commission established an officially nominated Network of Country Correspondents on Certification and Certified Forest Products Markets. The authors of this chapter did not survey the entire network, but rather obtained information for some key markets from some correspondents in the network, as well as from other key players in the market. There are currently no official statistics for trade in CFPs, as confirmed by the FAO/UNECE Working Party on Forest Economics and Statistics in May 2006, reflecting the fact that CFPs do not feature in the Harmonized Commodity Description and Coding System (HS) maintained by the World Customs Organization. Nevertheless, there are alternative sources of information. Unless otherwise attributed, all estimates and opinions in this chapter are from the authors' interpretations

This chapter will provide a basis for an exchange of ideas on CFP markets at the joint Timber Committee and International Softwood Conference Market Discussions on 8-9 October 2007. Following last year's market discussions, a policy forum was held on "Public procurement policies for wood and paper products and their impacts on sustainable forest management and timber markets"[98.] Some government procurement policies and some company procurement policies require certified wood products as evidence of sustainability and legality. The forum examined the complexity of new public procurement policies in Europe, and new green building policies in North America, e.g. how to assess different certification schemes and how to avoid creating trade barriers. Public procurement and green building policies are strong drivers for CFPs.

It is a pleasure to thank once again Mr. Florian Kraxner,[99] expert in CFPs, International Institute for Applied Systems Analysis, Laxenburg, Austria, who led the production and wrote most of this chapter. Mr.

Kraxner is a member of the UNECE/FAO Team of Specialists on Forest Products Markets and Marketing, and presented CFP markets at the last Timber Committee Market Discussions. Dr. Catherine Mater,[100] President, Mater Engineering, Ltd. and Senior Fellow, The Pinchot Institute, Corvallis, Oregon, US, contributed especially to the North American analysis. We thank once again Dr. Toshiaki Owari,[101] University of Tokyo, for his perspective on Asian CFP markets.

10.1 Introduction

The UNECE region's CFP markets have been analysed in a chapter of the UNECE/FAO *Forest Products Annual Market Review* since 1998. This year's chapter provides an in-depth statistical overview of the market and trade of CFPs and also concentrates on policy-related aspects of certification in the forest sector. CFPs bear labels demonstrating, in a manner verifiable by independent bodies, that they come from forests that meet standards for sustainable forest management (SFM). Consumers might find labels on furniture and wood products, while manufacturers can verify the sources through the certification scheme's chain-of-custody (CoC) procedures. Non-independently (third-party) certified forests such as the Malaysian Timber Certification Council[102] (MTCC) or the Indonesian Ecolabelling Institute[103] (LEI), and their CFPs, are not included in this analysis, although their certified products are imported into the UNECE region. Process certification schemes such as ISO[104] 14001 are not included in this comparative analysis. The chapter focuses on certification systems based in the UNECE region.

---

[98] Proceedings at: www.fao.org/docrep/009/a0914e/a0914e00.htm

[99] Mr. Florian Kraxner, expert in certified forest products markets, International Institute for Applied Systems Analysis, A-2361 Laxenburg, Austria, tel: +43 2236 807 233, fax: +43 2236 807 599, email: kraxner@iiasa.ac.at, website: www.iiasa.ac.at/Research/FOR

[100] Dr. Catherine Mater, President, Mater Engineering, Ltd, 101 SW Western Boulevard, Corvallis, Oregon 97333, US, tel: +1 541 753 7335, fax: +1 541 752 2952, e-mail: Catherine@mater.com, website: www.mater.com

[101] Dr. Toshiaki Owari, Lecturer, Forest Business and Management, University Forest in Hokkaido, Graduate School of Agricultural and Life Sciences, University of Tokyo, Yamabe, Furano 079-1561, Japan, tel: +81 167 42 2111, fax: +81 167 42 2689, e-mail: owari@uf.a.u-tokyo.ac.jp

[102] http://www.mtcc.com.my/

[103] http://www.lei.or.id/english/index.php

[104] http://www.iso.org

This year's chapter contains:

10.2 Supply of CFPs

10.3 Demand for CFPs

10.4 Policy issues

10.4.1 Public procurement and governance in North America

10.4.2 Sustainable forest management and illegal logging

10.4.3 Certification in the Russian Federation

10.4.4 Developments in the Japanese and Chinese markets for CFPs

10.4.5 Biomass for bioenergy – biofuel potential and its certification

10.4.6 Certification and forest plantations

10.4.7 Non-wood forest product certification

10.5 References.

10.2 Supply of CFPs

By May 2007, the area of certified forest worldwide totalled 294 million ha, approximately 7.6% of the world's forests (3.9 billion ha (FAO, 2007)), a relatively steep and constant increase since the first third-party certification of forest area took place in 1993 by the Forest Stewardship Council (FSC). However, compared with some of the previous survey periods (e.g. May 2004 to May 2005), the annual rate of increase in certified area has fallen by more than half to some 12% during the period May 2005 – May 2006 and to only 8.3% during the period May 2006 to May 2007. Approximately 1.5 million ha in Europe (mostly Sweden) and another 0.8 million ha in North America (mostly Canada) are double certified by two different systems (graph 10.2.1).

"Double certification" or "dual certification", i.e. the certification by two or multiple third-party schemes at the same time for the same forests and the same products, is a new trend in forest and CoC certification. This tendency originates from the desire for mutual recognition by the major certification schemes, strongly requested by forest industry and consumers alike. Nevertheless, full or partial recognition between FSC and the Programme for the Endorsement of Forest Certification schemes (PEFC) is not feasible in the near future due to controversies between them. Full mutual recognition exists e.g. between the Sustainable Forestry Initiative (SFI) (PEFC-umbrella) and the American Tree Farm System (ATFS). Consequently, under the SFI system, ATFS-certified (raw) material is considered equivalent to SFI-certified material and vice versa (figure 10.2.1).

GRAPH 10.2.1

Forest area certified by major certification schemes, 1998-2007

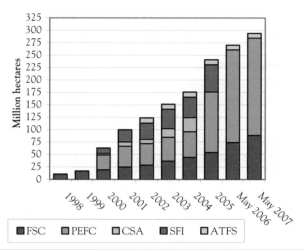

Notes: As of May 2007, approximately 2.3 million hectares have been certified by more than one scheme. These are not deducted from any scheme. The graph therefore shows a slightly higher amount of total forest area certified than exists in reality. FSC=Forest Stewardship Council; PEFC=Programme for the Endorsement of Forest Certification schemes; CSA=Canadian Standards Association Sustainable Forest Management Program (endorsed by PEFC in 2005); SFI=Sustainable Forestry Initiative (endorsed by PEFC in 2005); ATFS=American Tree Farm System.

Sources: Individual certification systems and the Canadian Sustainable Forestry Certification Coalition, 2006.

FIGURE 10.2.1

Examples of certification logos based in the UNECE region

Source: Nordic Family Forestry, 2007.

Since 2000, the certified forest area has increased every year, mainly due to certification by:

- ATFS.
- Canadian Standards Association Sustainable Forest Management Program (CSA, endorsed by PEFC in 2005).
- Forest Stewardship Council (FSC).
- PEFC, formerly known as the Pan European Forest Certification System.
- SFI, endorsed by PEFC in 2005, in the US and Canada.

PEFC endorsed the two biggest certification schemes in North America – the CSA system of Canada at the beginning of 2005, as well as SFI by the end of 2005. Allowing CSA to bear the PEFC label means including another 73 million ha (May 2007) and a further 54.4 million ha – in the case of SFI - under the PEFC umbrella, which now totals 196.3 million ha of certified forest area worldwide. In North America, the forest area certified under the PEFC umbrella has grown as a result of a 5.4% increment of the CSA scheme, whereas there was no increase of SFI certified area during the last 12 months until May 2007. Worldwide, the PEFC umbrella performed an increment rate of 5.2%, or 10.2 million ha in absolute figures, during this survey period (May 2006 to May 2007). PEFC managed to keep the same increase in absolute numbers of additionally certified ha (not by endorsement of other existing schemes and their ha), as during the previous survey period.

Additionally, 10 forest certification systems are currently undergoing the PEFC endorsement process. Lithuania and the US (ATFS) have submitted their systems for endorsement. Latvia and Switzerland have submitted their systems for re-endorsement. For the endorsement assessment, the national certification systems for Estonia, Gabon, Italy, Poland, Slovenia and the United Kingdom have been going through a public consultation process and will consequently be endorsed by the PEFC Board of Directors and a vote by the PEFC members on endorsement or otherwise.

FSC listed a total of 88.4 million ha in May 2007, an increase of more than 14.5 million ha, or 16.4%, during the last 12 months. FSC's increment rate slowed down by more than half during this period compared with the survey period May 2005-May 2006.

The third major system of North America is ATFS, which has remained relatively stable throughout the last five survey periods. After a slight drawback during the survey period, the smallest third-party certification scheme in North America could grow again, totalling slightly more than 9.3 million ha in the US only. ATFS is currently undergoing an endorsement process with PEFC

and might join the umbrella within this year. Officially, the ATFS and SFI labels are already mutually recognized, which allows for fast endorsement negotiations with PEFC.

In terms of share of certified forest area, the market is clearly divided (graph 10.2.2). Due to the endorsement of SFI and CSA by PEFC, the portfolio of major certification schemes has been reduced to 3 systems only. The PEFC umbrella accounts for slightly more than two thirds of the area certified globally. With a share of 30%, FSC is the second largest scheme and ATFS currently still holds 3% of the certified area worldwide. Due to a higher increase by FSC (plus some 2%), the PEFC umbrella lost about 3% (of its relative share in the total) during the present survey period (May 2006-May 2007). This loss might be compensated soon by the endorsement of ATFS, anticipated in 2007.

GRAPH 10.2.2

Share of certified forest area by the three major schemes, 2007

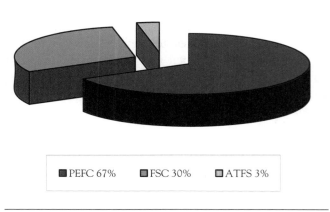

| ■ PEFC 67% | ■ FSC 30% | □ ATFS 3% |

Notes: If a forest has been certified to more than one standard, the respective area has been counted in each of the certifying schemes involved. The total of certified forest area in this graph therefore shows a higher amount, approximately 1.5 million hectares more, than exists in reality. As of May 2007.

Sources: Individual certification systems, Forest Certification Watch and the Canadian Sustainable Forestry Certification Coalition, 2007.

Relatively unchanged from the last survey period, most of the PEFC-certified forest area lies in the northern hemisphere, i.e. non-tropical (boreal and temperate) zones, with more than two thirds of it outside Europe (graph 10.2.3). The majority of this certified area (65%) is in North America. Approximately one third is located in the EU and other countries of western Europe (European Free Trade Association (EFTA)). There is still no forest area certified by PEFC in Russia. The share in the tropics is less than 1%, located only in Latin America.

PEFC currently has no certified forest area in either Africa or Asia. However, Gabon will soon be the first African country producing wood under the PEFC label.

GRAPH 10.2.3

Regional distribution of certified forest area by the PEFC and PEFC-endorsed systems, 2007

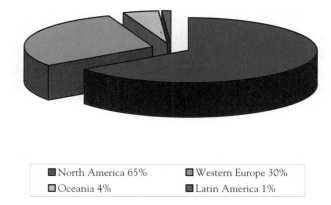

| ■ North America 65% | ■ Western Europe 30% |
| □ Oceania 4% | ■ Latin America 1% |

Notes: Distribution of the certified forest area within the PEFC system, including the endorsed CSA and SFI in North America. As of May 2007.
Sources: PEFC, CSA and SFI, 2007.

A different situation is shown by the diverse geographical spread of forests certified by FSC, even though the majority of the area certified still lies in the northern hemisphere (graph 10.2.4). Compared with the distribution of the last survey period (May 2005-May 2006), areas such as western Europe, North America, Latin America and Oceania have lost in their share of global certification, while eastern European and CIS (mainly Russia) managed to increase their share by some 6%, totalling 23%. The geographical division of forest area certified under FSC shows three to four regions that are clearly dominating the distribution. One third is located in North America, approximately 28% in western European countries, 23% in eastern Europe and CIS countries and 11% in Latin America. Other tropical regions such as Africa and Asia remained unchanged in their shares at 3% and 2% respectively. Oceania has dropped to 1% within the FSC distribution.

GRAPH 10.2.4

Regional distribution of certified forest area by FSC, 2007

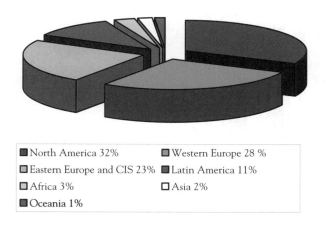

■ North America 32%	■ Western Europe 28 %
□ Eastern Europe and CIS 23%	■ Latin America 11%
□ Africa 3%	□ Asia 2%
■ Oceania 1%	

Note: As of May 2007.
Source: FSC, 2007.

More than 84% of the world's certified forest is located in the northern hemisphere with more than half (56%) located in North America and 28% in western Europe. However, as a logical consequence of having certified most of their forest area during the past decade, all these regions are starting to lose their share of total certified forest to other regions in the world.

North America dropped from 58% to 56% (compared with the last survey period, May 2005-May 2006) and western Europe lost 5% since 2005. Relative to these losses, the proportions of eastern European and CIS countries have increased from 3% to 7% over the last two years. However, even with this change, the area certified outside North America and western Europe still only accounts for 16% of the global total (graph 10.2.5). The least change could be noted in Africa and Latin America during the past two years. This tendency of decreasing shares in North America and western Europe might be a first indicator for the upcoming years when forest management certification is expected to boom in Russia and probably also in Asia (China and Japan drive the entire Asian region).

Nevertheless, this latest trend does not promise any change in the unbalanced distribution of certified forest area within the northern hemisphere (temperate and boreal) and the southern hemisphere (mostly sub-tropical and tropical). While the original driver for certification was uncontrolled deforestation in the tropics, in practice, certification has been far more successful in the north than in the south, and in the developed world than in the developing world.

GRAPH 10.2.5

Geographical distribution of total certified forest area, 2005-2007

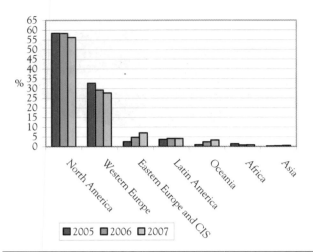

Notes: All major certification schemes combined. As of May 2007.

Sources: Individual certification systems, Forest Certification Watch and the Canadian Sustainable Forestry Certification Coalition, 2007.

With the exception of Oceania, which had a constant annual increase of 1% during the last three years, the new trend still appears to rather emphasize the disparities between the hemispheres, taking into consideration the ambitious certification efforts currently under way in the world's most forest-rich country, Russia.

In western Europe, slightly more than half of the total forest area is certified, compared with more than one third in North America. The rate of increase in percentage of certified area to the total forest area in these two regions is relatively small but constant. One reason for this marginal increment, especially in the case of Europe, might be that the commercial forest areas in these countries are mostly certified, and significant further certification can be realized only by double certification, which will not be visible in the statistical calculations (graph 10.2.6).

Apart from western Europe and North America, only Oceania (5%) and eastern European countries and CIS (2%) exceed 1% of their total forest area under certification and these trends also mirror the statistical developments or non extension of their certificates. Some African forests experienced delays in gaining certification, or have not had their certificates extended, due to mismanagement or other problems.

The potential roundwood supply from the world's certified forests in 2007 is estimated at approximately 387 million m³. This is some 4% more than during the

last review period (May 2005-May 2006) and shows that the increment rate in roundwood provided from certified resources dropped by half (table 10.2.1). This potential production equates to approximately one quarter of the world's production of industrial roundwood, or about 42% of the industrial roundwood production of North America and western Europe, where 84% of certified forests are situated. Concerning roundwood production from certified forest area, the UNECE regions' average annual removals on forests available for wood supply are multiplied by the percentage of the regions' certified forest area. According to the UNECE/FAO definition, roundwood is composed of industrial roundwood and fuelwood; however, the latter was not considered in this estimation.

GRAPH 10.2.6

Certified forest as a percentage of total forest area by region, 2005-2007

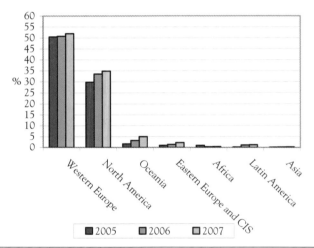

Notes: The forest area is based on FAO's *State of World's Forest 2007* data, excluding the category "other wooded land". As of May 2007.

Sources: Individual certification systems, Forest Certification Watch, the Canadian Sustainable Forestry Certification Coalition, 2007 and FAO, 2005.

North America has the largest area of certified forest, as it has had during the last four years (graph 10.2.7). Canada, accounting for 127.4 million ha of certified forest, ahead of the US with 36.7 million ha. Even though the rate of increase in certified forest area has slowed further, Canada's certified area still grew by almost 5.5% during the survey period May 2006-May 2007.

TABLE 10.2.1.

Certified forest area and certified roundwood production by region, 2005-2007

Region	Total forest area (million ha)	Total certified forest area (million ha)			% of total forest area certified			Estimated industrial roundwood produced from certified forest (million m³)			% of estimated industrial roundwood from certified forests (from global roundwood production)		
		2005	2006	2007	2005	2006	2007	2005	2006	2007	2005	2006	2007
North America	470.6	140.2	157.7	164.2	29.8	33.5	34.9	180.6	201.8	210.1	11.4	12.7	13.2
EU/EFTA	155.5	78.5	78.9	80.8	50.5	50.7	52.0	160.1	162.5	166.4	10.1	10.2	10.5
CIS	907.4	8.8	13.0	20.6	1	1.4	2.3	1.6	2.3	3.6	0.1	0.1	0.2
Oceania	197.6	3.4	6.4	9.9	1.7	3.3	5.0	0.9	1.6	2.5	0.1	0.1	0.2
Africa	649.9	6.2	2.1	2.6	1	0.3	0.4	0.7	0.2	0.3	0.0	0.0	0.0
Latin America	964.4	2.3	11.1	12.1	0.2	1.1	1.3	0.4	1.9	2.1	0.0	0.1	0.1
Asia	524.1	0.8	1.1	1.6	0.2	0.2	0.3	0.4	0.5	0.7	0.0	0.0	0.0
World total	3 869.5	240.2	270.3	291.8	6.2	7.0	7.5	344.6	370.8	385.7	21.7	23.4	24.3

Notes: The reference for forest area (excluding "other wooded land") and estimations for the industrial roundwood production from certified forests are based on FAO's *State of the World's Forest 2005* data. Concerning roundwood production, the subregions' annual roundwood production from "forests available for wood supply" is multiplied by the percentage of the regions' certified forest area (i.e. it is assumed that the removals of industrial roundwood from each ha from certified forests is the same as the average for all forest available for wood supply). However, not all certified roundwood is sold with a label.

Sources: Individual certification systems, Forest Certification Watch, the Canadian Sustainable Forestry Certification Coalition, 2007, FAO, 2005 and the authors' compilation. As of May 2007.

More than half of PEFC-certified forest and almost one quarter of FSC certified area were in Canada. After a loss of certified forest area in 2005, the certified forest area in the US grew by 6% during the last 12 months until May 2007 as a result of an increment of FSC and ATFS.

There was minor change in certified forest areas in Finland (22.6 million ha, PEFC only), Sweden (17.5 million ha) and Norway (9.2 million ha). With a 65% increase, Russia (14.7 million ha, FSC only) now ranks fifth and became the country with the second to the most forest area certified by FSC after Canada. Only Australia (9 million ha, PEFC only) and Brazil (5.7 million ha, FSC only) showed similar increase rates at 60% and 32% respectively. Belarus (2.5 million ha), Croatia (2 million ha), Ukraine (1.4 million ha) and the Baltic countries show higher increase rates on lower certified forest area.

In most of the listed countries there is a clear tendency towards a single certification scheme. Canada, Finland, Norway, Germany, Australia and France are clearly dominated by PEFC or PEFC-endorsed systems. In Russia, Poland and Brazil, FSC is the predominant system. The US and Sweden have several schemes certifying almost equal amounts of forest.

In sub-tropical and tropical areas, FSC has issued most of the certificates that are adding up to some 4 million ha in Africa, Latin America and Asia.

GRAPH 10.2.7

Five countries' certified forest area, 2004-2007

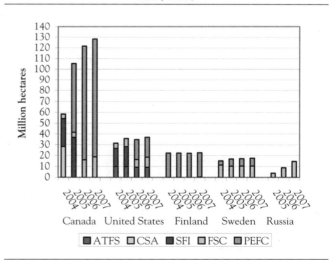

Notes: The graph contains no overlap from double certification. Forest Management certification in Russia, Australia and Brazil only started in 2005. As of May 2007.

Sources: Individual certification systems, country correspondents, Forest Certification Watch, Canadian Sustainable Forestry Certification Coalition, 2007.

10.3 Demand for CFPs

Some major European wood-producing countries such as Finland and Austria have already reached 100% certification of their managed forests. This means that in these countries the entire roundwood production could bear a certification label from one of the major approving schemes. However, due to low consumer awareness and the resulting frequent lack of demand by final consumers, on the one hand, and lack of incentive for the producer (i.e. no clear market advantage such as a price premium), on the other, the vast majority of these products, as in previous years, is marketed without any reference to certification.

Netherlands seem to be an exception, with the consumer being the driving force for CFPs. A 2005 survey of the Dutch market shows that FSC is the most important on-product label. The total share of timber from FSC-certified sources in the Netherlands is about 12.2%, with 9.3% sold as labelled product and 2.9% without any label. The marketed timber sourcing from PEFC certified forests has a share of 22% on the Dutch market, but only 3.9% is sold as labelled, whereas 18.1% is sold without any label. When looking at the Dutch pulp and paper market, the situation appears to be upside-down. PEFC's share in the totally marketed pulp and paper is 21.9% at a labelling percentage of 19.3% and non-labelled selling of 2.6%. The share of pulp and paper derived from FSC-certified sources is 5.7%, of which 4.3% is labelled and 1.4% is not labelled. For sawn softwood, already more than 50% of the market is sustainable in the Netherlands. However, a major effort will be necessary to lift the market share of sustainable tropical hardwood and sustainable temperate hardwood to the same level. Within the sawn softwood market, major growth is still possible in the packaging and pallet industry, a largely untapped market for sustainable timber (Leek and Oldenburger, 2007).

In the UK, a market survey found in 2006 that the insistence on the supply of certified goods is more prevalent among the larger industrial user (e.g. timber frame construction). Certification has yet to feature as an essential requirement among smaller companies where there appears to be a lower awareness and, significantly, fewer public procurement processes in place. In 2005,it was estimated that of all imported goods, just over 10% were subject to specific customer requests with the majority of these goods supplied by the larger sawnwood and panel suppliers (Timbertrends, 2007).

Downstream industries do not usually need commodity products to be certified; hence potential supply of CFPs exceeds actual demand in many markets, especially of PEFC-certified CFPs. An additional constraint impeding awareness of CFPs among the public

is that most companies do not communicate that their products are certified (Owari et al., 2006). By not labelling certified products, any possible link is missed between consumer demand for assurance of SFM and producers' tremendous expenses for certifying forests and establishing CoC.

FSC CFPs from tropical wood are increasingly appearing on the shelves of do-it-yourself retailers and even supermarket chains selling furniture from tropical wood in western and central Europe.

CFPs remain difficult to quantify due to the lack of official figures and trade classifications. This fundamental issue – independent, compatible and accurate data collection and management as a tool for a reliable market assessment – was also stressed by several key speakers at the UNECE Timber Committee Market Discussions (3-4 October 2006, Geneva). So far, one practicable tool for describing market characteristics and developments of the amount of CFPs in business-to-business markets is the number and type of CoC certificates, serving as a crucial indicator.

Since 1998 the number of such certificates has increased immensely (graph 10.3.1). Between May 2006 and May 2007 the rate of increase was 19.5%, which was about the same rate as during the previous survey period (May 2005-May 2006). By May 2007 the number of certificates worldwide totalled 8,600, of which 63.4% were by FSC and 36.6% by PEFC.

GRAPH 10.3.1

Chain-of-custody certification trends worldwide, 1998-2007

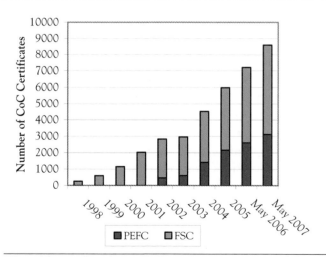

Notes: The numbers denote CoC certificates irrespective of the size of the individual companies or of volume of production or trade. As of May 2007.

Sources: FSC and PEFC, 2007.

This has not changed significantly during the last three survey periods, indicating that both systems have increased at the same rate (20%) over the last years in terms of certificates issued. Prior to that, PEFC had enjoyed a much higher rate than FSC.

Both the SFI and CSA systems in North America have developed logos, licensing procedures and on-product labelling, but have not yet issued CoC certificates. FSC and PEFC remain the only schemes on the market offering full CoCs for CFPs. By May 2007, FSC CoC certificates were active in 71 countries and PEFC CoC certificates were active in 27 countries.

Using the total number of CoC certificates issued per country as an indicator for business-to-business demand for CFPs, within the UNECE region France (1,061 certificates) leads the UK (1,046 certificates) and Germany (1,007 certificates). France had certificates from both schemes, PEFC accounting for 90% of all certificates issued in the country and FSC accounting for 10% (graph 10.3.2). The UK is now rated second, with 65% of its certificates issued by the FSC system, and 35% by the PEFC system. In third position is Germany, with 59% of its certificates issued by PEFC and 41% by FSC, ahead of the US and Switzerland. Poland lost its position to Switzerland owing to the renewing of the Swiss Q-label, which had been suspended during the last survey period (May 2005-May 2006) due to a non-conformity with the PEFC regulations. This ranking illustrates that in most countries' markets, with the exception of Germany, Belgium and Spain, there is an obvious dominance of one system, tending to converge towards one of the certification schemes. However, within the UNECE region both certification schemes could issue about the same amount of certificates (57% FSC certificates and 43% certificates issued by the PEFC system).

In countries outside the UNECE region, almost all companies holding a CoC certificate obtained their certificates from FSC (97% certificates by FSC and 3% issued by PEFC). Japan leads with 384 certificates and is followed by China, with 262 certificates, which took over Brazil, with 202 certificates in May 2006 (graph 10.3.3). The important market growth for CFPs for Asia is illustrated over the last year by the dominant position of Japan, the 77% growth in CoC certificates in China and the large number of certificates issued in Viet Nam (119), Malaysia (66) and Indonesia (34). Growth in Asia is rising in parallel to some countries in South America. However, companies in these regions are most often exporting to North America and Europe, rather than supplying their domestic markets, which have not yet demanded certified products.

GRAPH 10. 3.2

Chain-of-custody certificate distribution within the UNECE region, 2007

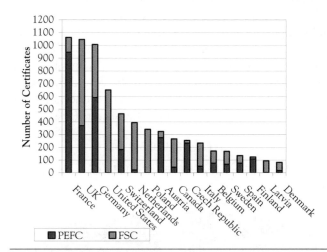

Notes: Countries with fewer than 50 CoC certificates are not shown. The numbers denote CoC certificates irrespective of the size of the individual companies as of May 2007.
Source: FSC, PEFC and authors' compilation, 2007.

GRAPH 10.3.3

Chain-of-custody distribution outside UNECE region, 2007

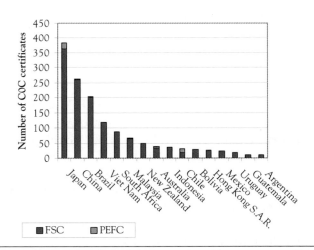

Notes: The graph only includes countries with ten or more CoC certificates. The numbers denote CoC certificates irrespective of the size of the individual companies as of May 2007. As of May 2007, neither SFI, CSA nor ATFS have CoC certificates.
Sources: FSC, PEFC and authors' compilation, 2007.

The distribution of CoC certificates across the product range illustrates that companies from all wood-based industries and trade sectors hold CoC certificates. Companies holding CoC certificates of FSC (64%) cover a relatively wide product range (graph 10.3.4). The distribution of FSC-issued CoC certificates among industry sectors changed somewhat over the last year.

The main reason for the change in the allocation might be the statistical system by FSC, which is undergoing a modification affecting mainly the product category definitions. Hence, roundwood and other primary forest industry, together with panels and sawnwood producers, hold approximately half of the CoC certificates, with relatively equal shares of between 15-18%. Pulp and paper, together with furniture producers, account for the next quarter at approximately even shares and the fourth quarter is divided by window and door producers (10%), wood manufacturers (10%) and other sectors (5%).

GRAPH 10.3.4

FSC chain-of-custody distribution by industry sector, 2007

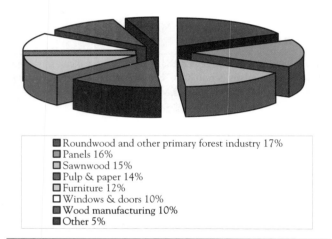

■ Roundwood and other primary forest industry 17%
□ Panels 16%
□ Sawnwood 15%
■ Pulp & paper 14%
□ Furniture 12%
□ Windows & doors 10%
■ Wood manufacturing 10%
■ Other 5%

Note: Some overlap between the industry sectors is possible.
Source: FSC, 2007.

Generally, the distribution of PEFC-issued CoC certificates (36% of the total) did not change over the last year (graph 10.3.5). PEFC CoC certificates are mainly issued for timber trade and sawmilling, with almost the same shares, approximately one third of the total. These two PEFC CoC main sectors are followed by other primary forest industries (13%). The wood products trade and retailing sector and the secondary wood manufacturing sector each hold some 10% of the PEFC CoC certificates' spectrum. The rest is distributed among pulp and paper (6%), other forest industry sectors (2%) and the construction sector (1%). Different accounting and product groupings do not permit a direct comparison between the industry sectors and products certified by the schemes.

GRAPH 10.3.5

PEFC chain-of-custody distribution by industry sector, 2007

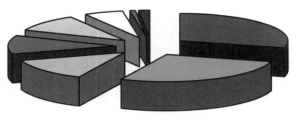

■ Timber trade 29%
■ Sawmill 28%
□ Other primary forest industries 13%
■ Wood products trade/retailers 11%
□ Wood manufacturing 10%
□ Pulp and Paper 6%
■ Construction 1%
■ Other 2%

Note: Some overlap between the industry sectors is possible.
Source: PEFC, 2007.

10.4 Policy issues

10.4.1 Public procurement and governance in North America

Six major trends connected to public lands certified wood procurement and governance either currently affect or are likely to soon affect the growth of certified supply and market demand for CFPs in the US.

10.4.1.1 Continued growth of public forestland certification and impacts on private forestlands

Of the 250 million ha of forestland in the US, approximately 37% is public, private non-industrial ownership is about 45% (Butler et al., 2003). There are over 10 million non-industrial forestland owners across the US who are expected to provide 60% of the US timber supply by 2030 and who often rely on public land managers for forest management information and access to markets (Zhang et al., 2005). Public forestland managers and public agencies throughout the US are proving to be significant catalysts in both the growth of certified wood supply and growth of market demand for certified wood product. In 2007, public land certifications under the SFI system were slightly over 6.4 million ha, equal to 12.5% of the total SFI certified area in the US (SFI, 2007). Public land certification comprised 71% of all FSC certified volume in the US, equal to 6.6 million ha of a total of 9.2 million ha (FSC-US, 2007).

Initial discussions of certification of public forestlands began in 1997, and with the states of Minnesota and Pennsylvania becoming FSC-certified in 1998. By 2006, over 3.6 million ha of state forestlands in ten states[105] were certified either by FSC, SFI, or both (Mater, 2006).

In March 2006, the USDA Forest Service authorized the country's first official pilot projects in forest certification assessments. National forests comprise some 78 million ha of forestland throughout the country and are significant contributors to overall wood flow in many regions across the US. FSC assessments have so far been conducted on about 2 million ha of national forestlands in the states of Oregon, Pennsylvania, Wisconsin and Florida. Results of these FSC assessments will be released to the public in mid-2007, but first results indicate that FSC-US currently lacks specific standards to certify national forests. However, if FSC developed the necessary standards, then part or all of the national forests could be certified. This could open up geographically dispersed market supply channels, which could also benefit non-industrial private forestland owners (NIPFs) across the US, who typically have trouble accessing certified markets due to their smaller offer.

10.4.1.2 *Paper purchasers driving growth in market demand for certified supply*

Major environmental challenges to users of uncertified paper products began in 2002, which resulted in an unprecedented acceleration of certified wood coming from public forestlands. Starting in 2003, the world's largest magazine company had set time-bound targets for achieving over 85% certified (FSC or SFI) content in their annual paper purchases (600,000 tons/year) by 2006. This resulted in certification of state forests in Michigan, Wisconsin, and Maryland.

In 2006-2007, a nationwide speciality retailer of high quality home products combined with the largest publishing company in the UK and a worldwide computer manufacturer to set time-bound limits for using certified paper in their catalogues. These three companies alone have a combined purchasing volume of over 250,000 tons of paper per year.

Out of the 781 CoC certificate holders in the US, 55% are paper manufacturers, printers, and merchants (FSC, 2007). In Canada, 51% of FSC CoC certificate holders are paper manufacturers, printers and merchants located throughout all Canadian provinces (FSC-Canada, 2007).

10.4.1.3 *Impact of green building growth impact and Leadership in Energy and Environmental Design*

The unprecedented growth of the green building market in the US, spearheaded by the US Green Building Council and the Leadership in Energy and Environmental Design (LEED) programme, has significantly impacted both awareness and purchase power for FSC-certified wood in building construction. Interestingly, it is public agencies across the US that drive a substantial portion of that market demand, as LEED allows for credits in using wood only sourced from FSC-certified supplies. As of May 2007, LEED initiatives including legislation, executive orders, resolutions, ordinances, policies and incentives are found in 55 cities, 11 counties and 22 states across the US.

Awareness and use of certified wood in housing construction appears strongest in west coast states in the US. In 2006, Washington State-based Cintrafor released the results of a survey they conducted with 240 residential builders from across the US (Ganguly, 2006). Results showed that 77% of builders in west coast states were aware of certified wood and had home buyers who were willing to pay premium for a home built with certified wood. 70% of those west coast builders who were aware of certified wood actually use certified wood in the homes they build, with over 56% of their softwood framing material coming from certified supply. Builders in the central states and the east coast were less aware of certified wood, but even those percentages were markedly higher than responses to similar surveys conducted just five years earlier (Ganguly, 2006).

10.4.1.4 *Removal of woody biomass from public forestlands for reduction of catastrophic wildfires and use in green energy and green biofuels products*

In 2005, the US adopted legislation to reduce fuel loads and catastrophic wildfires on public forestlands. The area burned in 2006 was 131% greater than that which burned in 2000, and for 2006, the USDA Forest Service spent $1.5 billion in suppression costs on over 0.8 million ha burned. Nearly half of the Forest Service's 2008 budget is allocated to fire suppression (USDA Forest Service, 2007).

The US Congress established an interagency programme called CROP (coordinated resource offering protocol) to help meet fuel load reduction goals on an area of 12 million ha of federal land by increasing private investment in producing wood products, energy, and biofuels through inter-agency coordination, levelization, and contracting of annual biomass supply to be removed. Energy and biofuels investors, as well as biotechnology companies, have been particularly interested in the

---

[105] In addition to Minnesota and Pennsylvania, Maine, Maryland, Michigan, New York, North Carolina, Tennessee, Washington and Wisconsin.

CROP results, given the national push toward green energy and green fuels.

In 2007, several political levels in the US proposed that the country should produce more than 100 million tons per year of biofuels by 2017. The Energy Policy Act already requires that 20 million tons per year of biofuels be produced by 2012. The higher requirement forces woody biomass to be included in the feedstock mix. At the same time, this push towards woody biomass removal from public lands has fostered new environmental concerns over sustainable, well-managed biomass removal, and looks certain to foster certification of biomass removal and standards development for public lands.

10.4.1.5 Woody biomass in carbon sequestration projects and their certification requirement

Public forestland managers in the US and Canada are now actively reviewing the potential for gaining carbon credits and payments for carbon offsetting from management of their lands, and forest certification is looking to be an important element. Global carbon markets have doubled in size over the last year and current estimates place regulated markets at $21.5 billion and voluntary markets at about $100 million for the first three quarters of 2006 (Bayon et al., 2007). The prospects for continued growth in carbon markets are strong due to the strength of growing voluntary carbon markets. Whereas most regulatory carbon markets currently do not allow for reporting carbon sequestration by forestry practices, the voluntary carbon markets do.

In the US, there are two regional carbon registries that not only allow for reporting of carbon sequestration by forestry practices, but also include FSC and SFI certification as a requirement for forest-based offset verification. The Eastern Climate Registry (ECR) – only considering afforestation and deforestation projects for registry listing, and the California Climate Action Registry (CCAR) – allowing for certified sustainable forest management projects for registry listing. As a consequence, certification is more likely to help facilitate sales of carbon credits in the US – a fact likely to gain attention from public land managers.

10.4.1.6 Introduction of certified hybrid poplar supply into solid wood and biofuel markets

In 2002, FSC certified the first fast-growing, short-rotation hybrid poplar plantation (6,000 ha) in the US. The plantation was transitioned from a fibre focus to a sawlog focus, and in 2007 approximately 100,000 m³ of FCS-certified solid wood is to be produced. This production flows into North American markets established for the "new" wood species for both certified solid wood and biomass supply (Mater, 2007).

The Pacific Northwest is likely to serve as a strong catalyst for hybrid poplar plantation certification across the US. Currently, there are approximately 36,400 ha of hybrid poplars grown throughout the US for fibre use (Bioenergy Feedstock Information Network, 2007). The certified hybrid poplar wood flow is expected to spark certification of additional plantations across the US.

In addition, 2007 study results from the US Department of Agriculture revealed that when compared with the lifecycle of gasoline and diesel, ethanol and biodiesel from corn and soybean rotations reduced greenhouse gas emissions by nearly 40%, reed canarygrass by 85%, and switchgrass and hybrid poplar by 115%.

10.4.2 Sustainable forest management and illegal logging

It is difficult to estimate the exact scale of illegal logging; but this problem is still rampant or even growing, according to an International Experts Meeting on Illegal Logging held in March 2007, in Tokyo. In order to follow up on the G8 Action Plan "Climate Change, Clean Energy and Sustainable Development" that was formulated in Gleneagles, UK, in 2005, and to prepare for the G8 summit in 2008 in Japan, the Japanese Foreign Ministry invited 17 major timber-producing and timber-consuming countries[106] and representatives/researchers from relevant international organizations and institutions[107] who are actively dealing with the topic to meet together and to collectively work on possible solutions to resolve this complex issue.

Regarding certification, the experts noted that while there were high hopes, the rate of expansion of total certified forest area in tropical supplier countries was slow. Participants discussed whether certification could be considered an instrument for tackling illegal logging, with some considering that certification could best be used to verify SFM and build on existing initiatives. Regarding the social factor – which has high impact on the issues of need-based and greed-based illegal logging, the experts stated that certification might hence be seen as one powerful tool for fighting illegal logging. There is a distinct link between the relative share of certified forest

---

[106] Australia, Canada, China, Cameroon, Democratic Republic of Congo, France, Germany, Indonesia, Italy, Japan, Malaysia, Netherlands, New Zealand, Papua New Guinea, Russia, UK, US, and EU.

[107] Center for International Forestry Research (CIFOR), FAO, Institute for Global Environmental Strategies (IGES), International Tropical Timber Organization (ITTO), National Institute for Environmental Studies (NIES), International Institute for Applied Systems Analysis (IIASA) and the World Bank.

area in percentage of the total national forest area and those areas which have the highest illegal logging; the tropical regions of the southern hemisphere are lacking certification (the darker the green area, the higher the share of forest area certified) (figure 10.4.1). At the same time, forest-rich countries that are showing light green or white areas have highest potentials for future increase in certified forest area, which might – once certification is established – tackle and curb illegal logging to a certain degree (Kraxner, 2007a).

FIGURE 10.4.1

Global distribution of certified forest area as a percentage of total forest area by countries, 2007

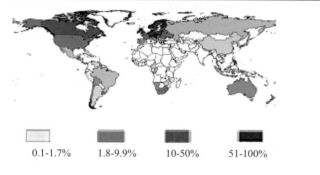

| | | | |
| 0.1-1.7% | 1.8-9.9% | 10-50% | 51-100% |

Note: Relative share of certified forest in percent of the countries' total forest area. The forest area is based on FAO's *State of the World's Forest 2007* data, excluding the category "other wooded land." Intervals for forest area certified as percentage of total forest area are determined by frequency distribution (natural breaks).

Sources: Individual certification systems 2007, Forest Certification Watch, the Canadian Sustainable Forestry Certification Coalition, 2006 and FAO, 2007.

Several producer countries described their experience with certification and participants noted that attention should also be paid to the independently developed certification schemes that now exist in some tropical supplier countries. It was further pointed out that certification must be balanced against other initiatives with respect to costs and impacts.

Combining findings by Nilsson (2006) and the results from table 10.2.1 above, the volume of industrial wood from illegal sources (350-650 million m³/year) is estimated at least as high as the volume of industrial wood deriving from certified forests (385 million m³/year). The total share of illegal logging is estimated at 20-40% of the total global industrial wood production. In addition to these high figures it has to be considered that according to the certification percentage revealed in the figure above, the main share of the wood production from certified forest originates from the northern hemisphere, while a huge part of illegal logging is happening in the southern hemisphere.

The volume of illegally harvested wood is substantial and it affects the prices of industrial wood. Illegal logging is responsible for vast environmental damage for certain industry sectors in both developing and developed countries, but the damage is also economic, i.e. through reduced prices for legal timber, which must compete with illegal timber in a distorted marketplace. The impact of illegal logging on the American wood market is estimated to be a price reduction of 7-15% (Brack, 2005). The global annual loss has been estimated at approximately $15 billion, taking account of losses to Governments and to legal competitors (World Bank, 2006a).

Using a small share of this $15 billion for the certification of the most endangered forest areas might have a multiple positive effect. On the one hand (assuming that certification is an appropriate tool for tackling illegal logging) the monetary damage could be reduced drastically and on the other hand certified sustainable forest management might protect the forest areas at risk from being cut illegally or burnt down for other incentives. The direct certification costs vary from $1 up to several dollars per ha (Hansen et al., 2006) which means that for instance some 150 million ha of endangered forest might be certified (for more than one year) when calculating at an average ha price of $10 for direct certification and using only 10% of the annual monetary damage of illegal logging.

At the expert meeting in Japan, it was stated that discrepancies in trade statistics continue to be a problem, which both exporter and importer countries were encouraged to take steps to address. It was also noted that although certification is a market-based instrument, there are no data on the total volume of wood certified globally, and that such a data system is urgently needed. The FAO/UNECE Working Party on Forest Economics and Statistics reached the same conclusion at their 2006 session. In addition to the ecological damage caused by illegal actions in the forests there might be also a link between illegal logging and wood supply (Nilsson, 2007). Hence, detailed knowledge of the wood markets is definitely an asset when discussing the illegality issue. The drivers for certification were identified as market access, demonstration of good forest stewardship and membership in associations that promote certification.

10.4.3 Certification in the Russian Federation

In November 2006, the new Forest Code of the Russian Federation was adopted by the State Duma. Under chapter 1, article 1, one of the first principles mentioned is the enhancement of SFM and biological diversity (World Bank, 2006b).

Since 1999, approximately 15 million ha of forest area have been certified in Russia, so far exclusively by FSC.

The great majority of this area is in the European part of the Federation, but there are also some certified forests in central Siberia, eastern Siberia and the Altai region, where markets show less sensitivity to the value of sustainable forestry than in the European part (Tysiachniouk, 2004). From 2005 to 2006 the certified area in Russia has almost tripled and during this year's survey period, the area almost doubled. Russia has the largest forest area in the world, with 763.5 million ha, or 22% of the world's forests, and with an annual harvest of about 168 million m³. The total amount of certified forest area is still fairly low (less than 2%); however, the growth rate of certified forest area as well as CoC certificates issued, which almost doubled from 27 to 49 (all FSC) during the survey period May 2006-May 2007, mirrors the enormous potential of Russia and justifies special focus on its development.

PEFC started its process in Russia in 2004 and established in September 2006, a "Partnership on the Development of PEFC Forest Certification", which reunites and represents the two Russian forest certification initiatives in the PEFC Council. These are: the National Council of Voluntary Forest Certification in Russia (RSFC), and the Russian National Council for Forest Certification. Both initiatives have revealed that they will submit their certification systems for PEFC endorsement in due course. The approach Russia has taken by uniting two independent forest certification systems under one umbrella organization is similar to the example of the SFI and the ATFS: both PEFC member systems through their US member organization in PEFC, the Sustainable Forestry Board.

10.4.4 Developments in the Japanese and Chinese markets for CFPs

Japan and China are the driving economies for the regional CFP market in Eastern and Southeast Asia, mainly because of their importance on the global wood market. The dominating CoC scheme in both Japan and China is FSC. Although FSC is also the only scheme for forest management certification in China, the National Forest Certification Scheme of China is under development and will be formally launched within the year 2007 (Lu, 2007). PEFC has not yet issued certificates in Japan or China but has established a PEFC Asia Promotions Office in Tokyo.

In Japan, paper industries have constituted the majority of CoC certification holders (368 (FSC) and 24 (PEFC) CoC certificates by May 2007), receiving two thirds of the certificates issued. The main certified products sold were paper for plain paper copy and printing, wood chips as raw paper material, and printed material such as environmental reports and calendars (Owari and Sawanobori, 2007). Among the customers,

large Japanese corporations, mainly in the manufacturing industry, have been driving the demand for certified paper. As the use of recycled paper becomes the norm, Japanese customers consider certified paper an environmentally friendly substitute. Along with the public procurement policy, the revised purchasing guidelines for printing and copying papers by the Green Purchasing Network (GNP) led corporations to use certified paper. By labelling printed material with certification logos, they can communicate their sense of responsibility to stakeholders. In contrast, the development of a market for certified wood products has been stagnating in Japan. Do-it-yourself chains and house builders seem to have little interest in certified products. The lack of demand from both retailers and end-users has resulted in a small market for CFPs (Owari and Sawanobori, 2007).

The share of government procurement is estimated at 2-3% of the total wood demand in Japan (Morita, 2007). According to the amended Green Purchasing Law, contractors of government procurement are responsible for verifying the legality and sustainability of wood and wood products. The target items include paper, stationary, office furniture, interior fixtures and beddings, and wood material for public-work projects (Goho-Wood Navi, 2007).

In China, FSC had granted 284 CoC certificates by May 2007 (77% growth from the last year's survey), most of which were in partnership with foreign companies. The main certified product was small furniture for export to Europe. The certified companies were mainly located in Guangdong, Hong Kong, and Zhejiang, where the economy is relatively developed. Large foreign furniture retailers such as B&Q, IKEA, and Home Depot plan to obtain certified material from China's domestic forests, resulting in growing attention to forest management certification in the country. However, certification of forests has been limited due to high costs and difficult communication (Wang and Xu, 2006).

As of May 2007, PEFC has issued four CoC certificates in China. Complementary to the Promotion Office in UK and the recently established office in Japan, PEFC also launched an office in China, which is considered to be a key area in international globalization and trade. The aim of the PEFC China Office is to build market awareness and acceptance of PEFC-CFPs in Asian markets. This also involves Chinese public and corporate procurement policies choosing certification systems endorsed by PEFC, as an assurance of legal and sustainable supply (PEFC, 2007).

The 2006 Timber Committee Market Discussions had a theme of "China's influence on forest products markets in the UNECE region". It was stressed that China's total forest resources remain largely unknown with respect to extension and quality, and that special attention regarding forest management certification will have to be put on forest plantations in China. Additionally, socio-economic factors such as population dynamics and GDP development, as well as future environmental and climate policies, will have a strong influence on certification in that country with respective consequences on the global market development.

Participants in the Timber Committee also agreed that only an improved and centralized data collection and data management system on CFPs would lead to better market evaluation and prediction in the field of SFM and CoC certification.

10.4.5 Biomass for bioenergy – biofuel potential and its certification

Considering new governmental renewable energy policies, high shares of biomass in the global energy portfolio are predicted for the coming decades. A huge volume of this biomass for bioenergy will be transformed into and applied as liquid biofuels, which consequently makes the transport sector an important driver of this development. Under the auspices of Germany's leading automotive and transport industry, an expert workshop on "Sustainable biofuels – How to certify them?" was held in February 2007 in Berlin. It was stressed that under current technical and socio-economic conditions, and given the uncertainties of the climate change impacts, the growing demand for biofuels could only be satisfied by using sustainably produced woody biomass (Kraxner, 2007b). Results of a global bioenergy model presented at the workshop show biomass production in 2100 will be concentrated in the tropical zones, North America, Europe, China and Russia.

These findings might put additional pressure on the remaining natural forest areas, especially in the tropical regions. When comparing the regions of high forest certification (shown in figure 10.4.1) to the areas with the highest potential of biomass for bioenergy production, it is easy to detect high correspondence (figure 10.4.2). Consequently, certification of forest area and the resulting product chain, such as biofuels, should go hand in hand in order to assure protection from e.g.. illegal logging and unsustainable production (Kraxner and Obersteiner, 2007). The certification schemes are going ahead in the areas mentioned. Taking into account these findings, certification is lacking from some of the forests where it is most needed.

The existing systems for forest certification might serve as a pool for experience, or even as a partner, when designing a special certification system for biofuels. Parts of the certification regulations from FSC or PEFC might be taken as foundations and could be adapted accordingly

and extended with CO_2 (GHG) balance and further socio-economic criteria and indicators (Woods, 2007). Experts especially stressed the importance of legitimacy and credibility of such a new certification system for biofuels (Müller, 2007).

FIGURE 10.4.2

Accumulated biomass for bioenergy production, 2000-2100

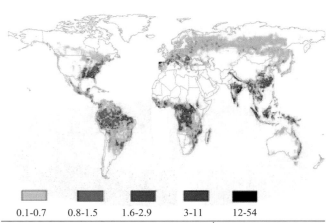

| 0.1-0.7 | 0.8-1.5 | 1.6-2.9 | 3-11 | 12-54 |

Note: Spatially explicit cumulative biomass production for bioenergy between 2000-2100 in Exa Joules per grid.
Source: Rokityanskiy et al., 2006.

The recent development of biofuels certification is mainly driven by the transport industry, NGOs, the education sector, and national initiatives. The Energy Center at the Ecole Polytechnique Fédérale de Lausanne(EPFL) in Lausanne, Switzerland, just announced the launch of a multi-stakeholder Roundtable on Sustainable Biofuels, to draft global standards for sustainable biofuels production and processing. Founding Steering Board members include, among others, WWF, FSC, Toyota, BP, the National Wildlife Federation, Shell, the Dutch and Swiss Governments, the UN Foundation, Petrobras, the World Economic Forum, and Friends of the Earth Brazil. Areas of interest will include protecting biodiversity, water resources, and labor and land rights, as well as encouraging biofuels' contribution to economic development in rural areas (ISEAL, 2007; EPFL, 2007).

10.4.6 Certification and forest plantations

Together with the new topic of biofuels certification, certification of forest plantations is considered crucial for the future development of labeled marketing of forest management and wooden products.

By March 2007, FSC reported that of all forests under its scheme, 8% were plantations (graph 10.4.1). Totaling almost 50% of FSC certified forest area, including the categories semi-natural and mixed plantation and natural forest (39%), certification of plantations makes up an important part of this certification scheme. Assuming that the relative distribution by forest type might be similar within other certification schemes, and taking into account the different definitions of forest types by the schemes, up to half of the globally certified forest areas might be plantations or mixed plantation, and semi-natural/natural forest.

GRAPH 10.4.1

Percentage of total FSC certified area by forest type, March 2007

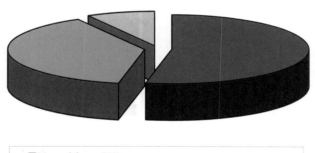

- ■ Natural forest 53%
- ■ Semi-natural and mixed plantation & natural forest 39%
- ■ Plantations 8%

Notes: Due to missing statistics and varying definitions of plantation forestry by the different certification schemes a comparison of certified area by forest type and certification system was not feasible by May 2007. FSC has been selected as an example.
Source: FSC, 2007.

Plantations and monocultures are controversial regarding their environmental impacts, e.g. potential lack of biodiversity, occasional use of non-native species and fertilization. Hence, certification of large-scale plantations is a complicated topic with possible damage to the image of individual schemes (Langmack, 2006).

Natural and plantation forest management in sensitive regions in the world, should be of particular interest for certification activities. Fast-growing species such as eucalyptus, pine, bamboo, or hybrid poplar are required by both the biomass for bioenergy sector, as well as for the wood and paper processing. Plantations are seen as a major contributor to satisfying the predicted high demand for forest resources in the future (Kraxner, 2007b).

10.4.7 Non-wood forest product certification

PEFC now provides a new option for non-wood forest products (NWFPs), as part of PEFC's international CoC. NWFPs can be PEFC-certified since November 2006; however, only a few examples are on the market. The new PEFC requirements allow companies to market products such as berries and mushrooms, which come from PEFC-certified forests, with the PEFC logo. For certification NWFPs neither include forest-related services, such as tourism and sports, nor products whose origin cannot be linked to a specific forest property, such as animals, birds, air and water (PEFC, 2006).

Among the NWFPs that are already on the market, there is certified cork in Spain and Portugal, essential oil in Italy (Pinus mugo essential oil) as well as honey, chestnuts and berries. The potential for certified NWFPs is considered to be high and soon there will also be certified truffles and mushrooms from PEFC-certified Italian forests, on the market. Furthermore, there are plans to market PEFC-certified meat from certified forest in Italy, France and Spain. Meat from game requires special hunting plans and fenced forest areas are prerequisites for this type of NWFP (Brunori, 2007).

10.5 References

AF&PA. 2007. Sustainable Forestry Initiative. Available at: www.afandpa.org/Content/NavigationMenu/ Environment_and_Recycling/SFI/SFI.htm

American Forest & Paper Association. 2007. Available at: www.afandpa.org

American Tree Farm System. 2007. Available at: www.treefarmsystem.org

Bioenergy Feedstock Information. 2007. Popular Poplars – Trees for Many Purposes (Poplar Pedigree). May 2007. Available at: bioenergy.ornl.gov/misc/ poplars.html.

Brack, D. 2005. Illegal Logging. Briefing Paper, Chatham House. Available at: http://www.illegal-logging.info

Brunori, A. 2007. PEFC Italy. http://www.pefc.it

Butler B. and Leatherberry E. 2003. USDA Forest Service, Forest Inventory and Analysis: National Woodland Owner Survey. Available at: www.fs.fed.us/ woodlandowners/publications/nwos_draft_tables_june_2003

Canadian Sustainable Forestry Certification Coalition. 2007. Available at: www.sfms.com

Canadian Standards Association. 2007. Available at: www.csagroup.org

Center for International Forestry Research. 2007. Available at: www.cifor.cgiar.org

Cao, Z. 2007. Temporal and Spatial Variation of Soil Organic C in Phyllostachys Praecox Stands with Intensive Cultivation Management and its Role in CO_2 Sequestration. Presentation given at the Sino-German Workshop on Study of Eurasian Forest as a Pool of Carbon Dioxide. 20-26 May 2007, Hangzhou, China.

Ecole Polytechnique Fédérale de Lausanne. 2007. Biofuels. Available at: http://cgse.epfl.ch/page65660-en.html

FAO. 2007. State of the World's Forest 2007. Rome, Italy. Available at: www.fao.org/forestry

FAO. 2005. Global Forest Resources Assessment. Rome, Italy. Available at: www.fao.org/forestry

FAO. 2004. Trade and Sustainable Forest Management – Impacts and Interactions. Rome, Italy. Available at: www.fao.org/forestry

FAO, 2005. Estudio de tendencias y perspectivas del sector forestal en America Latina. Informe Regional. Borrador. Available at: www.fao.org/forestry

Forest Certification Resource Center. 2007. Certification Systems. Available at: http://www.metafore.org/

Forest Certification Watch. 2007. Available at: http://certificationwatch.org/

Forest.ru. 2007. Available at: http://www.forest.ru/eng/sustainable_forestry/certification/fsc-russia.html

Forest Stewardship Council. 2007. Available at: www.fscoax.org/coc/index.htm

Forest Stewardship Council - Canada. 2007. Available at: www.fsccanada.org

Forest Stewardship Council - Germany. 2007. Available at: www.fsc-info.org

Forest Stewardship Council. 2007. FSC certified forests (March 2007). Available at: www.fsc.org

Forest Stewardship Council. 2007. News and Views. Available at: www.fsc.org

Forest Stewardship Council - US. 2007. Available at: www.fscus.org

Ganguly, I. 2006. Material Substitution in the US Residential Construction Industry: 1995-2005; Cintrafor News; winter 2006. Available at: www.cintrafor.org

Global Forest and Trade Network. 2007. Available at: www.panda.org/about_wwf/what_we_do/forests/our_solutions/responsible_forestry/certification/gftn/members/gftn_participants/index.cfm

Goho-Wood Navi. 2007. Available at: www.goho-wood.jp

Hamilton, K., Stewart, E., Waage, S., Bayon, R., Rau, A. and Hawn, A. 2007. Carbon Offsets Report; Voluntary Carbon Market. Available at: www.bsr.org/meta/BSR_Voluntary-Carbon-Offsets.pdf

Hansen, E., Washburn, M. P. and Finley, J. 2006: Understanding Forest Certification. Available at: Sustainable Forests Partnership. http://sfp.cas.psu.edu

International Tropical Timber Organization. 2007. Available at: www.itto.or.jp

ISEAL. 2007. ISEAL Alliance. Available at: http://www.isealalliance.org/index.cfm?nodeid=1

Kraxner, F. 2007a. Forest Certification and Certified Forest Products: A Market Overview for Identifying Tools to Curb Illegal Forest Actions. Background paper presented at the International Experts Meeting on Illegal Logging, 5-6 March 2007, Tokyo, Japan.

Kraxner, F. 2007b. Aspects of Global Biofuels Production. Presentation given at the Econsense Workshop Sustainable Biofuels – How to Certify Them?, 9 February 2007, Berlin. Available at: http://www.econsense.de/_veranstaltungen_bilder/_veranstaltungen_bilder/

Kraxner, F. and Obersteiner, M. 2007. Aspekte einer globalen und nachhaltigen Biokraftstoffproduktion. Background paper for the Econsense Workshop Sustainable Biofuels – How to certify them?, 9 February 2007, Berlin.

Langmack, F. 2006. Marketing Research for FSC – Results. Presentation by FSC. LEED Initiatives in Governments and schools. MetaFore, www.metafore.org

Leek, N. and Oldenburger, J. 2007. Sustainable timber on the Dutch market in 2005. Stichting Probos. Available at: http://www.probos.net

Lu, W. 2007. China's efforts for timber verification. Paper presented at the International Seminar in Tokyo for Tackling Illegal Logging. Available at: www.goho-wood.jp/event/event1/China_BE.pdf

Mater, C. 2006. Market Shifts and Certification: Implications and Innovations. Presentation given at Design for Global Forum. Oaxaca, Mexico. January 2006.

Mater, C. 2007. Teleconference with Potlatch Corporation and Greenwood Resources; May 2007.

Morita, K. 2007. Meaning and guidelines of the procurement policy of the Government of Japan. Keynote speech at the International Seminar in Tokyo for Tackling Illegal Logging. Available at: www.goho-wood.jp/event/Keynote_Japan.pdf

Müller, M. 2007. Legitimacy of Certification. Presentation given at the Econsense Workshop Sustainable Biofuels – How to Certify Them? 9 February 2007, Berlin. Available at: http://www.econsense.de/_veranstaltungen_bilder/_veranstaltungen_bilder/

Nilsson, S. 2006. Forests: Conflict and Security. Presentation at IIASA Day in Sweden, 10 May. International Institute for Applied Systems Analysis, Laxenburg, Austria.

Nilsson, S. 2007. Changing Patterns of Supply – Illegal Logging. Keynote paper prepared for the Meeting on Forest Governance and Trade: Exploring Options. 24 January 2007, Chatham House (Royal Institute of International Affairs).

Owari, T., Juslin, H., Rummukainen, A. and Yoshimura, T. 2006. Strategies, Functions and Benefits of Forest Certification in Wood Products Marketing: Perspective of Finnish Suppliers. Forest Policy and Economics. (in press).

Owari, T. and Sawanobori, Y. 2007. Analysis of the certified forest products market in Japan. Holz als Roh- und Werkstoff, 65: 113-120.

Owari, T. and Sawanobori, Y. 2006. Analysis of the certified forest products market in Japan. Berlin / Heidelberg, Germany, Springer, Holz als Roh- und Werkstoff. (in press).

PEFC Czech Republic. 2007. Available at www.pefc.cz/register. PEFC, 2006: Annual Review. Available at: http://www.pefc.org/internet/resources/5_1177_1628_file.1908.pdf

Programme for the Endorsement of Forest Certification Schemes (PEFC). 2007: Available at www.pefc.org

Rokityanskiy, D., P.C. Benítez, F. Kraxner, I. McCallum, M. Obersteiner, E. Rametsteiner and Yamagata, Y. 2006. Geographically explicit global modeling of land-use change, carbon sequestration, and biomass supply. Technological Forecasting & Social Change. (in press).

Sustainable Forestry Initiative. 2007. SFI Update January 2007. Available at: www.sfi.org

Status of FSC Certification – Canada. 2007. Available at: www.fsccanada.org

Sustainable Green Ecosystem Council. 2007. Available at: www.sgec-eco.org

Timbertrends. 2007. Measuring Timber Certification. Industry sector: timber importing & trading. Timbertrends; Independent industry analyst.

Tomaselli, I. 2006. Perspectives on the forest export industries (in Portuguese). Presentation given at the International Congress on Solid Wood Products from Forest Plantations, November 2006, Curitiba, Brazil.

Tysiachniouk, M. 2004. Forest Certification in Russia. Paper presented at the Symposium Forest Certification in Developing and Transitioning Societies: Social, Economic, and Ecological Effects. Yale School of Forestry and Environmental Studies, New Haven, Connecticut, US. 10-11 June 2004.

US Department of Agriculture – Forest Service. 2007. Overview of FY 2008 President's Budget; FY 2008 Budget: Current Management Landscape, Responsive Strategy, Management Efficiencies to Date; February 2007. Available at: www.fs.fed/publications/budget-2008/fy2008-forest-service-budget-justification.pdf

Wang, D. and Xu, P. 2006. The movement toward the promotion of forest certification in China. Mokuzai Joho 183: 22-23.

Woods, J. 2007. Sustainability Criteria for Biofuels. Presentation given at the Econsense Workshop on Sustainable Biofuels – How to Certify Them?, 9 February 2007, Berlin. Available at: http://www.econsense.de/_veranstaltungen_bilder/_veranstaltungen_bilder/

World Bank. 2006a. Available at: http://www.worldbank.org/

World Bank, 2006b. Forest Code of the Russian Federation. (Unofficial translation from Russian). Available at: http://wbln0018.worldbank.org/ECA/ForestryAR/Doclib.nsf/b55973402562047d8525657700 5afa2f/afdf1af50d73f60685257228007 90886/$FILE/ForestCode-3rdReading-061108-eng.pdf

Worldwide Fund for Nature. 2007. Available at: www.wwf.org

Zhang Y., Zhang D. and Schelhas J. 2005. Small-scale non-industrial private forest ownership in the US: Rationale and implications for forest management. April 2005.

Chapter 11

Increasing global demand benefits value-added trade, but downturn in US housing hurts engineered products: Value-added wood products markets, 2006-2007[108]

Highlights

- World furniture consumption and trade is continuously expanding, including in some developing countries, which are becoming consumers of high quality furniture.

- Europe's tightening supply, and consequent rising prices of roundwood, is one factor driving imports of value-added wood products from cost efficient suppliers, e.g. from Asia.

- Innovative furniture manufacturers in the UNECE region are finding ways to keep manufacturing cost competitive, e.g. by paying attention to delivery times and resource utilization.

- Anti-dumping measures have proved ineffective to reduce rising furniture imports into European markets and a new wave of barriers to trade is expected by market participants.

- Creation of a World Furniture Federation is expected in 2007 to alleviate trade problems by improving cooperation between industries in different parts of the world.

- China has become the world's largest furniture exporter, overtaking Italy in export value, and Malaysia is the world's largest tropical furniture exporter.

- In the United States, builders' joinery and carpentry (BJC) and profiled wood markets have seen the wave of southern-hemisphere, plantation-based softwoods arrive; however, Europe is still dominated by local softwoods.

- Slowing US housing construction may not be catastrophic for profiled wood and BJC markets; owners will stay longer in their houses and invest more in renovation and maintenance.

- After an extended period of growth, weakness in US housing construction resulted in a drop in production for all engineered wood product (EWPs) in 2006, particularly I-beams and laminated veneer lumber (LVL), as 75% of these products are consumed in new residential construction.

- Forecasts call for continued weakness in North American EWPs markets through 2007, in tandem with the residential market, with a turnaround expected sometime in 2008.

- New generation EWPs such as oriented strand lumber (OSL) will compete with LVL and glulam in various end uses including structural beams and headers over windows and doors.

---

[108] By Mr. Craig Adair, APA – The Engineered Wood Association, US; Mr. Tapani Pakasalo, Indufor, Finland; Dr. Al Schuler, USDA Forest Service, US.

Secretariat introduction

Value-added wood products (VAWPs) and engineered wood products (EWPs) are an indication of the demand side of the equation for some primary wood products presented in the previous chapters. VAWPs are produced from commodity primary products, and are often driven by national and trade association policies to earn greater returns. Developing countries' policies to produce VAWPs are working, as evidenced by increasing tropical VAWPs imports by UNECE region countries.

This chapter is divided into two sections: value-added furniture and joinery products, and EWPs. As some of the production of primary products is not accounted for in statistics when integrated processing occurs, the chapter gives an indication of production and consumption through the trade statistics.

We sincerely appreciate the continuing collaboration with the three chapter authors. Mr. Tapani Pahkasalo,[109] Market Analyst, Indufor Oy, analysed the value-added markets in the first section. He has presented the findings at previous Timber Committee Market Discussions. He is a member of the UNECE/FAO Team of Specialists on Forest Products Markets and Marketing and was a marketing assistant on the *Forest Products Annual Market Review* in 2003. His analysis focuses on the top five countries' imports to capture the changes of trade flows between importing countries and supplier regions. Intra-regional trade is also important. The VAWPs section covers both market developments and policy developments.

The section on North American EWPs is by Mr. Craig Adair,[110] Director, Market Research, APA–The Engineered Wood Association, and Dr. Al Schuler,[111] Research Economist, USDA Forest Service. Dr. Schuler is a member of the UNECE/FAO Team of Specialists on Forest Products Markets and Marketing. The section focuses on North America, as similar production and trade statistics are not available yet for other regions. Innovations and new market applications for EWPs are one part of the "sound use of wood" policy, as recommended by the UNECE Timber Committee and FAO European Forestry Commission.

---

[109] Mr. Tapani Pahkasalo, Market Analyst, Indufor Oy, Töölönkatu 11 A, FIN-00100 Helsinki, Finland, tel. +358 9 684 01115, fax +358 9135 2552, e-mail: tapani.pahkasalo@indufor.fi, www.indufor.fi

[110] Mr. Craig Adair, Director, Market Research, APA–The Engineered Wood Association, P.O. Box 11700, Tacoma, Washington, USA 98411-0700, tel. +1 253 565 7265, fax +1 253 565 6600, e-mail: craig.adair@apawood.org, www.apawood.org.

[111] Dr. Al Schuler, Research Economist, Northeast Forest Experiment Station, USDA Forest Service, 241 Mercer Springs Road, Princeton, West Virginia, USA 24740, tel. +1 304 431 2727, fax +1 304 431 2772, e-mail: aschuler@fs.fed.us, www.fs.fed.us/ne.

11.1 Introduction

EWPs, builders' joinery and carpentry (BJC), profiled woods and wooden furniture all belong to the classification of value-added wood products (VAWPs), also called secondary processed wood products in the tropical timber chapter. Demand for VAWPs arises from housing construction, housing renovation, maintenance and improvement (RMI), and in housing decoration.

Trade in VAWPs has been increasing rapidly in the past years since production costs are high in most of the UNECE region countries, and, emerging producer countries have policies to promote their domestic value-added production. VAWP consumption increasingly takes place in other regions than their production. Furniture manufacturers, and also other VAWP manufacturers to a smaller extent, have shifted production to low-cost Asian countries. Closing production facilities within the UNECE region causes local and regional employment loss and economic hardship and has led to severe trade disputes.

World furniture market demand continues to grow along with corresponding trade. Market liberalization has opened up new possibilities for both emerging market producers and lately also for industrialized country manufacturers. Global demand has clearly augmented, as the emerging markets are also increasingly demanding more and higher quality furniture. Emerging countries are therefore potential customers for middle and upper-middle range furniture produced in the industrialized countries (CSIL Milano, 2007). However, production of lower-end furniture has inevitably moved to low-cost labour countries.

Some UNECE region furniture manufacturers are finding ways to compete with the ever-increasing imports of lower-priced Asian furniture. Since design can be copied, labour costs are definitely lower overseas, and even raw material can be imported to make "genuine" furniture in Asia, companies in the UNECE region have been changing production philosophies and reducing delivery times. Since they cannot compete on unit labour cost, furniture manufacturers are focusing on labour productivity, material cost and availability, freight costs, shipping time and overall production time (Chavez, 2007). Customers' demands for more specialized and custom furniture are being met quickly, saving on expensive resources, inventory, warehousing and delays.

The slowdown in North American housing construction will raise the importance of RMI and may actually not be so catastrophic as for commodity building components such as sawnwood and panels as for the profiled wood and BJC markets. More money is spent per product in RMI than in new house construction as the owners prepare to stay longer in their current houses.

Energy efficiency, environmental concerns and product quality have become increasingly important when making choices of window frames and other VAWPs.

11.2 Imports of value-added wood products in 2005 and 2006

11.2.1 *Wooden furniture imports in major markets*

11.2.1.1 *Market development*

World furniture exports are forecast to surpass the $100 billion limit in 2007, including all furniture traded in the international markets (CSIL Milano, 2007). Wooden furniture accounts for the majority of this trade, with some regional variation. Largest furniture importers are the US, Germany, France, UK and Japan. Wooden furniture imports by the top five importers were worth $33 billion in 2006, growing some 4% from the earlier year. Yet, import growth has halved every year since 2003, when the growth in imports was still over 15% per annum. China has become the world's largest furniture exporter (wood and non-wood together), followed by Italy and Germany. Malaysia is the world's leading exporter of tropical furniture and Indonesia ranks second in this category.

The US is by far the world's largest furniture importer. China is the largest exporter of wooden furniture to US, representing already 46.5%, or $7.9 billion, of total imports of $17.1 billion. Asia strengthened its position as the leading supplier, while all other regions lost some of their market share and imports decreased from the previous year (graph 11.2.1 and table 11.2.1). Chinese furniture export growth to the US slowed: there was only a $1 billion or 15% increase from 2005, compared with 20% growth from 2004 to 2005. This reflects the slowing US housing market. The top five US furniture exporters list has now changed as Viet Nam grew to be the third largest furniture exporter to the US in 2006. Mexican and Canadian exports to US have remained stable since 2004 and Canada continues as the second largest sources of US furniture imports. Viet Nam doubled its US furniture exports in 2005 and further increased exports by 30% in 2006, passing Mexico in exporter ranking. Malaysia continues in fifth place, while Italy has increased exports to US and has almost reached the Malaysian value.

German wooden furniture imports decreased slightly in 2006, by $122 million, down to a total of $4.7 billion. Intra-European imports declined most, by $196 million. Imports from Asia continued climbing by $80 million, reaching $648 million or 13.9% of total imports. Poland continues as the leading source to Germany, strengthening exports by $80 million, followed by Italy and Denmark. China holds the forth position, increasing exports by $50 million to a total of $240 million.

Wooden furniture imports by the UK increased by over 6% to a total of $4.9 billion in 2006. Imports from Asia, mostly China, soared to $1.9 billion, increasing $380 million from the previous year as European sources declined.

Wooden furniture imports by France grew slightly, reaching $3.9 billion in 2006. Both Asia and Europe increased exports to France, while Asia's share has grown to 17.2% and Europe's share has modestly decreased to 78.9%.

GRAPH 11.2.1

Furniture imports for the top five importing countries, 2002-2006

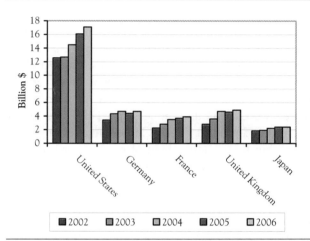

Sources: Eurostat, Trade Statistics of Japan by the Ministry of Trade and Customs, International Trade Administration, Under-Secretary for International Trade of the US Government, 2007.

11.2.1.2 *Asian furniture industry continues growth*

China is not only a producer and exporter but also a huge consumer of wooden furniture. Kitchen furniture demand in China was approximately 500,000 units just two years ago and this demand has now almost doubled to nearly 1 million kitchen furniture units (CSIL Milano, 2007). Several internationally known, brand-name furniture manufacturers have opened their own stores in China and are actually importing furniture manufactured in North America and Europe. China eliminated furniture import tariffs, which accelerated this market development. Apparently demand for high-end furniture in China is increasing rapidly. While the volumes are currently modest, this trend is important.

TABLE 11.2.1

Wood Furniture imports for the top five importing countries, 2005-2006

(Market shares in percent and values in US dollars)

Exporting regions	United States		Germany		France		United Kingdom		Japan	
	2005	2006	2005	2006	2005	2006	2005	2006	2005	2006
Asia	61.7	65.8	11.9	13.9	16.4	17.2	35.0	40.5	82.3	82.9
North America	17.6	16.4	0.1	0.2	0.4	0.4	1.9	2.2	1.7	1.5
Europe	11.8	10.0	86.5	84.5	79.1	78.9	59.9	54.4	15.8	15.4
Latin America	8.5	7.5	0.7	0.6	3.1	2.5	2.1	2.2	0.0	0.0
Others	0.4	0.3	0.8	0.8	1.1	1.0	1.2	0.6	0.1	0.1
Total imports in billion $	16.1	17.1	4.8	4.7	3.8	3.9	4.6	4.9	2.4	2.4
Of which furniture parts, billion $	1.9	2.1	0.9	1.0	0.6	0.6	0.7	0.8	0.5	0.5

Sources: Eurostat, Trade Statistics of Japan by the Ministry of Trade and Customs, International Trade Administration (ITA), Under-Secretary for International Trade of the US Government, USDA Foreign Agricultural Service, 2007.

Raw material availability is becoming a more critical issue in China as the Russian Federation has announced increases in the roundwood export tariffs. Nevertheless, the Chinese wood products industry has deep vertical integration and is therefore better able to absorb the increased wood costs and, at least partially, push them through to end-product prices. Chinese market operators are small but form a long chain of producers within the country. Furniture enterprises tend to be relatively large in scale and already highly efficient in their production.

Other southeast Asian furniture manufacturers are increasingly facing shortages of raw materials and corresponding roundwood price rises. This has put significant pressure on manufacturing costs and therefore also on furniture prices. In Viet Nam, for example, wood prices have increased over 30% in the past three years following neighbouring countries' logging bans and decreased sawnwood exports. Viet Nam is dependent on roundwood and sawnwood imports since logging quotas from its natural forests are low and plantation-based wood is not yet available in sufficient quantities. Its forests provide only 20% of the domestic wood demand.

Asian imports of sawn hardwood from North American have increased significantly and even sliced veneer is being imported. Imports of hardwood logs have almost entirely been replaced with trade in sawnwood and veneers. China, Viet Nam, Thailand, Indonesia and Malaysia import significant quantities from the US, especially oaks, both white and red. This wood is typically used by the furniture industry and then exported back to the US as furniture.

11.2.1.3 Policy development

The major and rapid structural changes over the last few years in world furniture markets has led to two apparently contradictory policy reactions: conflict between "winners" and "losers", notably through trade policy measures of a protectionist nature, and the search for cooperation and partnership, whether through discussion forums or international investment (e.g. US furniture companies investing in China and neighbouring countries). As furniture companies becoming increasingly multinational, it becomes harder to analyse the significance of statistics based only on political boundaries rather than on companies.

In mid-2004, the US Department of Commerce (DoC) imposed anti-dumping duties ranging from 2.3% up to nearly 200% on Chinese bedroom furniture, depending on the degree of alleged "unfair pricing". The American Furniture Manufacturers Committee for Legal Trade, which requested the duties, restated its position in September 2006 and advised the DoC to remove taxes from certain products. Recently, however, the Chinese bedroom furniture dumping issue in the US has been reduced to a smaller group of products as the DoC announced that certain products imported from China have been excluded from anti-dumping levies from January 2007.

European furniture manufacturers, led by Italian and German producers, were rumoured in 2006 to be preparing a complaint against Chinese furniture dumping. However, the European Commission has not received a petition nor has any news from manufacturers since the end of 2006. EU Trade Commissioner, Mr. Peter Mandelson, has stated that European industries should not look to anti-dumping measures as a shield to protect them from legitimate competition. Additionally, the EU will not provide a *carte blanche* to protectionists in Europe who seek to avoid the effects of competition. There are countries in Europe who would like to see increased protection for European industries.

The World Furniture Congress, which took place in May 2006 in Palma, Spain, decided to proceed with the formal creation of the World Furniture Federation. The next Congress will be held in Shanghai, China, and the Federation is expected to be created in September 2007

(UEA Press Release, 2007). The new global Federation is expected to promote better international relations in the sector, as also stated in last year's *Review*. The initiative has been led by the Union Européenne de l'Ameublement (UEA).

The Italian furniture manufacturers association, Federlegno-Arredo, and several Chinese furniture manufacturers associations have signed an agreement on the protection of intellectual property rights. Signed in Beijing, it stipulates that the two sides should abide by fair competition rules and clearly identify priority areas such as counterfeiting, brand and patent protection and protection of intellectual rights. This is seen as a leap forward in advancing relations with the Chinese manufacturers and establishing rules of fair trade; however, the effects will only be seen later (ITTO MIS, 2007).

American-owned companies in China account for nearly 60% of wooden furniture exports. This fact divides the American furniture industry on the issue of imported Chinese and other Asian furniture. In the aforementioned 2004 bedroom furniture anti-dumping case, this dilemma was already present. However, some companies loudly opposed any anti-dumping measures against Chinese furniture imports since the companies were themselves importing significant quantities of bedroom furniture. In Europe the situation is somewhat similar as some large and influential retail stores depend heavily on imports from Asia. Furniture manufacturers' associations are evidently losing power in the on-going globalization process when the largest multinational companies have their financial interests spread between domestic production, manufacturing abroad and imports.

Technical standards and requirements could be tightened in the EU for imported products, including furniture. Some see this as an alternative strategy to control ever-increasing Asian imports. Tightened standards lead to increased production costs and recalls of products. Technical barriers of trade can be very effective if they are implemented. The Government of France has submitted a legal request to the European Commission related to the safety of upholstered furniture. It would forbid producing, importing and selling upholstered furniture and mattresses in France if they are not fire-resistant. Acceptable products would have to pass the test of resistance to flammability from a cigarette. The UEA is considering the feasibility and acceptance of such legislation at the EU level (UEA Newsletter, 2007).

11.2.2 Builders' joinery, carpentry and profiled wood markets

11.2.2.1 Market development

The US is the dominant importer of builders' joinery and carpentry (BJC), where over 60% comes from Canada (graph 11.2.2 and table 11.2.2). Total US imports grew by 6% to $2.85 million in 2006. BJC products are mainly made of softwoods: countries rich in pine plantations, such as Brazil and Chile, are strong exporters to US markets, holding third and fourth position after Canada and China. China is a large-scale producer of BJCs, where the production is largely based on imported Russian softwoods. Asian imports to the US increased by 31% between 2005 and 2006 and Latin American imports increased by 18.5%.

European BJC imports followed the same development. Imports from Asia and Latin American have rapidly increased, while those from adjacent regions declined or rose only modestly. The UK and French BJC import markets expanded strongly in 2006, by 12% and 9% respectively, while German imports of BJCs continued their decline by 1%. Latin American exports to Germany increased by 185%, to France by 85% and to the UK by 33%; imports from Latin America are currently at a low level but could be an emerging trade flow as exporters search for alternative markets in the light of the US housing market slowdown. European BJC imports are mainly from European producers, with the exception of the UK, where China is the largest source followed by Indonesia. Asian exports of BJCs stand at around 10% in Germany and France but represent already almost a quarter of UK imports.

GRAPH 11.2.2

Builders' joinery and carpentry imports for the top five importing countries, 2002-2006

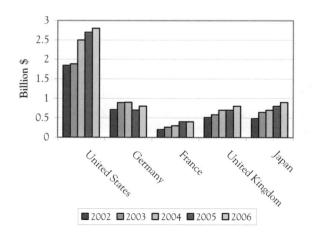

Sources: Eurostat, Trade Statistics of Japan by the Ministry of Trade and Customs, International Trade Administration, Under-Secretary for International Trade of the US Government, 2007.

TABLE 11.2.2

Builders' joinery and carpentry imports for the top five importing countries, 2005-2006

(Market shares in percent and values in US dollars)

Exporting regions	United States		Germany		France		United Kingdom		Japan	
	2005	2006	2005	2006	2005	2006	2005	2006	2005	2006
Asia	12.8	15.8	9.0	11.1	10.8	11.2	20.8	23.9	54.9	56.6
North America	67.3	63.2	0.3	0.4	1.0	1.4	9.9	9.2	8.1	5.7
Europe	5.8	6.2	89.8	87.3	84.4	81.9	57.2	57.2	30.5	32.0
Latin America	12.6	14.1	0.1	0.4	3.0	5.0	5.0	6.0	0.1	0.1
Others	1.5	0.7	0.9	0.9	0.8	0.5	7.1	3.7	6.4	5.6
Total imports in billion $	2.7	2.8	0.8	0.8	0.4	0.4	0.7	0.8	0.8	0.9

Sources: Eurostat, Trade Statistics of Japan by the Ministry of Trade and Customs, International Trade Administration (ITA), Under-Secretary for International Trade of the US Government, USDA Foreign Agricultural Service, 2007.

TABLE 11.2.3

Profiled wood imports for the top five importing countries, 2005-2006

(Market shares in percent and values in US dollars)

Exporting regions	United States		Germany		France		United Kingdom		Japan	
	2005	2006	2005	2006	2005	2006	2005	2006	2005	2006
Asia	28.4	27.7	18.9	21.6	13.1	15.8	37.8	46.0	75.7	77.3
North America	20.4	17.7	1.2	1.4	0.5	0.5	6.4	5.3	6.7	7.1
Europe	4.8	2.9	76.7	72.3	61.6	60.5	53.5	45.9	12.0	11.0
Latin America	43.6	49.5	1.7	2.7	22.2	21.4	1.8	2.2	4.6	3.5
Others	2.8	2.1	1.6	2.0	2.5	1.7	0.5	0.5	1.1	1.1
Total imports in billion $	1.6	1.7	0.2	0.2	0.2	0.2	0.3	0.3	0.3	0.3

Sources: Eurostat, Trade Statistics of Japan by the Ministry of Trade and Customs, International Trade Administration (ITA), Under-Secretary for International Trade of the US Government, USDA Foreign Agricultural Service, 2007.

Japanese BJC imports increased by 13%, with European exporters' share rising remarkably (18.6% overall increase, with imports from Finland increasing by 40%). Nevertheless, Asian exporters control an 83% market share of the Japanese market. Philippines and China are the leading sources, followed by Austria, Finland and Sweden. North and Latin America have lost some of their market share in Japan.

Profiled wood import markets expanded in all top five importer countries, with the largest growth of 22% in the UK (table 11.2.3 and graph 11.2.3). Latin American exporters enjoyed the fastest growth in their trade while the Asian countries have also increased their exports to all markets. Half of the profiled wood imported by the US came from Latin American countries, while in Germany and France the profiled wood comes from the intra-regional European markets. The UK market differs from the other European markets as only half of the imports come from Europe, with Asian exporters gaining important market share.

Some 60% of the imported profiled woods in US markets are softwoods, with the remaining 40% being hardwoods. The main suppliers of profiled softwood to the US are Chile and Brazil, in almost equal values. Canada occupies the third spot, with significantly smaller quantities than the Latin American plantation pine producers.

In Europe, the trade in softwoods is basically intra-regional, as the largest profiled softwood suppliers are the Nordic countries, followed by Germany, Poland, Italy and Austria. Only in the UK is China an important supplier of profiled softwoods. In Europe the share of imported profiled softwood varies between 21% and 27% of all imported profiled woods; this is the opposite of the US.

Source: APA – The Engineered Wood Association, 2007.

GRAPH 11.2.3

Profiled wood imports for the top five importing countries, 2002-2006

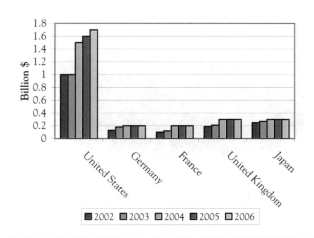

Sources: Eurostat, Trade Statistics of Japan by the Ministry of Trade and Customs, International Trade Administration, Under-Secretary for International Trade of the US Government, USDA Foreign Agricultural Service, 2007.

11.2.2.2 Policy development

With the tightening roundwood supply in Europe, VAWP imports will continue to rise. Cost efficient suppliers, whose advantage is mainly based on low-cost labour and materials, are likely to benefit from the tight supply and higher prices of roundwood in Europe. Wood product end-users seem indifferent to the origin of their wood products; moreover profiled woods and BJCs have not been central in the illegal logging discussion. Importers may source their wood raw material from sustainably managed, even certified, forests and the UNECE region's concerns are in fact more related to employment and local value-adding losses than environmental issues. The value-added processing industry is a key employer and taxpayer in several local economies within the UNECE region.

Environmental communication increasingly targets building architects to specify natural materials over plastic. As the markets become environmentally sensitive, sustainable wood campaigns hope to bear fruit finally in sales. Wood is perceived as more environmentally friendly than plastic-based products, especially in window frames and doors. Energy efficiency, health issues and environmental soundness have become increasingly important during the last years, all assets of wood. Also, wood product manufacturers have worked to improve product quality and good products are now more readily available.

The slowdown in the US housing markets is not necessarily detrimental for the BJC and profiled wood markets. RMI investments are, by definition, made to

enhance the current situation. Often, this means RMI investments are made to higher quality and more expensive products and more dollars are spent per piece. Ageing houses will need more RMI in the future, as the owners will now stay longer in their current homes. Rising energy costs provide an incentive to make houses more energy efficient, which will also spur RMIs. This is changing the spending structure to more long-term RMI investments, which are becoming increasingly important demand drivers in all markets.

11.3 Engineered wood products market developments

11.3.1 North America

US housing markets, after peaking in the autumn of 2005, fell 13% in 2006 and are expected to decrease another 17% in 2007. The total decline between 2005 and 2007 is forecast to exceed 27%. EWPs are oriented towards new residential construction, which is the market for 61% of glulam production, 77% of I-beams, and 75% of LVL. Consequently, the following tables and figures show the extent of the downturn in these markets, paralleling the slowdown in housing. The EWP analysis is based on North American data because it is the only information available in the UNECE region. Owing primarily to the prevalence of wood-frame residential construction in North America, the bulk of EWP production occurs there. That said, there is, nevertheless, increasing usage of EWPs elsewhere. For example, Japan is using increasing volumes of EWPs (glulam and laminated lumber) for use in pre-cut, post and beam construction. Post and beam, a labour-intensive technology, is the prevalent wood frame construction in Japan, but growing skilled labour shortages and stricter building standards are forcing the trend to factory-made pre-cut technology.

11.3.1.1 Glulam timber

Gleam manufacturers weathered the 2006 housing downturn quite well, with production declining only 1% (graph 11.3.1 and table 11.3.1). Residential glulam declined 7% and use in non-residential construction increased about 10%. While demand for beams in non-residential construction is expected to advance 5% in 2007, residential market demand could decline by15%. Overall, glulam production is expected to retreat 7% in 2007 to 698 million cubic metres.

Over 60% of glulam is used for new residential construction, with 39% used in non-residential, remodelling, and export (graphs 11.3.2 and 11.3.3). The bulk of glulam is consumed in new single-family housing.

GRAPH 11.3.1

Glulam production in North America, 2002-2007

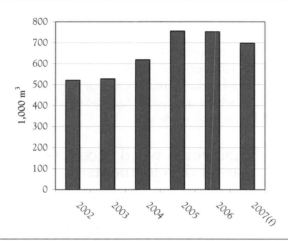

Notes: f = forecast. Conversion factor: 650 board feet per cubic metre.
Source: APA – The Engineered Wood Association, 2007.

TABLE 11.3.1.

Glulam consumption, production and trade in North America, 2005-2007

(1,000 m³)

	2005	2006	2007(f)	% change 2005-2007
United States				
Consumption				
Residential	487.7	453.8	387.7	-21%
Non-residential	187.7	206.1	215.4	15%
Industrial, other	33.8	35.4	33.8	0%
Total	709.2	695.4	636.9	-10%
Exports	15.4	15.4	23.1	50%
Imports	-10.8	-1.5	-1.5	-86%
Production	713.9	709.2	658.5	-8%
Canada				
Consumption	26.1	26.2	21.5	-18%
Exports	16.9	15.4	18.5	9%
Production	41.5	41.5	40.0	-4%
Total North American production	755.4	750.8	698.5	-8%

Notes: f = forecast. Conversion factor: 650 board feet per cubic metre.
Source: APA – The Engineered Wood Association, 2007.

GRAPH 11.3.2

North American residential glulam end uses, 2006

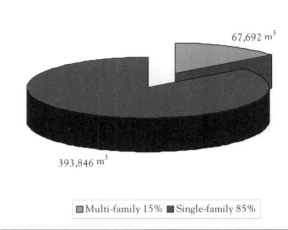

67,692 m³

393,846 m³

☐Multi-family 15% ■Single-family 85%

Source: APA – The Engineered Wood Association, 2007.

GRAPH 11.3.3

North American non-residential glulam end uses, 2006

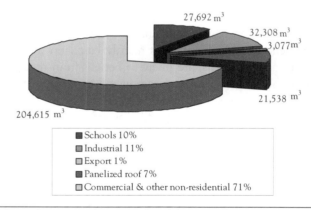

27,692 m³

32,308 m³

3,077m³

21,538 m³

204,615 m³

☐ Schools 10%
☐ Industrial 11%
☐ Export 1%
☐ Panelized roof 7%
☐ Commercial & other non-residential 71%

Notes: Conversion factor: 650 board feet per cubic metre. Industrial includes bridges, utility structures, marine and other.
Source: APA – The Engineered Wood Association, 2006.

11.3.1.2 I-beams.

In North America, the key I-beam market, i.e. raised residential floors, market share increased from 43% in 2004 to 45% in 2005 and fell back in 2006 (graph 11.3.4). Open web floor joists (beams) increased from 13% in 2004 to 14% in 2005. These two products took share away from solid sawnwood, which declined from 40% in 2004 to 38% in 2005. The housing downturn resulted in less production in 2006 (graph 11.3.5). Market share came down a notch, as some cost-conscious builders switched back to sawnwood beams, which are less expensive on a linear basis according to the North American Home Builders (NAHB) Research Center survey for 2006. I-beam market share will also retreat slightly in 2007.

GRAPH 11.3.4

US I-beam market share, 2001-2007

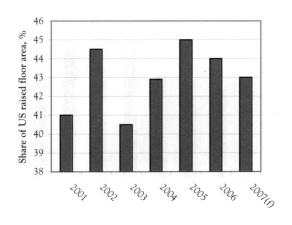

Note: f = forecast.
Source: APA – The Engineered Wood Association, 2007.

GRAPH 11.3.5

I-beam production in North America, 2001-2007

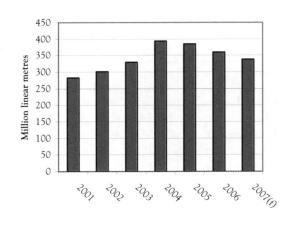

Notes: f = forecast. Conversion: 3.28 linear feet per metre.
Source: APA – The Engineered Wood Association, 2007.

I-beams still have the advantages of predictable performance and quality with less waste compared with solid sawn floor beams. With the continued consolidation in home building (the top ten builders now build over 20% of single family homes in the US, compared with 10% a decade ago), growth prospects for I-beams, and EWPs in general, are good. Builders seeking a competitive advantage are leading the transition from "site-built" homes to more efficient, higher quality homes built with more factory-built components. The advantages of factory-built components (e.g. roof trusses, engineered wall panels, and EWPs) include less site waste, reduced

labour content, and better quality control, which reduces potential for "callbacks" from unsatisfied customers.

I-beam construction is changing as a result of economics. For example, in 1994, 74% of I-beams used LVL for flanges, but today that number is closer to 50%. Some manufacturers are substituting less expensive solid sawnwood. However, in the short term, I-beam manufacturers are expected to maintain the current ratio of LVL and sawnwood flanges.

Most of the I-beams are consumed in residential construction: 73% in new residential floors, 7% in renovation, and 4% in new residential roofs and walls (table 11.3.2 and graph 11.3.6). Only 16% goes to markets other than residential. However, the non-residential end uses are growing the fastest, in percentage terms – 55% from 2003 to 2007, compared with a 10% drop in new residential end uses. This drop is due to the weakness in new residential construction. Another significant part of the I-beam market development is the rapid growth in production in Canada – 29% from 2003 to 2007, versus a 5% drop in the US. One major manufacturer closed a plant in the US and increased capacity in Canada. Canadian production now accounts for 32% of North American production, compared with 23% just five years ago.

TABLE 11.3.2.

**Wooden I-beam consumption and production
in North America, 2005-2007**

(million linear metres)

	2005	2006	2007(f)	% change, 2005-2007
United States				
Demand				
New residential	298.8	256.1	210.4	-30%
Non-residential, other	84.5	85.4	86.9	3%
Total, domestic	383.2	341.5	297.3	-22%
Production	258.0	245.1	230.2	-11%
Canada				
Demand	42.1	42.4	38.1	-10%
Production	126.8	113.4	108.2	-15%
Total North American production	385.1	358.5	338.4	-12%

Notes: f = forecast. Conversion: 3.28 linear feet per metre.
Source: APA – The Engineered Wood Association, 2007.

GRAPH 11.3.6

I-beam end uses in North America, 2005

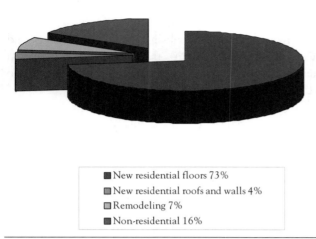

- New residential floors 73%
- New residential roofs and walls 4%
- Remodeling 7%
- Non-residential 16%

Source: APA – The Engineered Wood Association, 2007.

GRAPH 11.3.7

LVL production in North America, 2001-2007

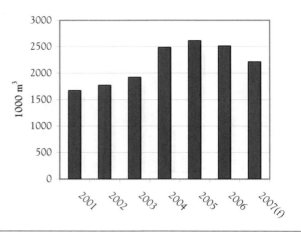

Notes: f = forecast. Conversion: 35.315 cubic feet per cubic metre.
Source: APA – The Engineered Wood Association, 2007.

11.3.1.3 *Laminated veneer lumber*

Laminated veneer lumber (LVL) production increased 5% in 2005 in response to housing starts and as a result of more building designers specifying LVL in their construction plans (graph 11.3.7 and table 11.3.3). Production declined in 2006 when the housing market declined and more I-beams were made with sawnwood flanges.

In the future, the demand for LVL beams and headers will continue to grow. However, the advent of new OSL production in late 2007 makes the LVL forecast less certain than in the past. While OSL will probably take market share from nailed-together sawnwood beams and headers, it may also take share from LVL.

The outlook reduces the rate of LVL growth from past forecasts to reflect housing weakness and the expectation that new beam and header products will be in the marketplace within a year or two.

Beams and headers now account for 59% of demand and I-beam flanges for 35% (graph 11.3.8). Industrial uses, such as scaffold plank, components of roof trusses, glulam tension lams, concrete form bracing, furniture and millwork parts, make up about 4% of overall LVL demand. Only about 2% is used for rim boards in I-beam floor construction.

TABLE 11.3.3.

LVL consumption and production in North America, 2005-2007

(1,000 m³)

	2005	2006	2007(f)	% change, 2005-2007
Demand				
I-beam flanges	945.9	897.8	841.1	-11%
Beams, headers, others	1 659.6	1 600.1	1 359.4	-18%
Total demand	2 605.5	2 497.9	2 200.5	-16%
Total production				
United States	2 387.4	2 268.5	1 954.1	-18%
Canada	218.1	229.4	246.4	13%

Notes: f = forecast. Conversion: 35.315 cubic feet per cubic metre.
Source: APA – The Engineered Wood Association, 2007.

GRAPH 11.3.8

LVL end uses in North America, 2005

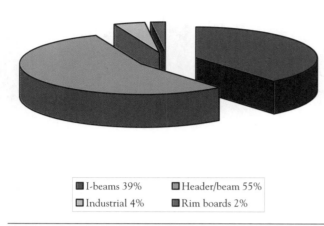

◼ I-beams 39%   ◼ Header/beam 55%
◻ Industrial 4%   ◼ Rim boards 2%

Source: APA – The Engineered Wood Association, 2007.

Source: APA – The Engineered Wood Association, 2007.

11.4   References

APA – The Engineered Wood Association. 2007. Structural Panel and Engineered Wood Yearbook. APA Economics Report E173. Tacoma, Washington.

Chavez, Jon. Toledo Blade. Overseas Competition Challenges Furniture Industry. March, 2007. http://www.toledoblade.com

CSIL Milano, World Furniture Outlook 2007.

EUROSTAT, External Trade, http://epp.eurostat.cec.eu.int/

International Trade Administration, Office of Trade and Industry Information, http://ita.doc.gov/td/industry/otea/

ITTO MIS. International Tropical Timber Organization, Market Information Service, April 2007.

Trade Statistics of Japan, Ministry of Finance and Customs. Japan Imports of Commodity by Country.

Union Européenne de l'Ameublement (UEA), Newsletter, 2007.

Union Européenne de l'Ameublement (UEA), Press Release. Paris. January, 2007.

USDA Foreign Agricultural Service, 2007.

Chapter 12
Lower tropical exports boost prices: Trends in tropical timber production and trade, 2005-2007[112]

Highlights

- For International Tropical Timber Organization (ITTO) producer countries as a whole, forest coverage declined from 52.7% of total land area in 1985 to 46.4% in 2005 primarily as a result of agricultural expansion.

- Softwood exports from tropical countries to advanced economies remain marginal, although pine plantations have grown strongly and steadily and will play a key role in the future as many countries (especially in Asia) restrict production from natural forests.

- Public procurement policies have entered into effect in many EU countries such as France, the largest EU log and veneer importer, where from 2007 50% of public procurement of timber is to come from certified tropical forests, rising to 100% by 2010.

- Malaysia is still by far the largest exporter of all tropical primary timber products, dominating the export of logs (41.2% market share 2007 forecast) and veneer (33% market share 2007 forecast).

- Chinese exports of tropical plywood have grown strongly over the last three years (from 0.7 million m³ in 2004 to a forecasted 1.3 million m³ in 2007) due to its booming plywood industry.

- China is by far the largest importer of tropical logs and sawnwood, although Chinese tropical log imports have decreased slightly over the last three years (from 7.3 million m³ in 2004-2005 to a forecasted 6.5 million m³ in 2007) as supplies tighten and Russian softwood log imports continue to increase.

- Decreasing exports from many tropical countries, together with a global economic expansion and improved consumer confidence in many markets, led prices for a majority of primary tropical timber products to strengthen in 2006.

- Brazilian suppliers of softwood plywood, still exporting half of their production to the United States despite an 8% import tax and an unfavourable exchange rate, are increasing exports to the EU and favouring domestic markets boosted by a flourishing construction sector.

- Secondary processed wood products exports from tropical countries exceeded $10 billion in 2005 for the first time, 5% more than the value of primary products and are forecast to continue growing because of competitive prices and labour costs, excellent timber quality and supportive policies.

- As only 5% of forests certified for sustainable forest management are in tropical developing countries, these countries are having difficulty accessing markets demanding certified wood products.

---

[112] By Dr. Steven E. Johnson, Dr. Jairo Castaño, Mr. Jean-Christophe Claudon and Mr. James Cunningham, all from the International Tropical Timber Organization, Japan.

Secretariat introduction

This analysis is possible thanks to continued close cooperation with our colleagues in the International Tropical Timber Organization (ITTO), whose 2006 *Annual Review and Assessment of the World Timber Situation* and bi-weekly *Market Information Service* (MIS) reports serve as the basis for this chapter. We thank ITTO's Dr. Steven Johnson,[113] Dr. Jairo Castaño, Mr. Jean-Christophe Claudon and Mr. James Cunningham (consultant) for contributing this analysis.

Some of the terminology in this chapter differs slightly from the rest of the *Review*. In addition, owing to data being unavailable for several countries, 2005 is the base year for the analysis. Where possible, information for 2005, 2006 and 2007 (ITTO Secretariat forecasts) are included. In keeping with the theme of this year's *Review*, a brief analysis of the production and trade of tropical softwoods is included. ITTO categorizes its 60 member countries[114] into 33 producers (tropical) and 27 consumers (non-tropical), which together constitute 95% of all tropical timber trade and over 80% of tropical forest area. Poland joined ITTO in 2007.

For a complete analysis of trends in the production, consumption and trade of primary and secondary tropical timber products in relation to global timber trends, see ITTO's *Annual Review and Assessment of the World Timber Situation – 2006*, available on www.itto.or.jp

12.1 Tropical forests and softwoods

In all three ITTO producer regions, forest cover has been declining since the inception of ITTO in the mid-1980s: in Africa, from 49.3% of total land area in 1985 to 44.2% in 2005; in Asia, from 41.4% in 1985 to 35.4% in 2005; and in Latin America from 59.4% in 1985 to 52.4% in 2005 (graph 12.1.1). For ITTO producer countries as a whole, the decline was from 52.7% in 1985 to 46.4% in 2005. Forest degradation was not measured, and in the case of natural forests, deterioration could progress far from pristine conditions before forest cover loss would be recorded. Forest loss is due principally to conversion to agricultural crops such as soya and oil palm, while degradation arises from factors such as fires and illegal logging. While the total area of tropical forest loss

---

[113] Dr. Steven E. Johnson (Communication Manager), Dr. Jairo Castaño (Market Information Service Coordinator), Mr. Jean-Christophe Claudon (Statistical Assistant) and Mr. James Cunningham (consultant), International Tropical Timber Organization (ITTO), International Organizations Center, 5th Floor, Pacifico-Yokohama, 1-1-1 Minato-Mirai, Nishi-ku, Yokohama 220-0012, Japan, tel: +81 45 223 1110, fax +81 45 223 1111, website: www.itto.or.jp, e-mail: itto@itto.or.jp.

[114] ITTO member countries available at: http://www.itto.or.jp/live/PageDisplayHandler?pageId=233&id=224.

---

continues to increase, FAO's recent *Forest Resource Assessment Report* (FAO, 2006) found that in most countries, the rate of loss is decelerating.

The movement to establish tree plantations in tropical countries, progressing rapidly in recent years, also carried risks that natural tropical forests might be cleared to make way for plantations. Plantations have grown by more than a quarter in Asian producer countries, jumping from 10.4 million ha in 1990 to 12.9 million ha in 2005. Despite almost doubling between 1990 and 2005, African producers' plantation area remains small – 583,700 ha in 1990, growing to 972,000 ha in 2005. Plantations have also grown steadily in Latin America, from 6.1 million ha in 1990 to 7.7 million ha in 2005. In some countries (e.g. Brazil) a majority of timber exports are now sourced from plantations.

GRAPH 12.1.1

Forest cover, ITTO producers, 1980-2005

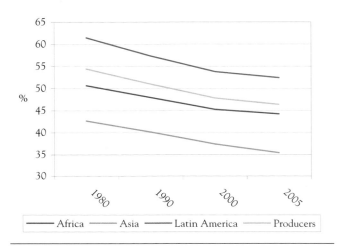

Source: ITTO, 2007.

According to a recent ITTO study, timber plantations (hardwood and softwood) in the tropics (including large areas in tropical China and Australia)) are estimated to cover 67 million ha, of which 10% to 15% are of softwood species, primarily pines. About 80% are in the Asia-Pacific region, 13% in Latin America-Caribbean and only 7% in Africa. ITTO African producers reported almost no softwood primary products production. Non-ITTO African tropical countries reported an estimated production of 3 million m³ of softwood industrial roundwood (most of it produced in Zimbabwe, Kenya, Tanzania) in 2005. They exported only a negligible quantity of softwood logs to the world (an estimated 21,250 m³) and only slightly higher amounts of the sawnwood, which was the main product arising from these softwood logs. Most of this trade was inter-African.

In Latin America, the 13 ITTO producers reported a production of 53 million m³ of softwood logs in 2005 (of an estimated total production of 54 million m³ from tropical America). Log production boomed over the last five years, with an annual increase of 5%. Brazil accounted for 83% of this production, mainly from its large pine plantations located in the non-tropical south of the country. It is not possible to disaggregate Brazil's tropical and non-tropical softwood timber production and trade. Only 100,000 m³ of softwood logs were exported from Latin America at an average price of $52/m³. The remaining logs were locally processed into softwood sawnwood, with Brazil and Mexico accounting for 90% of the 12.5 million m³ produced in 2005. Exports of sawn softwood by Latin American producers have decreased over the last four years (from 2.8 million m³ in 2002 to a forecasted 959,000 m³ in 2006) as a result of increased domestic consumption. Most sawn softwood is still exported to the US (75% for Brazil and 95% for Mexico). The slowing US housing market over the last four years has resulted in lower demand for sawn softwood (US sawn softwood imports decreased from 1.6 million m³ in 2002 to 1.3 million m³ in 2006), while non-tropical competitors such as Chile have increasingly focused on the US market. On the other hand, flourishing construction sectors in Mexico and Brazil have boosted domestic consumption of sawnwood, especially in Mexico, where $3.7 billion was invested over the last four years in diverse projects of housing, and urban development.

Latin American softwood plywood production almost doubled between 2002 and 2006 (jumping from 1.7 million m³ to 3.2 million m³, 90% from Brazil). Exports have remained stable at around 1 million m³ over this period. Brazil was virtually the only exporter of softwood plywood in the region. Owing to an 8% US import tax, Brazilian producers have diversified their exports to the EU (especially the UK, Germany and Belgium), which now accounts for 31% of their exports. However, despite the import tax, the US market still absorbs 50% of Brazilian softwood plywood exports.

Softwood log production almost doubled (from 3 million m³ to almost 6 million m³) in ITTO Asian producer countries from 2002 to 2007. Of the major producers, India has had constant production of about 3 million m³ over this period, while Indonesia and Fiji have been producing increasing amounts recently (1.8 million m³ and 300,000 m³ respectively in 2005). Few logs are exported (less than 2,000 m³ in 2005 for an average price of $143/m³). India processes all softwood logs into sawnwood (817,000 m³ in 2005) for the domestic market. In Indonesia, most softwood logs were processed into plywood (714,000 m³ in 2005), which was then exported primarily to Saudi Arabia (340,000 m³ for $253/m³), Bahrain and Yemen.

While natural softwood forests play an important role in providing species such as pines (e.g. Mexico, Honduras and Guatemala) and podocarps (e.g. Latin America and Asia) to tropical forest industries, it appears likely that softwood plantation areas will continue to grow strongly in the tropics and play an increasing role in wood supply. Many producer countries in the tropics are introducing more stringent regulations governing exploitation of natural forests, with resulting raw material shortages leading some to become large importers of wood. For example, by 2014, the Government of Indonesia proposes to completely forbid the use of timber from natural forests, which (even if this measure is only partially implemented) implies a need for a greatly expanded plantation area (including softwoods) if the country's forest industry is not to be decimated.

12.2 Production trends

Production of tropical industrial roundwood (logs) in ITTO countries totalled 127.1 million m³ in 2005 (125.6 million m³ from producer countries and 1.5 million m³ from consumer countries), a 6.4% decline from 2004 (table 12.2.1).

TABLE 12.2.1

Production and trade of primary tropical timber products ITTO total, 2005-2007

(million m³)

	2005	2006	2007ᶠ	% Change 2005-2006
Logs				
Production	127.1	140.6	142.5	10.6
Imports	15.4	15	14.7	-2.5
Exports	12.7	11.5	11.7	-9.4
Sawnwood				
Production	42.2	47.7	49.9	13
Imports	10.7	10.9	11.2	1.8
Exports	10.7	9.7	9.7	-9
Veneer				
Production	3.4	3.5	3.6	2.9
Imports	1.3	1.1	1	-15.3
Exports	1.1	1.1	1.1	0
Plywood				
Production	20.4	22.5	23	10.2
Imports	9.8	8.4	8.7	-14.2
Exports	9.8	10.4	10.5	6.1

Notes: Total of producer and consumer countries. f = ITTO secretariat forecasts.

Source: ITTO Annual Review and Assessment of the World Timber Situation – 2006, 2007.

ITTO producers represent about 85% of total tropical log production in the world, with similar or higher ratios for sawnwood, veneer and plywood. The largest non-ITTO tropical log producers are Viet Nam, Uganda, Tanzania, Kenya and Solomon Islands. In 2006, tropical log production rebounded to 140.6 million m³ (137.3 million m³ in producer countries, 3.3 million m³ in consumer countries), and the 2007 forecast is 142.5 million m³ (138.7 million m³ in producer countries, 3.7 million m³ in consumer countries).

The rebound in log production in 2006 is largely explained by developments in Indonesia in 2006. In 2005, the Government drastically reduced its allowable cut, generating a raw materials shortage for its entire forestry industry. Indonesian log production decreased by 22% and many wood product companies stopped operating, laying off employees and creating tremendous social problems. The Government appears (at least in practice) to have relaxed the allowable cut limit in 2006, leading to a strong rebound in log production (from an estimated 18 million m³ in 2005 to an ITTO estimated 26 million m³ in 2006). Other observers estimate even higher production, as high as 47 million m³. Log production in Indonesia is difficult to estimate owing to weak statistical infrastructure and high levels of illegal logging. African producers increased their log production by 6% in 2005 (mainly as a result of increases in Gabon and Cameroon), while Latin America decreased production by 7%.

Tropical sawnwood production by ITTO countries totalled over 42.2 million m³ in 2005 (41 million m³ in producer countries and 1.2 million m³ in consumer countries), a 4.5% increase from 2004. In 2006 sawnwood production jumped 13% to 47.7 million m³ (45.4 million m³ in producer countries and 2.2 million m³ in consumer countries), mainly because of an estimated rebound in Indonesian production. Sawnwood production is forecast to increase to 49.9 million m³ in 2007.

Tropical hardwood veneer production in ITTO countries held steady at 3.4 million m³ in 2005 (2.6 million m³ from producer countries and 0.8 million m³ from consumer countries). Production grew by 2.9% to 3.5 million m³ in 2006 (2.7 million m³ from producer countries and 0.8 million m³ from consumer countries) and is forecasted to grow another 1% to 3.6 million m³ in 2007. Tropical plywood production remained stable in 2005 at 20.4 million m³ (14.3 million m³ in producer countries and 6.1 million m³ in consumer countries), jumped by 10.2% to 22.5 million m³ in 2006 (16.1 million m³ in producer countries, 6.3 million m³ in consumer countries), and is forecast at 23 million m³ for 2007. The jump in production in 2006 was mainly due to estimated increases in Indonesia. Because of its strong impact on tropical timber markets, ITTO is working closely with the Indonesian authorities to obtain reliable estimates of its production and trade of timber products.

12.3 Export trends

Exports of tropical logs were nearly 12.7 million m³ in 2005 (12.6 million m³ from producer countries and 0.1 million m³ from consumer countries), a 1.5% increase from 2004. In 2006, exports were down 9.7% to 11.5 million m³ (11.5 million m³ from producer countries, 0.08 million m³ from consumer countries), with a forecast increase of 1.3% to 11.7 million m³ in 2007. Most of the 2006 drop was due to an 18% decrease in Malaysia's exports under a new conservation policy. Malaysia's exportable log surplus is likely to decline further in the future, as more logs will be domestically processed into value-added timber products. The top four exporters have combined to account for about 83% of total ITTO exports in recent years (graph 12.3.1).

GRAPH 12.3.1

Major tropical log exporters, 2004-2007

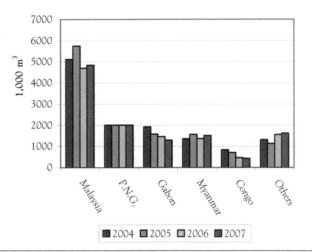

Note: P.N.G. = Papua New Guinea.
Source: ITTO, 2007.

The proportion of logs exported from Latin America and Asia for relation to the volumes processed in these regions is low (almost nil for Latin America and less than 10% in Asia), whereas Africa continues to export a higher proportion of unprocessed logs. However, the volume of log exports from Africa has been falling in recent years (from over 40% of production in the mid-1990s to under 20% today) and there is now a clear trend towards expanding processing capacity in Africa at the expense of log exports.

Tropical sawnwood exports rose 5.1% to 10.7 million m³ in 2005 (10.1 million m³ from producer countries, 0.5 million m³ from consumer countries) but fell back to 9.7 million m³ in 2006 (9.3 million m³ from producer countries, 0.4 million m³ from consumer countries), where they are forecast to remain in 2007. The decline in 2006 was attributable for the most part to a drop in Thailand's (-22%) and Malaysia's (-12%) exports of tropical sawnwood. This was mainly due to strong domestic consumption in both countries, boosted by their growing construction sectors. Among the major tropical sawnwood exporters, Malaysia and Indonesia account for about half of total ITTO exports (graph 12.3.2).

GRAPH 12.3.2

Major tropical sawnwood exporters, 2004-2007

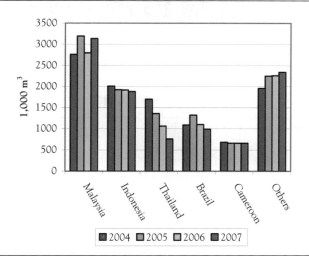

Source: ITTO, 2007.

Veneer exports increased by 7.1% in 2005 to 1.1 million m³ (1 million m³ from producer countries, 0.1 million m³ from consumer countries), stabilizing at this level in 2006 and in 2007. Tropical plywood exports increased by 1% in 2005 to 9.8 million m³ (8.3 million m³ from producer countries, 1.5 million m³ from consumer countries), rose 6.1% to 10.4 million m³ in 2006 (8.7 million m³ from producer countries, 1.6 million m³ from consumer countries) and are expected to ease by 1% in 2007 to 10.5 million m³. Plywood exports were boosted in 2006 partly by China, which has been expanding its share of many markets owing to quality improvements. Indonesian and Malaysian exports also expanded in 2006 (graphs 12.3.3 and 12.3.4). The top five veneer exporters account for three quarters of total ITTO exports, with Malaysia alone accounting for one third. For tropical plywood, Malaysia and Indonesia account for over three quarters of total ITTO exports. Chinese plywood exports have, however, been growing strongly, almost doubling from 0.7 million m³ in 2004 to a forecasted 1.3 million m³ in 2007. Chinese exports initially comprised mainly okoume plywood from imported African logs, but more recently China's mix of at least partially tropical export panel products has broadened to include a variety of combinations of different cores (often China-grown poplar) overlaid with face veneers of tropical woods such as bintangor or meranti. Chinese plywood products are comparatively lighter and cheaper than Southeast Asian products and their quality has improved noticeably in recent years. Interest in China's plywood products is rising in many markets, as demand outstrips available supplies from Southeast Asia.

GRAPH 12.3.3

Major tropical veneer exporters, 2004-2007

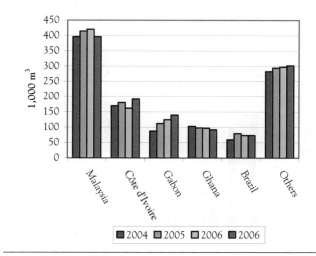

Source: ITTO, 2007.

GRAPH 12.3.4

Major tropical plywood exporters, 2004-2007

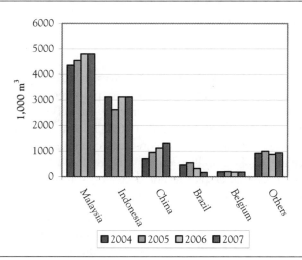

Source: ITTO, 2007.

12.4 Import trends

Imports of tropical logs stabilized in 2004 and 2005 at 15.4 million m³ (4.1 million m³ by producer countries, 11.3 million m³ by consumer countries) but declined by 2.5% in 2006 to 15 million m³ (4.3 million m³ to producer countries, 10.6 million m³ to consumer countries), with a 2007 forecast of less than 14.7 million m³ (graph 12.4.1).

Chinese tropical logs imports accounted for almost half of all ITTO members tropical logs imports at their peak in 2004-2005 before declining in the last two years. China's tropical log imports rose very steeply from the mid-1990s to their 2004 peak, with Malaysia, Papua New Guinea, Gabon, Myanmar and Congo the main sources. China's imports of non-tropical logs are huge and still growing, with Russia the main supplier. China's total log imports from all sources reached 31 million m³ in 2006, exceeding by far those of all other countries, and are projected to rise further in 2007, to almost 33 million m³.

GRAPH 12.4.1

Major tropical log importers, 2004-2007

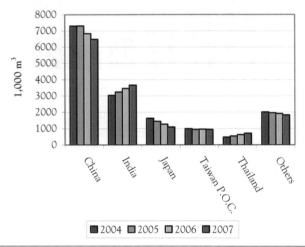

Note: P.O.C. = Province of China.
Source: ITTO, 2007.

Imports of tropical sawnwood decreased by 1.8% in 2005 to 10.7 million m³ (3.3 million m³ to producer countries, 7.4 million m³ to consumer countries) but rebounded by 1.8% to 10.9 million m³ in 2006 (3.6 million m³ to producer countries, 7.2 million m³ to consumer countries). A 2.7% increase to 11.2 million m³ is forecast for 2007 (graph 12.4.2). China, despite recent decreases, still accounts for about a quarter of total ITTO imports.

Total ITTO tropical veneer imports increased by 1.5% to 1.3 million m³ in 2005 (0.36 million m³ to producer countries, 0.94 million m³ to consumer countries), slumped by 15.3% to only 1.1 million m³ in 2006 (0.26 million m³ to producer countries, 0.84 million m³ to consumer countries) and are forecast at 1 million m³ for 2007 (graph 12.4.3). The drop in veneer imports was partially the result of the Government of Korea's imposition of higher taxes on persons owning more than one house in 2005. The aim was to stabilize the continuous rise of house prices. The new tax has had a dampening effect on the housing and interior sectors and consequently on veneer demand.

GRAPH 12.4.2

Major tropical sawnwood importers, 2004-2007

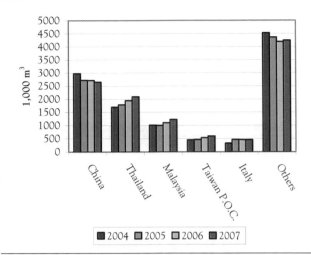

Note: P.O.C. = Province of China.
Source: ITTO, 2007.

GRAPH 12.4.3

Major tropical veneer importers, 2004-2007

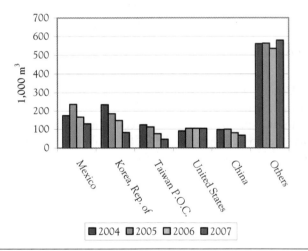

Note: P.O.C. = Province of China.
Source: ITTO, 2007.

Total ITTO imports of tropical plywood declined by 10.5% to 9.8 million m³ in 2005 (0.4 million m³ to producer countries, 9.4 million m³ to consumer countries) and continued falling to 8.4 million m³ in 2006 (0.4 million m³ to producer countries, 8 million m³ to consumer countries) (graph 12.4.4). This decrease in plywood imports was mainly due to the combined effect of plunging Japanese and Chinese imports (down 12% and 14% respectively in 2006). China's booming plywood industry has been producing more panels for the domestic market and for export from imported and domestic log supplies and therefore needs to import less, while the Japanese economy and building sector have remained subdued. A modest rebound in plywood imports to 8.7 million m³ is forecast for 2007.

Japan remains in number-one position among all ITTO importers of tropical plywood, despite the declining trend noted above. Imports will continue declining owing to its slow economy, declining population and progressive substitution of temperate and boreal conifers for tropical hardwoods, both in imports of plywood panels as such, and in the raw material feedstock for its shrinking primary wood-processing industries.

GRAPH 12.4.4

Major tropical plywood importers, 2004-2007

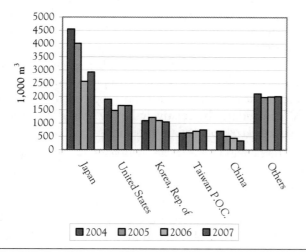

Note: P.O.C. = Province of China.
Source: ITTO, 2007.

In 2007, public procurement policies for timber began to be implemented in many European countries such as Denmark, France and the UK, while other countries (e.g. Japan) continued the development of such schemes. France is by far the largest European importer of tropical logs (accounting for 40% of total EU imports in 2006) and is also the largest EU tropical veneer importer (26% in 2006). From 2007, 50% of public timber procurement is to come from certified forests, and by 2010 this share should increase to 100%. It is estimated that public procurement accounts for 25% of the tropical timber imported by France. Problems foreseen in implementing the scheme include the lack of availability of products meeting requirements, the difficulty of correctly identifying the origin (temperate or tropical) of the products, and the difficulty in monitoring the actual effects of the policy. The lack of availability of certified tropical wood compared with certified temperate wood (only 5% of certified forests are in tropical developing countries) will likely be disadvantageous to tropical wood products seeking access to the French market. Efforts are therefore under way to help tropical countries improve sustainable forest

management and report on their progress. In 2006, France cancelled Cameroonian debt through a "debt for nature swap", which calls for Cameroon to invest around €20 million in sustainable forest management.

12.5 Prices

Prices for a majority of primary tropical timber products ended strengthened in 2006 or at least equal to their levels at the end of 2005, as exports of primary timber products declined, global economies expanded and consumer confidence improved in many markets. During 2006, African log prices mostly held on to gains made the previous year, with some species reaching new record highs in 2006 (graph 12.5.1). An ongoing degree of instability was seen, at least partially as a result of exchange rate fluctuations (prices sometimes declined in US dollar terms but were rising or stable in euros).

GRAPH 12.5.1

Tropical hardwood log price trends, 2006-2007

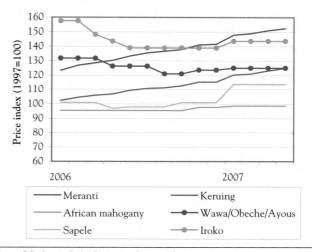

Note: SQ & up, L-MC are grade specifications.
Source: ITTO, 2007.

The improvement of log prices reflected greater demand (including from China and India), some continuing disruptions in log supply, and further tightening of log export restrictions in the region. Several African species are drawing increasing attention as substitutes for similar Southeast Asian species recently subject not only to rising prices but also to some instances of unavailability at quoted prices.

Log prices for some Southeast Asian species rose to 10-year and, in certain cases, all-time highs in 2006, as a result of further tightening supply of Asian logs, heightened by continuing toughness of law enforcement on logging operations and restrictions on log exports. Tropical log price increases were supported by active buyers from major Asian consumer countries, with the exception of Japan, where there was an increasing willingness to accept lower-priced substitutes such as softwoods.

Prices for sapele, a reddish brown timber from the Congo Basin found in countries from Liberia to Gabon, went through a cyclical trough in late 2005 and early 2006, at first seeming to fall from the upward trend tracked since 2001. But after dipping briefly in early 2006, sapele prices ratcheted upward for the remainder of the year. Recently, sapele prices have shown clear linkages with the prices for Asian meranti, an alternative red/brown timber, in both rising and falling cycles, so it is hardly surprising to see sapele currently riding the kite-tails of soaring meranti prices.

Similar 2006 price surges were also seen for keruing and meranti, which had already been climbing steadily though less dramatically since the end of 2003. Prices for keruing and meranti logs rose steadily through 2006, reaching nine-year and 13-year highs. Both seem poised to go on rising in 2007. In addition to shortages in Asian producers' log supplies owing to harvesting and export restrictions and some extraordinary weather episodes, continued strong demand from China and India fuelled the upward pressure. Both of these large-scale importers are now accepting wide ranges of sizes and grades. One result is that buyers from Japan have found difficulty competing for scarce supplies as they try to source larger sizes at exacting grading standards, yet wanted to obtain them at lower prices.

Prices for most Asian and African tropical sawnwood species were stable or rising in 2006 (graph 12.5.2). However, there were a few exceptions such as obeche sawnwood, which moved cyclically, showing firmness through the middle and latter parts of 2006 but not testing the highs of 2002 and 2004.

After reaching historical highs in 2005, iroko prices lost some ground in 2006 mainly owing to exchange rate fluctuations. Meranti and seraya sawnwood prices had been rising strongly during this period, with meranti continuing to post historical highs. Supply shortages and scarcity of offers were common in 2006, not only for traditionally strongly preferred sawnwood species such as dark red meranti (DRM) but also for others including rubberwood sawnwood.

Prices for Brazilian jatoba sawnwood firmed in early 2006 but declined gradually for most of the year as US demand slowed. In contrast, Latin American mahogany (*Swietenia macrophylla*) sawnwood prices kept reaching fresh record levels, driven upwards by harvesting and export restrictions linked with controls undertaken to meet the requirements of the species' Appendix II CITES listing. CITES is playing an increasing role in the tropical timber trade, with all 13 of the timber species currently listed in Appendix II being of tropical origin. Several more tropical species have been proposed for listing in 2007, including the relatively highly valued and widely used *Cedrela odorata* (Spanish cedar).

The demand for African mahogany (khaya or acajou, one of the continent's most valuable sawnwood export species) has been gaining strength and fuelling steady price gains ever since 2001. The US continued absorbing much of the African mahogany marketed, as the restrictions noted above curtailed the supply of South American mahogany.

Plywood export prices from all suppliers have been on a strong and steady upward track during the entire period from 2004 through the end of 2006 (graph 12.5.3).

GRAPH 12.5.2

Tropical sawnwood price trends, 2006-2007

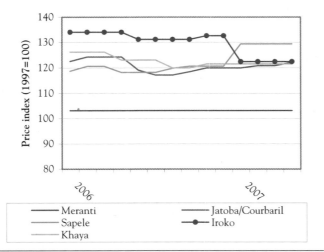

Source: ITTO, 2007.

GRAPH 12.5.3

Tropical plywood price trends, 2006-2007

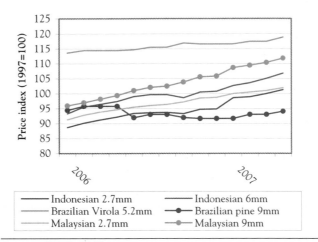

Source: ITTO, 2007.

Causative factors include scarce supply of large diameter peeler logs for plywood production, strong demand from North American and some European consumers, and problems in harvesting and shipping logistics, compounded in some cases by extreme weather conditions. Malaysia, where plywood mills are technologically better equipped, assumed price leadership in the market in 2005-2006, after overtaking Indonesia as the largest exporter to the key Japanese market in 2005. Malaysian exporters received another boost in January 2006 with the EU's reduction of its plywood import duty from 7% to 3.5%, while the EU maintained its 7% tariff on Indonesian and Chinese plywood. Indonesian panels have failed to benefit from the same price hikes seen in Malaysian panels, as buyers have lost confidence in the reliability of supply. Several Indonesian panel manufacturers have been unable to fulfil orders amid mill closures, lay-offs and declining exports. Additionally, Indonesia's export ban on logs and rough sawnwood introduced an additional level of bureaucracy, hindering the operations of legal exporters. Facing declining plywood supply from Indonesia, European and Japanese buyers have turned to Malaysia to replenish stocks but Malaysian mills were recently reported to be producing almost at full capacity. This has driven prices up further. In late 2006, importing countries were taking a second look at Indonesia and further increasing imports from China because of worries about the tight supply situation in Malaysia.

Source: FAO, 2006.

The Brazilian plywood sector has been undermined by the sustained strengthening of its currency, the *real,* and suspension in the approval of forest management plans. The suspension was due to a crackdown on illegal logging and to institutional changes in the forest authority. The plywood sector has been hardest hit by declining exports, which led to widespread layoffs. Brazilian exports of pine plywood plunged in the first half of 2006 as prices fell in the US and Europe and the exchange rate remained unfavourable. In the second half of 2006, the Brazilian

plywood sector was further affected by the slowdown in the US housing market. Tropical plywood benefited from higher prices owing to low supply in foreign markets, although price increases for white virola plywood have not been as steep as those for Southeast Asian plywood, as shown in graph 12.5.3. Brazilian pine softwood has lost competitiveness as the product continued to face loss of preferential tariff treatment it had enjoyed in both North American and European markets, as well as strong competition from Chinese plywood exporters, particularly on prices.

12.6 Secondary processed wood products

Exports of secondary processed wood products (SPWP) by ITTO producers continued their long-term upward trend in 2005. ITTO producer country exports of these value-added products rose by 7.1% in 2005, reaching almost $10.3 billion, exceeding the $10 billion mark for the first time. The leading producer country SPWP exporters in 2005 were Indonesia, Malaysia, Brazil, Thailand and Mexico. Each earned more than $1 billion from their 2005 SPWP exports, and all of them increased their exports from 2004 levels. Together, these five countries accounted for 89% of total ITTO producer SPWP exports in 2005. Much of Brazil's export furniture was made from solid pine and reconstituted panels from outside the tropics – it is impossible to disaggregate tropical SPWP from export statistics.

Japan and the US remained the two largest markets for SPWP from ITTO producers, with such products making up 31% and 22% of their total SPWP markets respectively in 2005. However, these shares had declined (from 35% in Japan and 25% in the US) since 2000, primarily as a result of competition from China, the world's largest SPWP exporter. The US was the main partner of ITTO producers in value terms ($4.8 billion in 2005) and its market continued to be the engine driving SPWP (mainly furniture) trade, growing almost four-fold in the last decade and up by 52% in the five years to 2005. In 2005, imports of SPWP by ITTO consumers from ITTO producers were worth a record $10.2 billion, exceeding the value of their imports of primary tropical timber products from these countries by almost 5%.

Reflecting the growing importance of SPWP to ITTO members, the 2007 Market Discussion (held on 9 May 2007, in conjunction with the 42nd session of the International Tropical Timber Council in Papua New Guinea) focused on "Trade in Secondary Processed Wood Products: Trends and Perspectives". An overview of the SPWP trade indicated that Asia-Pacific (69%) and Latin America (31%) were the dominant exporting regions in the tropics in 2005. Around 55% of the SPWP exports by

ITTO producers were furniture. However, producers faced intense competition from countries such as Viet Nam, Poland and particularly from China, which was the world's largest exporter of almost all SPWP categories in 2005, except builder's woodwork. Viet Nam, in turn, displaced Malaysia in 2005 as the largest tropical exporter of furniture. Although ITTO producers had made important inroads in SPWP trade, they had lost share to these countries in all key markets. This was despite the fact that China and Viet Nam imported most of their timber raw materials.

The discussion identified some prospects in the SPWP trade, including:

- Producers will continue expansion of exports and gain market share at the expense of industrialized countries.

- Growth will be driven by competitive prices, excellent timber quality (primarily from forest plantations) and supportive policies, among others.

- Producers' trade will remain below its potential, due primarily to product design deficiencies and tariff and non-tariff barriers.

- The recent elimination of furniture import tariffs by China will provide opportunities for producers in that huge market in spite of the country continuing to be a major competitor.

12.7 References

FAO. 2005. Global Forest Resources Assessment 2005. Available at: www.fao.org

ITTO. 2007a. Annual Review and Assessment of the World Timber Situation – 2006. Available at: www.itto.or.jp

ITTO. 2007b. ITTO Tropical Timber Market Report (biweekly). Available at: www.itto.or.jp

ITTO. 2007c. Status of Tropical Forest Management 2005. Available at: www.itto.or.jp

ITTO. 2007d. Tropical Forest Update. Available at: www.itto.or.jp

Annexes

Components of wood products groups

(Based on Joint Forest Sector Questionnaire nomenclature)

The important breakdowns of the major groups of primary forest products are diagrammed below. In addition, many sub-items are further divided into softwood or hardwood. These are all the roundwood products, sawnwood, veneer sheets and plywood. Items that do not fit into listed aggregates are not shown. These are wood charcoal, chips and particles, wood residues, sawnwood, other pulp and recovered paper.

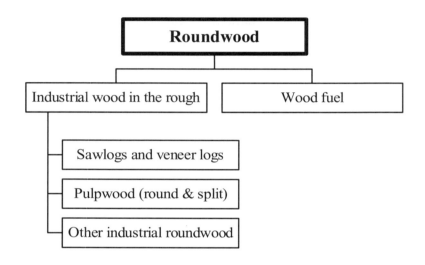

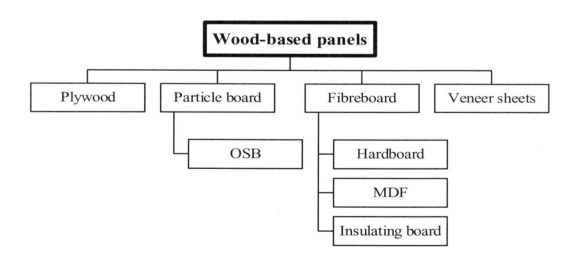

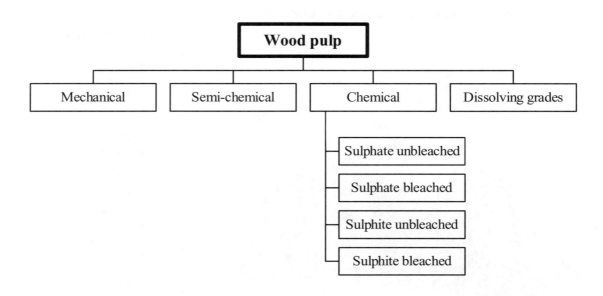

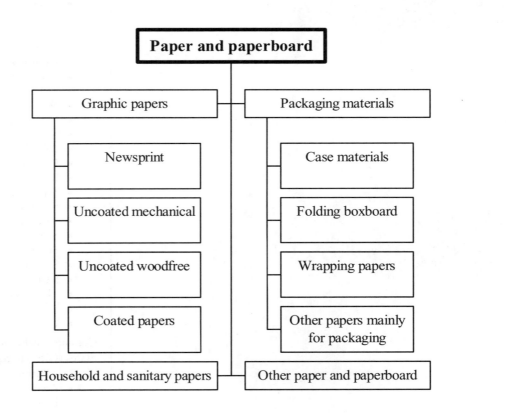

Countries in the UNECE region and its subregions

Europe subregion

Commonwealth Independent States (CIS) subregion

North America subregion

Europe subregion (EU *)
- Albania
- Andorra
- Austria *
- Belgium *
- Bosnia and Herzegovina
- Bulgaria *
- Croatia *
- Cyprus *
- Czech Republic *
- Denmark *
- Estonia *
- Finland *
- France *
- Germany *
- Greece *
- Hungary *
- Iceland
- Ireland *
- Israel
- Italy *
- Latvia *
- Liechtenstein
- Lithuania *
- Luxembourg *
- Malta *
- Monaco
- Netherlands *
- Norway
- Poland *
- Portugal *
- Romania *
- San Marino
- Serbia and Montenegro
- Slovakia *
- Slovenia *
- Spain *
- Sweden *
- Switzerland
- The FYR of Macedonia
- Turkey
- United Kingdom *

Commonwealth of Independent States (CIS) subregion
- Armenia
- Azerbaijan
- Belarus
- Georgia
- Kazakhstan
- Kyrgyzstan
- Republic of Moldova
- Russian Federation
- Tajikistan
- Turkmenistan
- Ukraine
- Uzbekistan

North America subregion
- Canada
- United States of America

Sources of information used in the *Forest Products Annual Market Review*

- APA – The Engineered Wood Association, United States, www.apawood.org
- Bureau of Labor Statistics, United States, www.stats.bls.gov
- Canadian Standards Association, CSA International, www.csa.ca
- Canadian Sustainable Forestry Certification Coalition, www.sfms.com
- *Commerce International du Bois*, France, www.ifrance.com/cib-ltb
- Council of Forest Industries, Canada, www.cofi.org
- Ecosecurities, United Kingdom, www.ecosecurities.com
- Euroconstruct, www.euroconstruct.org
- European Central Bank, www.ecb.int
- European Federation of the Parquet Industry (FEP), www.parquet.net
- European Panel Federation (EPF), www.europanels.org
- EUROSTAT – European Union Statistical Office, www.europa.eu.int/comm/eurostat
- Federal Statistical Office, Germany, www.destatis.de/e_home.htm
- Fédération Nationale du Bois, France, www.fnbois.com
- Finnish Forest Industries Federation, www.forestindustries.fi
- Finnish Forest Research Institute (Metla), www.metla.fi
- Finnish Sawmills, www.finnishsawmills.fi
- Forest Information Update, www.forestinformationupdate.com
- *Forest Products Journal*, United States, www.forestprod.org/fpjover.html
- Forest Stewardship Council (FSC), www.fsc.org
- *Hardwood Market Report*, United States, www.hmr.com
- *hardwoodmarkets.com*, United Kingdom, www.hardwoodmarkets.com
- *Hardwood Review Export*, United States, www.hardwoodreview.com
- *Hardwood Review Weekly*, United States, www.hardwoodreview.com
- *Holz Journal* (ZMP), Germany, www.zmp.de/holz/index.asp
- *Holz-Zentralblatt*, Germany, www.holz-zentralblatt.com
- *Import /Export Wood Purchasing News*, United States,
- www.millerpublishing.com/ImportExportWoodPurchasingNews.asp
- Infosylva (FAO), www.fao.org/forestry/site/22449/en
- International Forest List, groups.yahoo.com/group/ifl-tech2000
- International Monetary Fund, www.imf.org
- International Organization for Standardization (ISO), www.iso.ch
- International Tropical Timber Organisation (ITTO), www.itto.or.jp
- *International Woodfiber Report*, United States, www.risiinfo.com/risi-store/do/home/
- *Inwood*, New Zealand, www.nzforest.com
- *Japan Lumber Journal*, www.jlj.gr.jp
- *Japan Lumber Reports*, www.n-mokuzai.com/english.htm
- Japan Monthly Statistics, www.stat.go.jp/english/data/getujidb/index.htm
- Japan Wood-Products Information & Research Center (JAWIC), www.jawic.or.jp/english/index.php
- *La Forêt*, Switzerland, www.wvs.ch/topic5477.html
- *L'Echo des Bois*, Belgium, www.echodesbois.be
- *Maskayu*, Malaysia, www.mtib.gov.my/publication/publications.php

- Ministry of Forests and Range, British Columbia, Canada, www.gov.bc.ca/for
- Office National des Fôrets, France, www.onf.fr
- *PaperTree Letter*, United States, www.risiinfo.com/risi-store/do/home
- Programme for the Endorsement of Forest Certification schemes (PEFC), www.pefc.org
- Pulp and Paper Products Council, Canada, www.pppc.org
- *Random Lengths International/Yardstick*, United States, www.randomlengths.com/base.asp?s1=Newsletters
- RISI (former Paperloop), United States, www.risiinfo.com
- Smallwood Utilization Network, United States, www.smallwoodnews.com
- Statistics Canada, Canada, www.statcan.ca
- Stora Enso, Finland, www.storaenso.com
- Swedish Energy Agency, www.stem.se
- Swedish Forest Industries Federation, www.skogsindustrierna.org
- Swiss Federal Statistical Office, www.statistik.admin.ch
- Timber Trades Journal Online (*TTJ*), United Kingdom, www.ttjonline.com
- UN Comtrade, unstats.un.org/unsd/comtrade
- UNECE/FAO TIMBER database, www.unece.org/trade/timber
- US Census Bureau, United States, www.census.gov
- US Energy Information Administration, United States, www.eia.doe.gov
- USDA Foreign Agricultural Service, United States, www.fas.usda.gov
- USDA Forest Service, United States, www.fs.fed.us
- *Wood Markets Monthly*, Canada, www.woodmarkets.com/p_wmm.html
- *Wood Products Statistical Roundup*, American Forest and Paper Association, United States, www.afandpa.org

Some facts about the Timber Committee

The Timber Committee is a principal subsidiary body of the UNECE (United Nations Economic Commission for Europe) based in Geneva. It constitutes a forum for cooperation and consultation between member countries on forestry, the forest industry and forest product matters. All countries of Europe, the Commonwealth of Independent States, the United States, Canada and Israel are members of the UNECE and participate in its work.

The UNECE Timber Committee shall, within the context of sustainable development, provide member countries with the information and services needed for policy- and decision-making with regard to their forest and forest industry sectors ("the sector"), including the trade and use of forest products and, when appropriate, will formulate recommendations addressed to member Governments and interested organisations. To this end, it shall:

1. With the active participation of member countries, undertake short-, medium- and long-term analyses of developments in, and having an impact on, the sector, including those offering possibilities for the facilitation of international trade and for enhancing the protection of the environment;

2. In support of these analyses, collect, store and disseminate statistics relating to the sector, and carry out activities to improve their quality and comparability;

3. Provide the framework for cooperation e.g. by organising seminars, workshops and ad hoc meetings and setting up time-limited ad hoc groups, for the exchange of economic, environmental and technical information between governments and other institutions of member countries required for the development and implementation of policies leading to the sustainable development of the sector and to the protection of the environment in their respective countries;

4. Carry out tasks identified by the UNECE or the Timber Committee as being of priority, including the facilitation of subregional cooperation and activities in support of the economies in transition of central and eastern Europe and of the countries of the region that are developing from an economic perspective;

5. It should also keep under review its structure and priorities and cooperate with other international and intergovernmental organizations active in the sector, and in particular with the FAO (Food and Agriculture Organization of the United Nations) and its European Forestry Commission, and with the ILO (International Labour Organisation), in order to ensure complementarity and to avoid duplication, thereby optimizing the use of resources.

More information about the Committee's work may be obtained by writing to:

UNECE/FAO Timber Section
Trade and Timber Division
United Nations Economic Commission for Europe
Palais des Nations
CH-1211 Geneva 10, Switzerland

Fax: +41 22 917 0041
E-mail: info.timber@unece.org
http://www.unece.org/trade/timber

UNECE/FAO Publications

Forest Products Annual Market Review 2006-2007   **ECE/TIM/SP/22**

Note: *other market related publications and information are available in electronic format from our website.*

Geneva Timber and Forest Study Papers

Forest Products Annual Market Review, 2005-2006	ECE/TIM/SP/21
European Forest Sector Outlook Study: 1960 – 2000 – 2020, Main Report	ECE/TIM/SP/20
Forest policies and institutions of Europe, 1998-2000	ECE/TIM/SP/19
Forest and Forest Products Country Profile: Russian Federation	ECE/TIM/SP/18

(Country profiles also exist on Albania, Armenia, Belarus, Bulgaria, former Czech and Slovak Federal Republic, Estonia, Georgia, Hungary, Lithuania, Poland, Romania, Republic of Moldova, Slovenia and Ukraine)

Forest resources of Europe, CIS, North America, Australia, Japan and New Zealand	ECE/TIM/SP/17
State of European forests and forestry, 1999	ECE/TIM/SP/16
Non-wood goods and services of the forest	ECE/TIM/SP/15

The above series of sales publications and subscriptions are available through United Nations Publications Offices as follows:

Orders from Africa, Europe and the Middle East should be sent to:

Sales and Marketing Section, Room C-113
United Nations
Palais des Nations
CH - 1211 Geneva 10, Switzerland

Fax: + 41 22 917 0027
E-mail: unpubli@unog.ch

Orders from North America, Latin America and the Caribbean, Asia and the Pacific should be sent to:

Sales and Marketing Section, Room DC2-853
United Nations
2 United Nations Plaza
New York, N.Y. 10017
United States, of America

Fax: + 1 212 963 3489
E-mail: publications@un.org

Web site: http://www.un.org/Pubs/sales.htm

* * * * *

Geneva Timber and Forest Discussion Papers *(original language only)*

European Forest Sector Outlook Study: Trends 2000-2005 Compared to the EFSOS Scenarios	ECE/TIM/DP/47
Forest and Forest Products Country Profile: Uzbekistan	ECE/TIM/DP/45
Forest Certification – Do Governments Have a Role?	ECE/TIM/DP/44
International Forest Sector Institutions and Policy Instruments for Europe: A Source Book	ECE/TIM/DP/43
Forests, Wood and Energy: Policy Interactions	ECE/TIM/DP/42
Outlook for the Development of European Forest Resources	ECE/TIM/DP/41
Forest and Forest Products Country Profile: Serbia and Montenegro	ECE/TIM/DP/40
Forest Certification Update for the UNECE Region, 2003	ECE/TIM/DP/39
Forest and Forest Products Country Profile: Republic of Bulgaria	ECE/TIM/DP/38
Forest Legislation in Europe: How 23 Countries Approach the Obligation to Reforest, Public Access and Use of Non-Wood Forest Products	ECE/TIM/DP/37
Value-Added Wood Products Markets, 2001-2003	ECE/TIM/DP/36
Trends in the Tropical Timber Trade, 2002-2003	ECE/TIM/DP/35
Biological Diversity, Tree Species Composition and Environmental Protection in the Regional FRA-2000	ECE/TIM/DP/33
Forestry and Forest Products Country Profile: Ukraine	ECE/TIM/DP/32
The Development of European Forest Resources, 1950 To 2000: a Better Information Base	ECE/TIM/DP/31
Modelling and Projections of Forest Products Demand, Supply and Trade in Europe	ECE/TIM/DP/30
Employment Trends and Prospects in the European Forest Sector	ECE/TIM/DP/29
Forestry Cooperation with Countries in Transition	ECE/TIM/DP/28
Russian Federation Forest Sector Outlook Study	ECE/TIM/DP/27
Forest and Forest Products Country Profile: Georgia	ECE/TIM/DP/26
Forest certification update for the UNECE region, summer 2002	ECE/TIM/DP/25
Forecasts of economic growth in OECD and central and eastern European countries for the period 2000-2040	ECE/TIM/DP/24
Forest Certification update for the UNECE Region, summer 2001	ECE/TIM/DP/23
Structural, Compositional and Functional Aspects of Forest Biodiversity in Europe	ECE/TIM/DP/22
Markets for secondary processed wood products, 1990-2000	ECE/TIM/DP/21
Forest certification update for the UNECE Region, summer 2000	ECE/TIM/DP/20
Trade and environment issues in the forest and forest products sector	ECE/TIM/DP/19
Multiple use forestry	ECE/TIM/DP/18
Forest certification update for the UNECE Region, summer 1999	ECE/TIM/DP/17
A summary of "The competitive climate for wood products and paper packaging: the factors causing substitution with emphasis on environmental promotions"	ECE/TIM/DP/16
Recycling, energy and market interactions	ECE/TIM/DP/15
The status of forest certification in the UNECE region	ECE/TIM/DP/14
The role of women on forest properties in Haute-Savoie (France): Initial research	ECE/TIM/DP/13
Interim report on the Implementation of Resolution H3 of the Helsinki Ministerial Conference on the protection of forests in Europe (Results of the second enquiry)	ECE/TIM/DP/12
Manual on acute forest damage	ECE/TIM/DP/7

International Forest Fire News *(two issues per year)*

Timber and Forest Information Series	
Timber Committee Yearbook 2004	ECE/TIM/INF/11

The above series of publications may be requested free of charge through:

UNECE/FAO Timber Section
Trade and Timber Division
United Nations Economic Commission for Europe
Palais des Nations
CH-1211 Geneva 10, Switzerland
Fax: +41 22 917 0041
E-mail: info.timber@unece.org
Downloads are available at: http://www.unece.org/trade/timber